Broken Promises, Broken Dreams

About the Author

Alice Rothchild graduated from Bryn Mawr College in 1970 and began her study of the complex relationships between medicine, social justice, and politics while attending Boston University School of Medicine. She contributed to the first edition of *Our Bodies, Our Selves,* joined women's consciousness raising activities, and worked for health care reform. In 1973 she traveled to China, focusing on understanding the health care system, its relationship to political and social environments, and the role of Eastern medicine.

Alice did a medical internship at Lincoln Hospital in the South Bronx of New York City, working with community organizations in a unique effort to address the longstanding poverty and neglect in these devastated neighborhoods. She then did an obstetrics and gynecology residency at Beth Israel Hospital in Boston, again turning her attention to women's issues, focusing on efforts to educate and empower women and their families. She became Medical Director of the Women's Community Health Center in Cambridge, Mass. from 1977–1979. After completing her residency, she co-founded Urban Woman and Child Health, Inc. in Jamaica Plain, Mass., serving a unique mix of urban poor to middle class families from 1979 to 1988. She joined the staff of Beth Israel Hospital, now Beth Israel Deaconess Medical Center. In 1988 she became a member of the staff of Harvard. Community Health Plan which subsequently became Harvard Vanguard Medical Associates. Presently, she is also an Assistant Professor of Obstetrics, Gynecology, and Reproductive Biology at Harvard Medical School.

In 1997 Alice joined The Alliance to Defend Health Care and is currently president of the Alliance Board. In 2001, she traveled to Eritrea where she reviewed a health project for Grassroots International and assisted her daughter in developing a Girl Empowerment Workshop.

In 1997, through her involvement in the Boston Workmen's Circle, Alice turned much of her non-medical focus to understanding the Israeli/Palestinian conflict and its relationship to US foreign policy and American Jewry. She co-founded and co-chairs Visions of Peace with Justice in Israel/Palestine, now Jewish Voice for Peace, Boston, and co-organized the Jewish American Medical Project, now the JVP Health and Human Rights Project. She has co-developed four health and human rights delegations to Israel and the Occupied Territories and traveled to the region in 2004 and 2005. She has written and lectured extensively on issues related to women's health care and the Israel/Palestine conflict.

Please see website www.brokenpromisesbrokendreams.com for further information.

All book royalties will be donated to Jewish Voice for Peace, Boston.

Broken Promises, Broken Dreams

Stories of Jewish and Palestinian Trauma and Resilience

ALICE ROTHCHILD

Pluto Press

LONDON • ANN ARBOR, MI

First published 2007 by Pluto Press
345 Archway Road, London N6 5AA
and 839 Greene Street, Ann Arbor, MI 48106

www.plutobooks.com

Copyright © Alice Rothchild 2007

The right of Alice Rothchild to be identified as the author of this work has been asserted
by her in accordance with the Copyright, Designs and Patents Act 1988.

British Library Cataloguing in Publication Data
A catalogue record for this book is available from the British Library

Hardback
ISBN-13 978 0 7453 2597 2
ISBN-10 0 7453 2597 1

Paperback
ISBN-13 978 0 7453 2596 5
ISBN-10 0 7453 2596 3

Library of Congress Cataloging in Publication Data applied for

10 9 8 7 6 5 4 3 2 1

Designed and produced for Pluto Press by
Chase Publishing Services Ltd, Fortescue, Sidmouth, EX10 9QG, England
Typeset from disk by Stanford DTP Services, Northampton
Printed and bound in Canada by Transcontinental Printing

Contents

PART THREE   THE IMPLICATIONS OF KNOWING:
                       COMPLICITY AND DISSENT

Preface

For many Jewish families and friends in the United States, bringing up the topic of Israel and Palestine is a sure way to ruin a lovely dinner with the relatives or to stir up vitriolic passions on an otherwise moderately tolerant college campus. Indeed, often merely using the word "Palestine" is enough to flare tempers and to provoke strongly held emotional reactions in the most liberal of families or universities. I often hear secular as well as religious Jewish friends say, "It's too painful to talk about," or, "My family has decided we just won't mention it." Temple social action groups frequently report, "It's too divisive for our congregation," or "Arabs just want to drive Israel into the sea. What is there to talk about?" Rabbis confide that the presentation of outspoken views on Israel may threaten their contracts with their synagogues. Christian friends are often afraid of saying anything critical of Israeli policy for fear of being labeled "anti-Semitic" while left leaning Jews sometimes cringe at the lack of sensitivity to "Jewish sensibilities" voiced by their political allies. So why did opinions on this conflict, which is central to Jewish life as well as to the national discourse, become so taboo and controversial that it is often easier to discuss homosexuality, abortion, and torture in Abu Ghraib while asking your Uncle Morris to please pass the gefilte fish, than to utter the word "Palestinian?"

This book explores my personal transitions and changes in understanding by looking at individual experiences and by humanizing the players in this controversy while bringing the larger issues to a more accessible scale. I begin by sharing the voices of three Jewish women, two born in the Diaspora and one in pre-1948 Palestine. Each is grounded in and sympathetic to the long history of Jewish suffering and ongoing Jewish fears. Through a variety of different experiences during their lives, each fundamentally changes her vision of the conflict. Engaging in a personal search for justice rooted in Jewish humanism and political activism, these women ultimately cross the line and come to see Palestinians as fellow human beings, with their own suffering, blunders, aspirations, and historical narratives. In this process, old enemies become new friends and allies, and passionately held beliefs are challenged by the complexity and pull of disquieting insights. A Palestinian economist once said to me while describing her father, "Oh, he is a typical Palestinian." Flashes of angry, gun toting militants wrapped defiantly in checkered kaffiyas, touting the black, white, and green Palestinian flags with the red triangle rippling in the desert sun flashed before my eyes. She laughed and said, "They are all doctors or engineers. He's an engineer!" Such are the humbling moments on this unpredictable journey.

The remaining chapters of this book examine the complexity of Jewish-Israeli attitudes and then delve into the lives of a number of Palestinians living in the West Bank and Gaza. I had the unique opportunity to interview and work with Jews and Palestinians in the course of a medical and human rights project, collaborating with Physicians for Human Rights-Israel (PHR-I) and the Palestinian Medical Relief Society (PMRS). I invite you to join me on this intimate journey, acquaint yourself with the voices of people who suffer from different but mutually entwined trauma and conflict, and at the same time have an enormous resilience that is rarely appreciated. I invite you to examine the meaning of individual resistance, whether sipping coffee while sitting in a café that was recently the scene of a suicide bombing or staring defiantly into the eyes of an Israeli soldier at a checkpoint while he leafs through your permits.

So what happens when we refuse to be enemies? There are clearly personal and political consequences to crossing the line and bearing witness, to doing medical and political solidarity work in Israel and Palestine. For me, I began to re-examine US policy and the mainstream Jewish community's insistence on standing, unquestioning, behind Israeli policy. I was forced to stare directly into my private fears, my personal sense of entitlement, and my own racism towards Arabs. I began to wonder how all of these emotional and political forces and my new insights and sympathies shape my acceptance of narratives that are dissonant from my earlier cultural imprint.

Interestingly, the fault line of misunderstanding, fear, and hatred does gradually shift. No longer do I talk about the two sides, Israeli and Palestinian, but rather, of Jews and Palestinians who work for or against peace with justice in this region. Perhaps as you listen

to my first-hand narratives, you too will find starting points for a
different kind of conversation about Israel and Palestine. Perhaps these
discussions will help all of us begin the long walk to a future that is filled
with fewer demons and more possibilities for mutual acceptance and
respect between the descendents of the two sons of Abraham. Perhaps
a common need for survival, the dreaded weariness that comes with
the recurring spilling of young blood, and recognition of the physical
and psychic wounds that have passed from generation to generation
will change the political order. Maybe then empathy and forgiveness,
coupled with political activism, will enable us to bridge the chasms and
change the political course in this troubled area of the world.

Acknowledgements

As a physician, I have long felt that my central life work involves not only healing the individual patient but attending to the needs of society as a whole. For me, politics is not an abstract construct; it is grounded in a respect for the value and treasure of each unique human being. This book grew out of an effort to use my medical skills in order to hear individual narratives and to address the larger social issues that surround the tortured area of the world that is Israel and Palestine. I made this journey with a group of colleagues interested in health and human rights, the Jewish American Medical Project, now called the Jewish Voice for Peace, Health and Human Rights Project. I would like to thank all of my partners in this ongoing endeavor, in particular Seema Jilani, Howard Lenow, and Alan Meyers. I am also deeply indebted to all of the health care providers and other individuals in Israel, the West Bank, and Gaza who openly shared their stories and invited me and members of the medical project into their lives and their work. When I returned to the US, Amy Pett encouraged me to put this chronicle into words and was unfailingly supportive and cheerful when I felt filled with doubt. I thank her for her editing skills and for the comments of a number of readers including Carol Conaway, Roz Feldberg, Emma Klein, Karen Klein, Dorie Kraus, Alissa Rothchild, and Hilda Silverman. I am grateful for Elaine Hagopian's gracious willingness to share her knowledge over these many years and her enthusiastic support in finding a publisher for this book. I am also incredibly appreciative of Roger van Zwanenberg who convinced me that I had an important story to tell and that readers would be moved by my writing. Additionally, I would like to thank Jonathan Cook for granting permission to use his recently published map of the region. Lastly, I would like to thank my mother, Sylvia Rothchild, who shared with me her love of words and story-telling. As the doctor-daughter of a writer, I discovered the joy and fearlessness of creating a narrative and exploring its inner workings, of giving shape and meaning to the demons that have long remained silent in my life.

Abbreviations

AIPAC	American Israel Public Affairs Committee
GCMHP	Gaza Community Mental Health Program
HRW	Human Rights Watch
ID	Identity card
IDF	Israeli Defense Force
IMA	Israeli Medical Association
NGO	Nongovernmental organization
PHR-I	Physicians for Human Rights-Israel
PLO	Palestine Liberation Organization
PMRS	Palestinian Medical Relief Society (formerly Union of Palestinian Medical Relief Committees)
UNRWA	United Nations Relief and Works Agency
WHO	World Health Organization

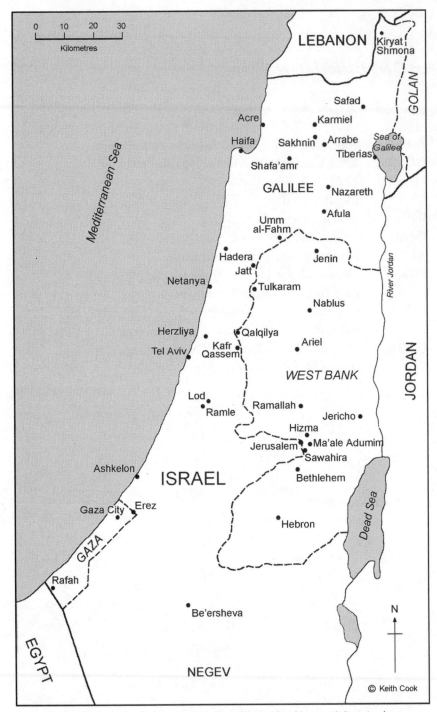

Source: Jonathan Cook, *Blood and Religion: The Unmasking of the Jewish and Democratic State*, London, Pluto Press, 2006.

To my husband, Daniel Klein, and my daughters, Emma and Sasha, who gave me the space to explore this troubled territory and joined me on this tumultuous journey. I hope that my daughters will draw strength from our commitment to Jewish humanism empowered by political activism and that they will continue the difficult task of challenging injustice and healing this wounded world.

Part One
Jewish Voices from Israel
and the Diaspora

1
My Own Story: Family Secrets

T HIS IS A BOOK ABOUT the unraveling of family secrets. It has been
a difficult journey, born of love and pain and tortuously leading
to questions, anger, and a desire to find a more honest place
and a more positive future. The difficulty in sharing this journey with
my family speaks to the depths of the trauma and the immense fear of
facing uncomfortable, dissonant truths. I am speaking not only about
my immediate family, even though they are significant players in this
drama, but also of the larger community that shaped my experience
of being Jewish in America. I was born in Boston in 1948 to first
generation parents and grew up with the State of Israel as my friend, my
pride, and ultimately my heartbreak. Thus, this is a story about losing
the beautiful myths of childhood and learning to stare open-eyed into
previously invisible contradictions, bringing voice to the unspeakable
ghosts that threaten both our foundations and our futures.

Diaspora Roots

Like many suburban Diaspora Jews growing up in the 1950s and
1960s, I went to Hebrew school three times a week and synagogue
services every Saturday morning. On Passover I sat quietly in the school
cafeteria, carefully unwrapping my matzo and avoiding the stares of my
classmates. These were all parts of the normal experience of crossing
back and forth between the world of public school and the religious
Brooklyn world of my grandparents. Even in my earliest memories, I
knew that we were different from Gentiles, that we could "pass" and
even succeed in "their" world, but ultimately the pull of Jewish cohesion

and difference would trump the seduction of total assimilation. After all, wasn't our separateness the key to our survival as a people?

I also grew up in the dark shadow of the Holocaust and the redemptive sunshine of the founding of the State of Israel, the heroic David miraculously fighting the goliaths of anti-Semitism and Arab hostility. I remember while in high school being drawn with horror and curiosity to the trial of Adolph Eichmann, a leader in the Nazi Gestapo, responsible for the extermination of 3 million Jews. The televised trial was deliberately held in Israel and prosecuted by Israelis rather than by an international tribunal. I can still recall being drawn to this malignant embodiment of evil who looked so ordinary with his dark glasses and high forehead, his headphones for translation and the protective glass box doubly framing his face. His trial was a central history lesson for my generation and etched the Holocaust into our consciousness.

Early on, I understood that Holocaust survivors were a special class of people, whether it was my red-faced Hebrew school principal screaming uncontrollably at a group of unruly students or the vulnerable rabbi's wife who always overdressed her children as if she could not protect them from some fierce internal cold. As a child, I knew that survivors needed our generous understanding and support. Their damage was deep and unimaginable. Although my family listened to the German composers, Wagner and Strauss, I remember that it was unthinkable to buy products made in Germany. In my teens, traveling in a Swiss sleeper car from Switzerland to Denmark, I heard my mother say clearly that she would not set foot in Germany. I have a hazy memory of dimly lit sepia colored German train stations, flashing by through the night with the grinding of brakes and the gentle rocking of the train. Despite the spacious wood paneled compartment with the crisp sheets on the foldout beds and the efficient but friendly conductor, German trains still had a lurking evil association for me. Even while touring Europe with a youth chorale in 1966, I looked into the face of every German man of a certain age and wondered what hideous crime haunted his Nazi past.

Embracing our status as the world's long-standing victims and living in a politically progressive family, I also proudly claimed another heritage: all the Jews who prominently defended the less powerful in the US through the labor, civil rights, and women's movements. Along with the legacy of Hebrew studies and Jewish history, to be Jewish in

America meant being an outsider and a survivor as well as a defender of the disenfranchised. We were chosen not only in the Biblical sense, but as my mother patiently explained, chosen to be responsible for the creation of a just world for everyone.

A Love Affair with Israel

When the country and I were both in our early teens, I visited Israel with my parents, younger sister, and brother. I fell in love with the exuberant beauty of the land, the olives and pomegranates, the terraced Judean hills, the red orange streaks of sand near the Dead Sea, the idealism of the kibbutzim, and the heroism of the soldiers. My carefully penned diary brims with youthful enthusiasm. There were detailed descriptions of Mediterranean beaches and a night-time bonfire with joyous singing and dancing. I was smitten with a lovely, doe eyed, Jewish Moroccan waiter named Hananya who shyly returned my attentions. My family explored the sandy white ruins of Caesarea. In my diary I noted: "Wandering along the walls and half uncovered buildings, it was fascinating to observe how each wave of inhabitants left their mark on the architecture. Gothic structures were intermingled with the marble steps brought from Rome and all this was topped by a tower that looked suspiciously like a minaret." We touched the fallen columns in Ashkelon and ran after darting lizards. We marveled at the Weizmann Institute of Science in Rehovot, an organization for scientific research where my father was consulting. I saw this as powerful evidence of the Israeli success story, a place for a smart, secular search for knowledge and discovery. "I was impressed by its idealistic purpose, truth for truth's sake. Men [sic] here spent their lives just looking for knowledge. The whole complex of buildings was all geared to the future. Everything looked new and promising."

At the same time, I was painfully conscious of the frailty and vulnerability of this nation-building project. Visiting the Galilee and Lake Tiberius, my diary describes "beautiful views of the checkered fields below us and the winding road above us. Sometimes we passed a lone sentry post battered with bullet holes and other times there were small kibbutzim nestled in the valleys." At the Sea of Galilee I noted, "The steep shore met the cool waters in the shade of the palm grove. The water was delightful and the bottom was covered with tiny shells and smooth rocks. On the other side were the pinkish purple hills of Syria." Another diary entry explains, "A half hour later we arrived in Safad after driving through the mountains to this hilltop city. From afar it looked like a sky blue mosaic. We parked the car and had a small lunch. We could see the crumbling Arab section, the poverty, the skinny cats, and the bullet holes on the police station from our table." After touring the artists' colony and *Sephardic* and *Ashkenazic* synagogues, I recorded,

> We strolled down thin, high-walled streets, broken by dark archways with old women and cats sitting in them. The stones of the street were large and smooth with a small gully in the middle. This being one of the major Jewish strongholds before Israel, there were many marks of war. Buildings were scarred by the patchwork of bullet holes, rolls of barbed wire remained and crumbling shattered houses stood in the rubble, a monument to bygone days.

Growing up in a house where even plastic guns were forbidden, I was intrigued with the idea of the Jew as an armed fighter rather than a frightened victim. One of my biggest thrills was when my father would stop the white Valiant rental car and pick up hitchhiking Israeli soldiers, invariably muscular, tanned, and radiating machismo. The Israeli Defense Force (IDF) was for me the Platonic ideal of an army: moral, invincible, principled, and Jewish. When we visited my parents' friends, General Ben Hur and his wife, my diary entry includes, "General Ben Hur had a battery of war stories, jokes, and other experiences at his finger tips. In the house his army uniform and guns hung on the wall." Later, they took us to Jerusalem on the winding Burma Road. I observed,

> Bedouins encamped next to their herds, camels standing in the shade, banana trees, orange groves, sugar cane, a memorial to the group of 14 and 15 year olds who defended a house against the Arabs and died doing so, small Arab villages tucked away, almost camouflaged in the scenery, and most of all the Judean Hills. These were most impressive, for if land could speak, they would tell a colorful, invigorating tale of courage, freedom, life, and spirit. These hills could have filled the Israeli fighters with bravery. We viewed the Jordanian border and spied on the Arab half of Jerusalem. Everywhere were the marks of war: bullet holes, barbed wire, sentry posts.

With the innocence and honesty of early adolescence, I also commented, "In Israel everyone has the right of way and maintains it."

My most powerful experiences occurred visiting kibbutzim, which were central to my understanding of the Israeli ethos. At Yad Mordecai, I wrote,

This was a kibbutz founded by Jews 43 years ago who had escaped from the Warsaw Ghetto. It was named after the man who had led the first revolt and thus this kibbutz symbolized the new Jew, the fighting Jew. The tour guide, talking constantly in Yiddish with Mom, led us down a white stone path towards a hill covered with luxuriant flowers. Because of the proximity to the border of the Gaza Strip, a special shelter was kept in readiness and each night a patrol went out to guard against Arabs. We were surrounded by green fields and forests until the end of the Israeli border. The Gaza Strip was a desert. These two regions were side by side and there was actually a distinct line where modern science and irrigation ended and the lands left to nature began. This was a true picture of the progress Israel had made in reclaiming the desert. On the hill there was a memorial and the graves of the 26 men and women who had died fighting against the Arabs in the original attack.

Approaching kibbutz Ayelet Hashachar, my diary includes,

With relief we saw the sign "Hotel Pension." We drove past much construction, turned down a driveway and there we were. Red, yellow, and white roses bloomed plentifully and bizarre shaped cacti filled a garden. We went wandering down an unpaved road, past new two story apartment houses, older wooden buildings, cement construction, small plots of corn, a calla lily, and numerous chicken houses. This was unbelievable. In the midst of the wilderness, near the troubled border, was a large and tempting pool. Walking back, we noticed children playing with parents, *Shabbat* candles lit in the windows, and we heard music playing. This was a small center of civilization.

An Uncomfortable Dissonance

Reading this diary more than 40 years later, I notice attitudes and assumptions that I now find troubling. I am struck by my sense of Eastern European superiority, unapologetic Jewish entitlement, and a stereotypic disdain for Arabs and *Sephardic* Jews. An entry on the way to Be'ersheva includes,

From the car, we could see many black-clothed Arabs. Mothers sheltered their children, and little boys herded flocks of black and white sheep and goats. Their dingy brown tents huddled in the distance and camels looked superciliously down upon each other. The streets were winding and often unpaved and lined with old shops. Chickens clucked from their cages and colorful scarves swayed in the infrequent sultry breeze. Arabs, dressed in long black robes and dirty head dresses walked everywhere. Little grey donkeys clopped delicately along, pulling heavy wagons behind them. Our next problem was to find a place to eat. We'd spy a place, but the dirty, greasy look of most everything made us lose our appetites. Falafel was sold from slimy looking stands managed by fat, unsanitary looking women. As you can see, the Arabs and Oriental Jews had had their effect on the city. At last we found a small, clean restaurant managed by a Yiddish speaking European Jew.

As a young Jewish teenager, I completely succumbed to the national mythos surrounding the 1948 Israeli War of Liberation, the militant, post-Holocaust Jew, and the superiority of Eastern European *Ashkenazi* culture with its educated, socialist, secular leanings. Like many in my generation, my fervor resonated with the emotionally uplifting 1958 Lean Uris novel and subsequent film (1960), *Exodus*, and the idealism and romance of the kibbutz movement. I am fascinated that despite my boundless adolescent curiosity and sensitivity for victims all over the world, I never asked what happened to the Arabs in those white stone houses with their dark empty archways or those towers that looked suspiciously like minarets. In my Israel, in the famous words of former Israeli Prime Minister Golda Meir, there was no Palestinian people. Like many in my family, there was also no *Nakba* or Palestinian catastrophe created when Jews founding Israel drove Palestinians off of their land. There was not even any doubt that this land was rightfully ours. Despite years of Hebrew school and a well-educated liberal family, I knew nothing of the philosopher and social activist, Martin Buber, or the rabbi turned professor, Yehuda Magnes. I was not exposed to their arguments for the creation of a secular bi-national state instead of a Jewish state and the vigorous debates that occurred within the early Zionist movements. A decade after the worst genocide the world had ever experienced, I had never heard of the expulsion and flight of 750,000 Palestinians, of the Deir Yassin Massacre, of the destruction of hundreds of Arab villages, of the victims that were created, in significant part, by my own people's victimization.

So how did my emotional and political transformation occur? In high school, my love affair with all things Israeli continued, woven into my obsession with the evils of the Holocaust and my private debates with the political theorist Hannah Arendt. I was fascinated by her analysis of the Eichmann trial and struggled over her depiction of Nazi behavior as exemplifying "the banality of evil," rather than as a unique manifestation of malevolent monsters. Celebrating the Israeli success story, I joined various Jewish youth movements and linked hands and scarves in a number of Israeli dance clubs. At my very WASP college, during freshman orientation I proudly attended temple services, which coincided with the Jewish holiday of Rosh Hashanah. Searching for my place in this new world, I founded a college Jewish discussion group, verbally sparred with private school graduates who had never before met one of my tribe, and started dating non-Jewish men who found me exotic. Into this adolescent cauldron, my own issues of inside/outside status, separation, and identity combined with the protests against the Vietnam War and the explosion of feminism. When I headed to medical school, my involvement in health care concerns, women's consciousness-raising, and economic justice continued to change my worldview, eclipsing my interest in and passion for Israel.

Gradually, I began to frame political conflicts in terms like colonialism, imperialism, and nationalism, and ask questions I had never previously imagined. I started to notice my discomfort with synagogue services, with all the familiar prayers that extolled the love of Zion and a yearning for the land of my forefathers. I developed a growing distress with the assumption of a uniquely chosen status for the Jewish people. Family Bar Mitzvahs became uneasy events, as I squirmed through rabbinical sermons that assumed an uncritical view of Israel. Seders, no longer the endless Yiddish chanting of my grandfather or the boisterous family happenings led by my father, became a battle ground not only around my relationship to my family and my Jewishness, but also about whether I could honestly sing "Next year in Jerusalem" at all. The childhood holiday of liberation felt to me unbearably ethnocentric and self-congratulatory. For years, my uneasiness had no vocabulary and little actual historical foundation beyond generalities. Increasingly alienated, unable to verbalize my own disappointment, I avoided the topic of Israel with a fierce defensiveness born of intellectual discord as well as gut-wrenching fear and lack of knowledge.

During the Vietnam War, I had learned to doubt official media as well as governmental spin. After the 1967 War in Israel and the occupation of the West Bank and Gaza, I started distrusting mainstream Jewish explanations as well. Like many Jews caught between long-standing loyalties and contradictions, I also became uncomfortable and distrustful of the relationship between my own government and Israeli policy. Because my relationship to Israel remained an important piece of my identity, this sense of unbalance and discomfort was not sustainable. I needed an historical memory and a context that merged my own personal history with the politics of the person I had become.

Finding My Anchor

In the mid 1990s, I finally began the painful unraveling of my Jewish family story, actively seeking dissenting voices in the US Jewish community and in Israel and discovering the narratives of a growing number of articulate and thoughtful Palestinians and Arab scholars. This work started in a more organized fashion appropriately enough on Yom Kippur, the Jewish Day of Atonement, 1997, as I sat on the pebbled shores of Jamaica Pond in Boston with a group of secular Jews from Workmen's Circle, a progressive secular Jewish cultural organization. We were talking about the service that we had created and celebrated, tossing bread (and our sins, regrets, and other disturbances) into the water amid the frenzy of excited, quacking ducks. We reflected on the meaning of repentance and healing the world, the possibilities for political work in the upcoming year, the place for progressive secular Jews. This informal reflection evolved into a group of Jews affiliated with the Workmen's Circle, Kahal B'raira (a secular humanist congregation), and New Jewish Agenda (a multi-issue progressive activist group founded in 1980). We met every few weeks to develop "A Forum on the Israeli/Palestinian Peace Process" for the larger 50th anniversary celebration of the founding of the State of Israel on the Boston Commons, sponsored by the Jewish Community Center of Greater Boston. We felt that these dissenting voices needed to be honored in an event focusing on Israel, which has its own indigenous peace movement and a complicated multicultural society.

Our group spent almost a year listening to the lesser heard narratives of American and Israeli Jews, Palestinians, Christian peace-makers, Mideast scholars, and rabbis, exploring what is rarely mentioned in the US media. We learned about events as described by Mideast scholars and the new Israeli historians, the narrative of the last 50 years from the point of view of Palestinians in the Diaspora, the political and social impact of the Israeli occupation, and the need for understanding, compassion, and accountability. At the 50th anniversary celebration, April 26, 1998, we were sandwiched between face painting and crowds singing the Israeli national anthem "Hatikvah," making bagels, and listening to a boisterous Israeli rock band. Our local Massachusetts congressman, Barney Frank, introduced the peace forum. A group of Palestinians, US and Israeli Jews, scholars, and rabbis shared their stories with over 200 people. The experience of learning about the complexity of the conflict and hearing history and personal experiences from people with whom I would usually not interact, gave me an exhilarating sense of wholeness. The pieces of this complicated puzzle were falling into place; my diffuse sense of anger, confusion, and injustice began to develop a framework. This empowered me to continue the dialogue and with my newly found friends, to establish an ongoing group, Visions of Peace with Justice in Israel/Palestine, build a website, and begin a more serious process of education and activism.

These were difficult months with endless agonizing about everything, starting with the name of the organization. Are we a Jewish group or Jewish/Arab? Are we about education, dialogue, coexistence, or activism? Is a vision of peace enough, does there have to be justice? What would justice look like? Do we as Jews use the word Palestine? Is that going to prevent us from reaching out to other Jews? When is it principled criticism to disapprove of the behavior of the Israeli government and when is it anti-Semitic? As if directed by our gene pool, the Talmudic tradition lived on, morphing our meetings into a detailed debate about framing the conflict, defining the principles, and developing a strategy. We realized we wanted to focus on educating other Jews and reaching out to the Christian and Muslim communities, to develop an independent Jewish voice that respected the suffering and aspirations of Jews and Palestinians, and to look critically at the role of our own government in this region.

This ongoing examination of narratives often feels overwhelming and painful. By immersing myself in the works of modern Israeli and US historians, I now know that Moshe Dayan, David Ben Gurion, and a host of other founding fathers were well aware that the land of Israel would be taken, one way or another, from an indigenous population and that an expansionist Jewish dream was present from the very beginning of this struggle. I now know that many pre-war

Jewish settlers felt a deep disdain and shame towards the survivors of the Holocaust and actively sought to create a different kind of Jew; powerful, self-sufficient, and militant. I find that it is a monument to post-Holocaust nation-building that the victors were able to create a relatively unchallenged story in which brave and rugged Jewish fighters valiantly struggled against a vast Arab enemy that had no human face and no human pain.

I now understand that buried in the wounds of my own people's near annihilation and the subsequent victories of war, another people's story was lost. This coexisting, unspoken, and interwoven tragedy is the opening chapter in a hidden but destabilizing family secret.

Listening to the Other

My most powerful educational moments came from exposure to the narratives of Israelis and Palestinians who are living the conflict. As potent examples, the stories of Ruchama Marton, an Israeli physician, and Gila Svirsky, a US-born woman who made *aliyah* to Israel, are detailed in the next two chapters. As an American-born Jew, I also never had the opportunity to meet with Arabs or Palestinians and to understand their personal and political histories. At a Visions of Peace meeting, Hilary Rantisi, now director of the Middle East Initiative at the John F. Kennedy School of Government at Harvard, gave me an intimate sense of the dark side of Israeli independence and the realities of occupation, while describing her own family story.

Hilary's father, Audeh Rantisi, was born in the city of Lydda, now called Lod, and now located in Israel. Church records from the town document her family living in Lydda since the fourth century. In July, 1948, when her father was eleven, with the city under curfew, Israeli soldiers came to his home and told the family to leave. Her grandmother, who had grown up in a German Lutheran orphanage, spoke Arabic, English, and German. She tried to talk with the soldiers in German and learned that the family of six children had five minutes to evacuate their home and were not allowed to take anything with them. Thinking that the soldiers were only searching the house, her grandfather grabbed the house key, and started with his family towards the church. In the street, Israeli soldiers blocked their way and they were directed towards the hills. Joined by the entire town, they were soon running with soldiers shooting over their heads. For three days, they marched to the Palestinian city of Ramallah, hungry, thirsty, and hot under the unrelenting Mediterranean sun. Her grandfather's cousin and his wife were killed by Israeli soldiers when they would not give up their precious gold jewelry. Hilary remembers her father telling a horrific story of watching a mother carrying a baby in each arm, pushed by a large Israeli vehicle, losing her grip, and watching one of her babies crushed to death by the vehicle. Once in Ramallah, the family lived in tents. Her grandfather was unable to find employment, shamed and broken by his inability to protect his family.

Hilary recounts that Audeh and his three brothers worked the streets, selling cigarettes and sweets. Her father was rescued by a Presbyterian minister, completed high school and ultimately attended college and became an Episcopalian minister. After marriage, he and his British wife started an orphanage for boys, driven by a desire to create the childhood that he had never had for boys who were now living in similar desperate circumstances. In 1972, Hilary was born in East Jerusalem and grew up in Ramallah under Israeli occupation. Her father became a respected leader and Deputy Mayor of the city. She remembers Israeli soldiers patrolling the streets, repeatedly occupying her home and breaking the windows, the frequent curfews where the family was confined to their home, and bullets flying into the kitchen. Her father was often detained, interrogated, and arrested, and lived under house arrest for a time. One of his crimes was organizing a ringing of church bells in 1988 when the Palestine Liberation Organization (PLO), based in Tunisia, declared Palestinian independence. As a child, Hilary recalls an imposing Israeli tank parked outside her home. Hilary grew up with a strong sense of national pride and emotional attachment. Today she lives in the Boston area, a woman with multiple identities and a commitment to the memory of her family's displacement. She holds a US Green Card, British citizenship, a West Bank Israeli military issued ID, a Palestinian travel document, and a United Nations Relief and Works Agency (UNRWA) refugee card. Her story was part of my introduction to the Palestinian narrative, to *Al Nakba*.

As I listen to the heart-breaking stories of Palestinians in the Diaspora, I am struck by the recurring themes of displacement, oppression, wandering, and yearning for a home. Palestinians have a strong sense of injustice and of a hostile world unconcerned with their fate, scattered in the Occupied Territories, refugee camps, and cities in the Western and Arab worlds. Strangely, these stories sound so familiar to me, at some basic level so like the Jewish stories that grounded my identity. I began to understand the ways in which our cultural legacies are parallel, reflections from opposite sides of the same mirror, and thus inextricably glued together. As my understanding deepened by reading and political discussions, I began to speak out publicly with other Jews and Arabs, Christians and Muslims. I published several editorials in the *Boston Globe* exploring the complexities of our relationships and the blinders with which our respective communities each view this conflict. I quickly discovered with my fellow activists that public criticism of the Israeli occupation and unquestioning US military support, and expressions of sympathy for Palestinians as fellow human beings, come with a heavy price. Along with the heartfelt discussions and notes of thanks I received, came vicious hate mail, hostile phone calls, outrageous accusations that I was a self-hating Jew and a supporter of terrorist organizations. Visions of Peace soon had increasing difficulties booking presentations at most Jewish venues and many community forums.

I was clearly bumping up against powerful agendas and deeply felt historical wounds. I began to understand that I was perceived as dangerous; a Jewish woman bringing critical attention, demanding a more complex, nuanced understanding of the injustices, missed opportunities, and human costs of current US, Israeli, and Palestinian policies. I found that for many, publicly stating that Jews could be victimizers as well as victims, and that Palestinians are equally human and deeply hurting, is unthinkable and a betrayal of Jewish loyalty and identity. This Jewish denial combined with the increasing brutality of the Israeli occupation is made possible by keeping Palestinians invisible as fellow human beings. Denying that they also love their children, want a decent life, and have compromised their national aspirations beyond our comprehension, is another dark corrupting secret that is now part of our painful family legacy.

Finding a New Jewish Voice

Since those days of nascent activism, I have witnessed a virtual explosion of US Jewish organizations working for a just peace in Israel and Palestine, in Boston and across the US. These organizations speak with a variety of voices, but from a different place than the mainstream Jewish community, which largely stands uncritically with Israeli policy. Instead we ask: does this work foster peace or hinder peace? We believe that for Israelis to be safe and secure, Palestinians need to be safe and secure, that to be "pro-Palestinian" or "pro-Israeli" is an artificial distinction. Thus, our Jewish dissent stems from an intense desire for justice and for a democratic future for Israeli and Palestinian people. I learned from secular as well as religious activists that the more we as a people take untenable stands, the more we risk losing what is most valued, cherished, and beautiful about our Jewish inheritance. In 2002, Rabbi Ben-Zion Gold, former Harvard Hillel director, a scholar and Holocaust survivor, said:

> At present the task of Jews who are committed to the welfare of Israel is to hold up the critical mirror for Americans and Israelis. We have to admit that not all of the people who criticize the way Israel has dealt with the Palestinians are anti-Semites. We have to recognize that not all who side with the Palestinians in their conflict against Israel do so because they dislike Jews. A nation as powerful as Israel has to accept responsibility for its policies and for its actions. It is not American Jewish criticism that has created sympathy for the Palestinians. It is the suppression of millions of Palestinians over 35 years that has done it.[1]

Another common theme for some of these Jewish peace organizations is the recognition that the creation of the State of Israel in 1948, which was an incredibly positive and joyous moment for Jews, was at the same time *Al Nakba* for Palestinians. I learned that there are two compelling sides to this story. I started to acknowledge that Arabs who were living in historical Palestine and Jews who emigrated there both have just claims and a deep attachment to the land. The Jewish people have treasured this memory for over 2000 years; the Palestinian people are descended from a vast Arab/Islamic empire dating back to the seventh century. With the shifts in colonial control, Palestinian national consciousness began to develop during the 400 years of Ottoman-Turkish domination which collapsed with the First World War. Thus, most Palestinian families were only uprooted a generation ago, and often still hold the keys to their family's homes, now occupied by Israelis. The question is not only who is the victor and who is the vanquished in this conflict, but what price Palestinians paid for the founding and flourishing of the State of Israel. Ultimately, I hope the question becomes, how can this land and its resources be shared, respecting and nurturing the human rights and aspirations of both of its peoples?

This tortured relationship between Jews and Palestinians has been further complicated by Israel's military occupation of the West Bank and Gaza since the 1967 War. At Israeli rallies, the Coalition of Women for Peace often carry banners that read, "The Occupation is Killing Us All." Israeli leaders have attempted to convince the press and the public that the West Bank is actually "disputed territories," or they use the more religious and expansionist term "Samaria and Judea," which implies that this area is rightfully part of Israel. I have come to understand that most of the world, except Israel and the US, considers the continued Israeli occupation of the territories captured in 1967 to be wrong and contrary to basic principles of international law. Even the former Prime Minister, Ariel Sharon, the father of the settlement movement, called this land "Occupied Territories." This occupation is not only damaging to Palestinians. Many Israelis recognize the corrupting consequences of attempting to maintain control over the territories seized in 1967. Some of the most eloquent critiques have been made by elite officers in the Israeli Defense Force who have refused to serve in the Occupied Territories. Guy Grossman, one of the early Israeli members of Courage to Refuse, stated in 2002,

> I refuse to fight for the continued occupation of Palestinian land. This war is unjust. It saps my country's sanity and morality and corrupts the soul. There is not and can never be a benign occupation. As a patriot, it is my duty to speak the truth and tell my people that this continued war of folly is undermining my country's long-term security. It erodes our legitimacy and the world's support.[2]

As my education progressed, I took my cues from dissenting Israeli voices, and began working with US Jewish peace groups that advocate an end to occupation. I now believe that ending the occupation has the potential to empower peace-seeking factions in Israeli and Palestinian communities to find a political solution. Thus, the current terrible cycle of fear and despair and terror may finally end. I understand that there is terror on both sides: the horrific acts of individual terrorism, like suicide bombers blowing themselves up in pizza parlors, as well as the acts of state-sponsored violence such as collective punishment, home demolitions, targeted assassinations, and the humiliation of an entire population. I understand the recent election of Hamas is partly a response to the gross inadequacies of the Fatah government. It is also a result of Israeli military destruction of thousands of Palestinian homes, the disproportionate killing of Palestinian civilians, the bulldozing of olive orchards, the checkpoints, the appropriation of land for settlements, bypass roads, and the separation wall. Palestinian violence and militant resistance occurs in a context that cannot be ignored and, much to my own disappointment and despair, that context is the outcome of Israeli governmental policies.

How Do I Know?

One of the benefits of joining and working with US peace organizations is the opportunity to share information, not only through literary and historical works, but also with the explosion of the internet. There is a huge network of email, list-serves, websites, publications, and lectures that provide a vivid alternative picture to the one to which the general public is exposed.

With broader sources of information I have become increasingly sensitized to what the media chooses not to report and the kind of bias this introduces into the general population's understanding of events. For instance, in May 2002, more than 100,000 demonstrators turned out for a peace rally in Tel Aviv. Sponsored by the Israeli group Peace Now, it was the largest peace rally since the Second Intifada. Peace Now spokesman Arie Arnon explained that the demonstrators were marching for a two state solution based on the return to the 1967 borders, the elimination of the settlements, and the establishment of Jerusalem as the capital of the two states.[3] Information about this major event for the Israeli peace movement was virtually shut out of the US media.

More recently, with the Gaza disengagement in 2005, there was extensive coverage of the sacrifice and anguish of the 8000 Jewish settlers who were forced to leave, albeit with compensation and assistance, the emotional conflicts for the Israeli soldiers, and the sensitivity training that was promoted for the soldiers. However, there was strikingly little reporting on the impact of these Jewish settlers on the 1.4 million Gazans who have lived for years in a virtual prison as a result of the settlements and the military that surrounded them. Months before the disengagement, 1600 Palestinian homes were demolished in southern

Gaza, in Rafah, to create a "buffer zone" along the border with Egypt. The fact that this was accomplished with Israeli bulldozers, Apache helicopters, little warning, and no compensation for the thousands of homeless families seems to have escaped the attention of much of the media and the sense of outrage or sympathy that Jewish settlers easily command. Commentators still refer to the end of the occupation of Gaza, ignoring the fact that Israelis control all border crossings, airspace, and ports, and thus the entire economy and movement of the population in and out of the Gaza Strip.

In another example, since March 2005, there are weekly nonviolent demonstrations involving Palestinians, together with Israeli and international activists, in the West Bank village of Bil'in protesting the construction of the separation wall, the confiscation of land, and the expanding Jewish settlements. Israeli authorities have repeatedly closed the village, confiscated half of the Bil'in land, and made multiple arrests. There has been an aggressive military response to the demonstrators, including planting stone-throwing provocateurs.[4] Palestinians are frequently told that resisting occupation in a nonviolent manner would improve their cause, but this weekly nonviolent effort receives almost no international media attention. These kinds of contradictions and double standards become increasingly difficult for me to ignore or to defend and are a source of growing outrage and frustration. They also result in an inaccurate portrayal of the vast majority of Palestinians who are more truthfully characterized by their enormous decency, moderation, and endurance. In 2002, Rabbi Gold, commenting on a proposed boycott by a variety of mainstream US Jewish organizations of America's leading media sources for having allegedly an anti-Israel, pro-Palestinian bias wrote:

> These people are saying "Don't tell us that thousands of houses were destroyed." "Don't tell us that civilians were killed." "Tell us the news as we like it." How pathetic! Expressions of sympathy for the suffering of Palestinians have become a major issue. I find it painful to see how much effort and money is spent on an attempt to impose on the media and on the American people an ideological spin on the conflict. It may well be that the prolonged immersion in the Holocaust and its misuse for political purposes has come back to haunt us with a vengeance.[5]

It is not acceptable to say that we do not know the consequences of the Israeli occupation. Uri Savir, one of Israel's chief negotiators in Oslo, revealed that during the negotiations he discovered that a Palestinian from the West Bank could not build, work, study, purchase land, grow produce, start a business, take a walk at night, enter Israel, go abroad, or visit his family in Gaza or Jordan without a permit from the Israelis. He noted that approximately one third of the Palestinian population had been detained or imprisoned by Israeli authorities and that the entire population had been humiliated by Israeli policies and soldiers. That was in 1998, and in 2006, the consequences of the Israeli occupation have deepened the collective Palestinian trauma and the strangulation of economic and social activity. According to the Israel Committee Against House Demolitions, some 65 percent of Palestinians live below the poverty line and an estimated 60 percent are unemployed. While I absolutely condemn their behavior, should we wonder why Palestinian teenagers turn to suicide bombing? Should we wonder why Israelis are justly afraid of this rage and hatred?

As I struggle to understand the recent Hamas victory and the terrible factional infighting, I am fearful of the militant destructiveness that has characterized this organization. At the same time I understand that Hamas has provided social services, health care, and educational facilities to a despairing and neglected population. I am also aware of the crippling desperation in the Palestinian population that has occurred at the hands of the Israeli occupying forces and the suffocating impact of the growing settlements, bypass roads, and restrictions of movement. I am aware that multiple Israeli incursions have destroyed the police stations and much of the civic and economic structure of Palestinian society. While I am totally appalled by violence of any kind, how can I not understand resistance? I frequently ask myself, if Jews were living under occupation, would we not also resist?

Unraveling Secrets

After years of listening to and supporting the voices of Jews and Palestinians, of struggling with the contradictions and competing histories, I finally felt compelled to return to the conflicted land of my childhood dreams. Working with a group of activists from Visions of Peace with Justice in Israel/Palestine, we developed a medical project, partnering with Physicians for Human Rights-Israel and the Palestinian Medical Relief Society. Armed with a desire to bear witness to voices that are rarely heard and to use my medical skills to both provide service and obtain an in-depth glimpse of both societies, I began my emotional journey exploring old demons and new possibilities.

What follows is an attempt to explore this painful, challenging reality using the words of the people involved, to unravel the secrets by humanizing the players, primarily through the lens of health care and human rights. I hope to face the contradictions of being both Jewish victim and victimizer and to explore the role of living in the Diaspora but bearing responsibility as a US citizen. As a physician, I have worked and talked with colleagues in Israel and the West Bank and Gaza, giving me a unique opportunity to ask difficult questions and understand the human impact of this conflict on Jewish Israelis and Palestinians in Israel and the Occupied Territories.

As a Jew, I come from a tradition with a long and understandable history of circling the wagons and hunkering down when it feels that all the world is against us. This simplistic and ultimately dangerous approach ignores the volatile combination in Israel and Palestine of psychological trauma, history, politics, and the self-destructive arrogance of Israeli military power. I worry that if US Jews remain silent, we become collaborators not only in the destruction of a Palestinian future, but also in a Jewish as well as Israeli survival that is filled with shame and acts as a lightning rod for Arab hatred and global anti-Semitism.

I have learned from Israeli peace activists that there are inspiring ways to frame this ongoing conflict. In the words of Jeff Halper, coordinator of the Israel Committee Against House Demolitions, "I am on the 'side' of Israelis and Palestinians who seek a just peace that addresses Palestinian rights of self-determination as well as Israeli concerns of security and regional integration. I am on the 'side' that stands for equality, human rights, democracy, peaceful co-existence and regional development."[6] The unraveling of secrets creates the possibility for empathy, forgiveness, and action which crosses old boundaries. Truth and reconciliation can change the political course in this troubled area of the world. Ignoring the secrets and the agonizing contradictions in this very human drama will have unpredictable and painful consequences for us all.

Somewhere in this journey, I began to see Israel not only as the victim of Arab hatred, but also as the neighborhood bully. I began to realize as the Israeli occupation continued and as Israel became a major military power backed primarily by the US, that Jewish suffering could not legitimize the excesses of Jewish power. Reading Marc Ellis's *Israel and Palestine – Out of the Ashes*,[7] I started to understand that an essential part of Jewish history and a just resolution to this tortured conflict requires understanding Palestinian as well as Jewish suffering. Behaving in a decent manner is both an act of survival and an opportunity to repair the legacy of the Holocaust as well as the Palestinian catastrophe, *Al Nakba*. Listening to the voices of the other is the first step in this painful and healing journey.

2
Dr. Ruchama Marton:
An Allergy to Lies

IN 1998, WHEN OUR NASCENT Israel/Palestine discussion group was searching for Israeli voices, Hilda Silverman, a longtime local activist who had been a fellow at the Bunting Institute of Radcliffe College in Cambridge, invited a newly appointed fellow to join us. She came to one of our planning meetings for the 50th anniversary celebration of the founding of the State of Israel. Israeli psychiatrist, Dr Ruchama Marton felt welcomed and immediately became friends with another group member, Elaine Hagopian. Elaine, an Arab-American, is an outspoken Professor Emerita of Sociology from Simmons College, a respected scholar and activist on Mideast affairs. Ruchama remembers at that first meeting, Elaine spoke of the possibility of a future where Jewish settlers in the Occupied Territories could live peacefully under Palestinian governance. Ruchama retorted, "How can you accept the settlers? I don't accept the settlers! The idea of grabbing the land!" Ruchama felt that an enduring peace in Israel and Palestine would require the evacuation of the Jewish settlements. The two women have been exchanging ideas ever since, all in the context of a deepening friendship and mutual respect. We novices watched these two "political heavies" and their verbal fireworks with anticipation and a growing understanding of how much we had to learn and how many storylines we had yet to unravel.

The First Meeting, the Beginning of a Long Relationship

I remember Ruchama arriving at my home that first evening in the early winter of 1998, grabbing a quick cigarette on the porch before joining the meeting upstairs. Angry, passionate, with a strident sense of moral urgency and personal outrage, she was my first real introduction to Israeli dissent. She became the touchstone for this small group of Boston area activists trying to make sense out of 50-plus years of complicated history and emotional confusion. We learned that Ruchama was spending a year as a Peace Fellow at the Radcliffe Bunting Institute at Harvard University, writing a personal and political memoir and networking with local activists. Ruchama spoke at the Israel 50th anniversary peace forum in 1998 and was a founding member of Visions of Peace with Justice in Israel/Palestine. In 2003, when a group of us began developing a project to examine the conflict through the lens of health care and human rights, it was obvious that we should work with Ruchama and the organization that she had founded in 1988, Physicians for Human Rights-Israel (PHR-I).

Visiting Ruchama in Tel Aviv

In 2004 and 2005 a number of us were able to meet with Ruchama in her home in Tel Aviv as part of the Jewish American Medical Project, a delegation that grew out of these early conversations. Like many of us, she was born into the Jewish story and developed her political identity through feminism and a growing awareness of the consequences of Israeli policy and Palestinian pain. In January 2004, she began our interview with her life story.

> I was born in Jerusalem, Palestine, almost ten years before the State of Israel was born and Jerusalem was then a little town, quite a nice one and a whole mélange of people were there. They managed to live really respectfully with each other, though some of them were extremely different, like religious, nonreligious. My parents were like this, nonreligious people from Poland. The next neighborhood was Mea Shearim; you cannot find more religious people than they are, not to mention Muslim and Christian Arabs. There was not big love and maybe therefore not big hate. People managed to live their lives and not to impose themselves on the other.

With tape recorder in hand, I look around Ruchama's living room which reminds me of somewhere in northern California. There are fresh flowers and pottery, lovely textiles and ethnically flavored artwork, as well as three framed posters that are particularly intriguing. One is a photograph of a cluster of people standing in drifts of sand. The scene is primordial Tel Aviv, 1903. In the second, a graceful silhouette of a tree frames a distant orange landscape and the dark outlines of the old city of Jerusalem with the caption "Visit Palestine," dated 1936. The third is a more modern photo by the Israeli photographer, Miki Kratzman, which depicts a concrete slab wall in the Jewish settlement of Gilo on the outskirts of Jerusalem. At the beginning of the Second Intifada, a series of concrete slabs were erected along the main street to protect the inhabitants from sniper fire from Beit Jalla, a neighboring Palestinian town. In the photo, on the concrete slabs, a pastoral scene has been painted that is continuous with the surrounding hills, and a pine tree and stones painted behind the wall give the concrete obstruction the appearance of invisibility.

The Family's Zionist Inheritance

Ruchama continues her narrative, rolling and lighting cigarette after cigarette, her gravelly voice intermittently intense and playful. Both of her parents left Poland in their late teens. Her mother, Bella, was a passionate Zionist and came to Palestine in 1929, but her father, Aharon, arrived a year later driven more by an unpredictable twist of circumstances. She explains that in Poland, there were four possible allegiances for Jews: Orthodox, Bundist, Zionist, and Communist. Her father was a Communist and desperately wanted to go to Russia with his comrades. He studied and worked and when he had saved enough Polish zlotys for the journey, his father caught him and made him take a vow. As Ruchama remembers, he told his son, "OK, you left God. You are going to leave me. It is breaking my heart. Don't go to Russia, you will be killed. If you must, go to America or Palestine." The young man kept his vow and headed south. In the 1930s all of his friends were assassinated in Russia and his father, two brothers, and beloved sister were later exterminated by the Nazis.

Ruchama lived with her parents and two other families in a three room apartment. Each family had a room, as was common in those meager times, until the family moved to Tel Aviv shortly before 1948. She explains that her parents were pioneers in the Zionist movement and she was brought up as a good Zionist, expected to finish primary school, and start working productively. She says that her role was to join the working class, marry, and have children. "They were stubborn,

I was not less. I managed to get a scholarship to the best high school in Tel Aviv and I finished high school with high grades. They were really unhappy about it [because they wanted me to] work and not become an intellectual which was against whatever they believed should be done." As was expected in 1955, Ruchama entered army service. "No one even raised the question of whether it's OK or not to go into the army. That was like a *mitzvah*, so like everyone else, I went into the army."

The Military as a Radicalizing Experience

Ruchama explains that in the army she had an experience that changed her life forever. "It was like a knife." She was working with a tightly bonded group of soldiers in her battalion, many of whom had fought for the establishment of the State of Israel in the Palmach. She explains she saw them as "the children of God, the myths of Israeli society," moral and humane as well as militarily effective. In 1956 during the Suez War, these Israeli reservists encountered a group of hungry, thirsty, unarmed Egyptian POWs and summarily murdered them. Ruchama felt, "I didn't have the mental equipment to put this horror into words. I felt I am not one of them any more. And *they* did it. It was more awful than awful." This incident became a cornerstone for her alienation, understanding, and future work in human rights.

In the military, Ruchama also had her first serious conflicts with authority. She was instructed to clean a room in the morning after a shift and had the audacity to ask why the four male soldiers did not have the same duty. Her commanding officer explained that this was because she was a female soldier. "So I said, 'Well that's right but this is not a good reason, or not good enough.' OK, so he said, 'Do what I told you.'" A complaint against the young recruit was made and passed from the lowest to the highest judicial levels.

> It took some time and everyone was really willing to help me. They didn't like the idea, "Just say sorry and everything will be OK." So I said I would say sorry if I would have a good reason for that, but I don't. So they kicked me out. In those years, it was in the year '57, it was unheard of, it was such a shame to be kicked out of the army. I personally didn't know even one person, unless it was a criminal thing. I didn't know what to do with myself but I survived it. One of the lessons – I mean the word feminism didn't exist then, for sure not for me – one of the things that I did understand, even then when I was so naïve and maybe even stupid, was that it is very bad to

fight alone, without support it is really awful. Since then, whatever I try to do – and I have a lot of fights – I try to have a group with me. Whatever, but not to fight alone.

Becoming a Physician and Maturing Politically

Prior to entering the army, Ruchama had passed the exams that would have allowed her to study medicine, but women in Israel were deprived of that privilege. When her army life was prematurely terminated, Ruchama was finally able to start medical school in Jerusalem at Hebrew University. There were eight women in a class of 80, filling the 10 percent quota that had been established in the interim. She found "there was a kind of attitude" towards the female students. "They didn't take us seriously." She was temporarily suspended for wearing trousers and had other conflicts during her medical school career. She married an engineer, and after graduation took a year off to take care of her newborn daughter, Orna. After a year-long foray into pediatrics, she settled on a career in psychiatry and has had an active practice ever since.

She describes her early political development, "I reacted spontaneously without any ideological background or any reading or nothing, it just came up." Towards the end of the 1950s and early 1960s she became involved with a tiny group that developed into Matzpen, the Compass, an anti-Zionist and anti-capitalist group with a few dozen members.

> They were wonderful people, they were extremely political people, and they were discussing and writing and reading. I liked their ideas very much. We were thinking that one state for both people, nonreligious, democratic, is the right, beautiful way to live here. Which I believe to this very moment but many things changed. So I took a very active part with this group but I didn't become a member out of feminist reasons, because all the speakers were young men. The young women there were preparing coffee and sex in those days. I mean everything was so free and easy, easier than now. And then came '67, the occupation, and the need for political activity became more and more necessary at least to my understanding.

Impact of the 1967 Six Day War

After the 1967 War, Ruchama felt compelled to see the newly Occupied Territories. She recounts how she took her cat Tula, her three-year-old daughter, "a lovely, stubborn baby, brilliant," piled them into her little Fiat 600, and went to see the lands that she remembered from her childhood. "And I was so convinced I could put my hand into the fire, that it's a question of days and we will give back all this land, we will trade the land and get peace. I couldn't think that there is another possibility. That was so clear. Now you can see how wrong one can be." Even Abba Eban, Minister of Foreign Affairs, announced on the radio that he was willing to return the land to the Arabs in exchange for peace. Ruchama remembers,

> In the first years the Palestinians were in a kind of shock, but they took the situation as it is, they didn't do anything against the occupation. That was so nice and easy for Israel, because we could do like this [she pats herself on the shoulder]. I mean, how nice we are, it is an enlightened occupation, no bloodshed, no nothing. They were working for less than half of the price, cheap good labor and we took something like half to two-thirds of their water, we took a lot of land, we didn't have to fix our borders, so why should we give up these beautiful conditions? That could go on forever and our Prime Ministers, one after the other, said that time works for us. Don't push, just because small not very effective political groups like us said it's about time to do peace, to give back the lands, and things like this. Time works for us. For us, I mean for the government, for the nation, and if the Intifada hadn't started, it could go on like this forever. Taking more land, taking more water, having the Palestinians like slaves more or less.

Ruchama sips her coffee, takes a long drag on another cigarette after reaching across the coffee table for her lighter. Cell phones ring, a cat walks across the carpeted living room. Ruchama's eyes sparkle with sarcasm, her face framed by short cropped hair. She goes on to describe the various political groups in which she was involved over the next two decades, a committee in the early 1970s opposing the closure of Birzeit University, north of Ramallah in the West Bank, a committee protesting the war in Lebanon in the 1980s. She recalls in 1981 a group, "the most sweet group I ever took part in," called "Liberated Territories," a name that inverted the meaning of the right-wing term for the Occupied Territories. This group wrote a weekly Friday column in *Haaretz*, a major liberal newspaper, paying a discounted 25 percent for the privilege of having the column published. "We wrote it together and that was fun. That was really fun."

The First Intifada

In the late 1980s, the First Intifada erupted and Ruchama's life took on a new focus. She explains that the word "intifada" does not actually mean "uprising," but rather "shaking off," the Palestinians were seeking "to shake us off their backs."

> In the very end of 1987, December, the First Intifada started, and it started spontaneously I can swear that was the case, in Gaza, in Jabalya Refugee Camp, and the Israeli army started all kinds of forceful actions against the riots. Rabin was Minister of Defense in those days, and he said, "We will break their bones and in three days everything will be quiet again." The Israeli army literally broke hands, legs, and heads, but the riot didn't go down, on the contrary, it became more and more. The Israeli media kept telling lies like always, but then, maybe more than always. You have a kind of allergy to cats? I have a kind of allergy to lies. I'm really starting to sniffle and I can't stand it. I can tell when one lies, especially if it is the government, and they *were* lying.
>
> So I called some friends in Gaza Strip and I asked them, what's going on? It was very hard to get phone contact with Gaza. I could dial like three hours to get a line, it was unbelievable, and no faxes in those days, no computers, forget it. So they started to tell me and then we came to the conclusion that the best thing if I really wanted to know, why don't I come and see for myself? Remembering the old lesson, I took a few people with me. I ask the Palestinians, "Is it safe because I am coming with a group?" They said, "Yes, please bring eleven people which we can house in one van and you are safe." And that's what I did; it was one *Shabbat*, January, we spent a whole day in Shifa Governmental Hospital in the city of Gaza in Gaza Strip and that was awful, really unbelievably awful what we saw.

Because the Israeli government had responsibility for the health care services in the occupied areas since 1967, the hospital Ruchama visited was an Israeli governmental hospital and the Palestinian physicians were employed by the Israeli government. She compared this institution to the medical services within Israel, a country famous for its social supports and the well-funded and advanced state of its health care system. "So it was our responsibility, our government, that this hospital should be run like an Israeli one, and it was a gap like thirty years at least, maybe more, equipment, level of medicine, no comparison. It was like Israel in the '50s." She couldn't believe the smell of urine and sewerage, the filthy water in the bathrooms, the cats roaming the hospital, and remembers being filled with shock and shame.

You could smell the hospital a mile ahead. I have pictures, I mean I can prove every word I am saying. The walls were covered with mold, pink, green, black, kind of yellowish, even in the operating rooms, it was unbelievable. Coming from our hospitals it was mind-boggling, I couldn't believe my eyes. .

The second point is the stories of doctors that were frightened because Israeli officers harassed them in many ways, some of them cruel and ugly, and the most frightening point for them was that they could be fired without giving any reason, like this [with a snap of a finger]. Not only are they at risk for losing their jobs, and there is nothing there in Gaza, but also they are losing all their social benefits that they were accumulating in the past.

The worst thing, the third one, was the stories we heard from the injured people there, and the people were young children up to 20 something, with broken hands, broken legs, unconscious from being beaten to their heads by clubs; that was a very personal war. I mean, I saw a child, he was 14 years old, and his hand was cast, so I asked him, "What happened to you?" and he wouldn't answer me. I mean my Arabic is far from perfect, my English is an Oxford one compared to my Arabic. He was looking like this, mute, speechless. So I ask someone next to me, "Please ask the boy what happened to him." He was still very frightened. He didn't say a word. He just took his plastered arm and did this kind of movement covering his head with his arm. So I did understand he was protecting his head. I saw his x-ray, his hand was broken in three different places which can happen only if one soldier … [she shakes her head, her lips tightening], never mind, it was awful, and this frightened face of this boy, that he was speechless, sorry to say, broke my heart. It was too much for me. And a lot of stories, including x-rays of inner parts of people that were shot by live ammunition which split into many particles, like dumdum bullets. .

The next week I took another eleven people to go to Mokassed, which is a Palestinian hospital, a private one in East Jerusalem. The conditions there were much better, overcrowded but clean, up-to-date, well-equipped.

During this first trip to Gaza, Ruchama met with Dr Eyad el Sarraj, a Palestinian psychiatrist. Two years later, Eyad asked Ruchama to join the board of directors of the newly formed Gaza Community Mental Health Program. Since that time, both physicians have shared a deep commitment to the promotion of health and human rights in Israel and the Occupied Territories.

The Physician as Human Rights Activist

The Association of Israeli and Palestinian Physicians for Human Rights was established by Ruchama Marton in the first months of the

Intifada. After visiting hospitals in the Occupied Territories, one of the Association's first activities was to protest against the use of medical care as a means of controlling the local Palestinian population and to protest against the participation of Israeli physicians in the torture of Palestinian detainees. They organized a controversial conference entitled, "Torture and the Case of Israel." The Israeli government and army vigorously countered their claims with arguments that Jews would not engage in torture and Palestinians could not be trusted as reliable witnesses. The Israeli Medical Association (IMA) denied that there was a systemic problem. Ruchama feels that the charges were too frightening, too threatening to the positive self-image of Israeli physicians, for them to analyze honestly the accusations and the data. The Association, which evolved into PHR-I, stated that its actions were based on universal principles of medical ethics as well as relevant international conventions relating to the safety of medical staff, access to health care delivery, and the treatment of patients, prisoners, and detainees.

A year later PHR-I established a weekly Saturday mobile clinic where Israeli volunteers, both Jewish and Palestinian, provide health care, usually to an isolated West Bank village in cooperation with their West Bank Palestinian counterparts. Still ongoing, this is both an act of solidarity, protest, and cooperation, a chance to provide desperately needed services, and an opportunity to understand first-hand the impact of the occupation as well as to negotiate different cultural attitudes. The mobile clinic prides itself in crossing the Green Line despite the political situation. In 1994, Israeli physician, Dr. Baruch Goldstein, killed 29 Muslims during their Friday prayers in the Cave of the Patriarchs or Ibrahimi Mosque in Hebron. He was beaten to death by survivors and rioting immediately followed, leading to 125 injured Palestinians and 26 deaths as well as nine Israeli deaths. A few days later, despite the high tensions, Ruchama remembers that PHR-I held a mobile clinic in Beit Ommar, just north of Hebron. The clinic was held in a private home and the health care providers did not finish until late in the afternoon. Despite feeling very hungry, because it was Ramadan and the Palestinian hosts were fasting, Ruchama recalls saying, "Don't feed us, it is the middle of Ramadan." The hosts explained that the Israelis were their guests and insisted that they eat a good meal. The Palestinians stood in a circle around the Israelis watching them as they ate and Ruchama noticed that there were no women present. When she inquired, she was informed that the women were all in the kitchen. When she asked why, she was told in a congenial manner, "It is not done." She responded with her usual spunkiness, "If they are not able to come to the upper floor, maybe I'll go to the kitchen to say thank you for a good meal." Three women from the Israeli contingent went downstairs to the kitchen and were warmly received.

> I can't tell you how happy the women were, speaking Hebrew, Arabic, a bit of English. The men up there well knew we have different ways of seeing life. There was no mood of disagreement. I blame the Palestinians for this good mood. It's a generality but they have a generous way of dealing with us. They are not harsh. Most of the smiling is real. After I went upstairs, this well-to-do man said, "I know what you meant, going down to the kitchen."

Such are the opportunities as well as the moments of irony that the mobile clinic provides to reach across the many divides that separate Israelis and Palestinians.

The Psychiatrist as an Agent of Social Control

Since those early visits to Gaza, Ruchama has continued to explore the issues surrounding the role of psychiatrists as agents of social control and as the establishers of social norms. In the book, *From the Margins of Globalization: Critical Perspectives on Human Rights*, Ruchama wrote a chapter based on a lecture given at the Tenth Annual Conference of the Israeli Psychiatric Society in 2000.[1] She argues that the recognition of human rights is intimately connected with the development of psychiatry. Psychiatrists now have quasi-judicial powers, determining who is mentally fit to stand trial, who is dangerous, who must be confined to mental institutions, and who has adequate intelligence and skill to be tried. Implicit in this responsibility is the upholding of the human rights of prisoners, particularly prisoners who suffer from mental illness. She explains that the ability of the psychiatrist to perform these critical tasks is directly related to the psychiatrist's awareness of his or her socio-political role and personal biases. Unless the physician is fully in touch and able to examine his or her "system of motives, emotions, fears and prejudices – as well as his or her rapport with the patient,"[2] there is a significant risk that the psychiatrist will become an agent of the state rather than a protector of the patient.

Ruchama finds that when Jewish Israeli psychiatrists are blind to their own subjectivity and the power of their own political needs and prejudices, they are at risk of seeing a Palestinian prisoner as "nothing more than a 'criminal,' an 'Arab,' a 'terrorist,' … nothing more than the representative of a group, with stereotypical characteristics."[3] The ultimate risk when the psychiatrist does not develop a sense of self-awareness regarding his or her own socio-political values and cultural concerns is the denial of the Palestinian prisoner, not only of basic human rights, but of the "right to madness."[4] In this analysis, there is no such thing as a neutral observer; rather the physician is required to recognize his or her preconceptions in order to evaluate adequately the patient/prisoner. If repeated self-analysis and processing of counter-transference is not done, then the psychiatrist is at risk for uncritically accommodating to the needs of the state and its worldview, rather than the emotional and human needs of the patient/prisoner.

> One should bear in mind that mentally ill prisoners are a minority within a minority, and they often suffer from very severe violations of human rights. When mentally ill prisoners are members of a different cultural and national group than that of their psychiatrist, the difference becomes a decisive factor in the diagnosis and treatment – which raises the question concerning the psychiatrist's personal stance when his patient is from a different culture or nationality. What is the psychiatrist's position when the patient is a Palestinian – not only a foreigner, but also the enemy? Is the psychiatrist aware of his subjective position, which perceives his patient as a "terrorist," i.e., as a real threat to society's security? Such a view might be so encompassing as to conceal all other parts of the patient's humanity. The specific role ascribed to Israeli psychiatry, to protect "public security," can obscure the boundaries between the psychiatrist's professional judgment and his political beliefs, and this may occur without sufficient self-awareness.[5]

Ruchama's publicly stated concerns that Jewish Israeli psychiatrists have made incorrect diagnoses of Palestinian prisoners due to the physicians' unconscious and unexamined values and allegiances have brought her into conflict with both the Israeli Psychiatric Association and the IMA. She documented that mentally ill Palestinian prisoners are often diagnosed as imposters or manipulators in order to uphold their ability to stand trial. After trial, solitary confinement is also used both for protective purposes and disciplinary action, the latter being forbidden under Israeli law and creating potential risk to the affected prisoner. "People usually do not die from solitary confinement – they simply become insane."[6] The unwillingness of the IMA to discuss these issues, she states, is related to the "socio-political need to see Palestinians as the enemy, as terrorists, and as dangerous."[7] She does not suspect that most psychiatrists are intentionally violating human rights, but rather, that the need to see Palestinians as the enemy is a critical unifying ideology for Israeli society. "The presence of the enemy is essential for maintaining the link and the interconnection between the patriotic Zionist discourse and the action deriving from this discourse – occupation, oppression, arrests and torture."[8]

The search for ethical guidelines is most urgent with regard to the use of torture and prisoners. In 1993, PHR-I asked the IMA to address the issue of physician participation in the examinations by the Israeli General Security Services. PHR-I alleged that the security services employed interrogation methods consistent with torture. Ruchama, along with journalist Michal Peleg and lawyer Tamar Peleg, found that physicians were required to examine the detainee before and during interrogations, to set guidelines and limits. Psychologists then assisted in developing techniques based on the detainee's mental and emotional vulnerabilities, the different clinicians all becoming deeply complicit in the act of torture itself. The IMA did not respond positively until 1999 when the Israeli High Court banned the use of torture. Ruchama states:

> Psychiatry can use its powers to determine norms that respect and accentuate the human rights of all people, patients and prisoners, or it can use its powers in a perverse manner, establishing and maintaining unethical and amoral norms.
>
> Tragically, in Israel, psychiatrists have frequently chosen to use their power in a perverse way. In order to do so, they have violated an unwritten rule of Western psychiatry – the rule which calls upon them to remove the mentally ill from the social sphere.
> [...]
> Within the power game managed by the state to silence the voices of the "other," the psychiatrist becomes complicit so long as he or she does not actively resist the prevailing mood.[9]

Ruchama ultimately called on the Israeli Psychiatric Association and its umbrella organization, the IMA, to recognize the political, cultural, and social influences that affect psychiatrists. She asked that they develop regulations regarding the protection of human rights, particularly for Palestinians and Palestinians with mental illness.

Impact of the Holocaust

As I listen to and read the words of Ruchama, a troubling and painful question keeps resurfacing. Jewish Israelis are often immigrants and have had the experience of oppression, ghettos, and racial hatred at the hands of dominant anti-Semitic societies. How have these Israelis moved to a place where they are able to do some of the same terrible things that were done to them? Returning to the living room discussion, Ruchama responds carefully with a deep sadness and sense of irony.

> If I would like to be cynical, which of course I don't want to be, I would say that we graduated a very good school and we learned very well how to do those things. Maybe the Holocaust, which I hate to do it, but I need to do it, was involved in this kind of turn of the whole concept of life, worldview, principles of life, that we Israelis moved from *how* to live, which is a moral question, how do I conduct my life, to the other question, *do* I live. For the sake of *do* I live, I am willing to do many things, including the things we did and the things we are doing. Then the moral questions become irrelevant and people like me and like us are mocked, are ridiculed, and in Hebrew they have a very specific word for it, "beautiful souls," but it is very pejorative ["bleeding hearts"].

She reminds us that there were movements within Zionism, like those dominated by Yehuda Magnes and Martin Buber, that conceived of a very different philosophy, but these movements were lost in the struggle for the creation of the state. The excessive use of power has become a very attractive and dominant ideology and this has intensified since the onset of the Second Intifada in October 2000. Much like the child of abusive parents, Israelis are capable of committing their own abuses in the name of security and in defense of their own sense of victimhood. Psychologically, a victim in this sense is both powerless and free of blame.

> We see ourselves as victims, even though we are for a very long time, not victims anymore. It's very useful, I'm afraid, because being a victim gives you a lot of license to do awful things and still you are right, at least in your own eyes. This is why many things in Israel, officially, are compared to the Holocaust and it's right by itself, in a very unfair way, because you cannot compare things that were done to us in the Holocaust to other things, but

if you do this comparison, then, ha, ha, nothing compares to this so we are right to do whatever we are doing. It is to protect ourselves that this Holocaust will not happen again. That's what Begin said time and again, and many others. Arafat is Hitler sitting in his bunker in Beirut. Come on.

In an article, "The Psychological Impact of the Second Intifada on Israeli Society," Ruchama clarified these ideas.

> Israelis have held on to their own historical victim status long past its salient historical time. The State of Israel is the strongest military power in the Middle East and possesses nuclear capacities, the strongest air-force and many other sophisticated weapons. Israel occupies Palestine and controls the lives of Palestinians, as well as their natural resources and economy. In spite of all this, Israelis maintain that they are the Palestinians' victims. Death and destruction caused by Palestinian suicidal-bombers in Israel serve to fuel these feelings.[10]

Ruchama sweeps her hand in a gesture of incredulity, takes a drag on her cigarette, and explains,

> People used to say we have six million licenses that go for the six million that were killed in Europe in the Second World War. Then we have our wonderful ideas about ourselves and everything goes together, empowering each other because being Jews we are by nature moral, by nature pure, by nature right and just, and maybe something else, and chosen that's for sure.

Disturbances of the Psyche

As a psychiatrist, Ruchama finds the defense mechanism of splitting is common within Israeli society and this leads to disturbances in the collective and individual psyche. Israelis often split the world into the *us*, "right, pure, moral, just, victimized," and the *other*,

> just the opposite of it and don't confuse me with facts because I am not willing to hear them or to understand them or to take them into consideration. It's a huge big denial of facts and it's very powerful. People in Israel, they have no idea of what's going on in the Occupied Territories, not because it's impossible to know, it's very easy to know. But they have their very good reasons not to know and they don't.

Members of the medical delegation have just been in the Occupied Territories and we have seen Israeli soldiers manning checkpoints, either as young recruits or as returning reservists. We are aware of the hundreds of thousands of Jewish settlers living beyond the Green Line. We wonder how it is possible to be unaware of the conditions. Ruchama explains that it is actually very easy, that most Jewish Israelis do not have interactions with Palestinians and that their Jewish sons do not talk about their army experiences. When they do, the discussion is frequently framed quite naturally in the context of the brave soldier dealing with the Arab terrorists and savages who want to kill him.

This mindset complements governmental decisions designed to acquire Palestinian land and transfer Palestinians away from that land. This coalesces with the messianic beliefs of 10 to 20 percent of the Jewish settlers and their supporters in Israel. Together this makes it possible not only to mistreat Palestinian civilians with impunity, but also to scar the ancient hills and landscape of the West Bank with military installations, bypass roads, and barbed wire, creating an endless armed camp. The Zionist movement along with the religiously motivated are willing to take these measures in order ultimately to claim all of the land. Ruchama urges us not to ignore the historical contribution of Israeli behavior to Palestinian violence that then makes it possible for Israelis to avoid taking responsibility for both the past and the future. She feels that there is an absence of historical memory in cause and outcome and a collective repetition compulsion "that may drive Israelis to do the unspeakable in the name of self-preservation; it has replaced every other moral or other thing." Security has become the unchallenged justification for governmental and civilian actions.

> We are living in a kind of isolated present, in a way, with no past, unless the very ancient past, but not what happened last week or last month, and with no vision of the future. People who are in the middle, in the present time, with no past and no future, are by nature very confused, because they have no horizon, no direction. The government really loves this condition, because people who are confused, it's easy to make them frightened, and scared, and people who are frightened, scared, and confused, those are the people who are the best for the government because they can be controlled. Frightened people just want a strong man to protect them. Whenever a bomb is happening here or there, ha, everyone is surprised. They don't remember that a few days ago we killed people in the Occupied Territories and this is a kind of revenge. One of the outcomes of the situation is that there is no critical thinking and no opposition to the government. Every time there is an explosion, a suicidal bomber, that is exactly where history begins.

Living in the "politics of the last atrocity," an expression from Northern Ireland, leads the population to seek more and more power and protection. Ruchama reminds us, "The word 'security' is the most holy word in Israel" and accounts for the popularity of men like Ariel

Sharon. Ruchama notes that Sharon's vision, like the governments' before him, involves emptying the land of the troublesome and treacherous Palestinian population.

> Sharon wants the Palestinians to get out of Palestine. He really believes in all kinds of transfer and to take more and more land and to kill more and more people, and those that can not be killed, let them suffer so much that they will prefer for their own good or for their own lives to go elsewhere. Then, believe it or not, the land will be "empty" again and we can take it. He wants the Greater Israel. I mean more land and less Palestinians, in one sentence. The ways to get to it are more or less the same, most of the time, killing, frightening, suffocating, destroying the civil society, and things like this.

Ruchama hesitates to talk about the future and she does not have a hopeful vision to share. Her analysis is complicated by the traumas she sees within Palestinian society. She suggests that the Palestinian Authority frequently acts as a "battered wife," trying to please the abusive husband, Israel, and at the same time trying to cause him pain. She notes that there are democratic forces within this society, such as the movement led by Dr. Haider Abd El Shafi and Dr. Mustafa Barghouthi, which "are working on self-empowerment, creating better society, not collaborating with Israel regarding security, and ending violence against Israel. I appreciate this, but Palestinians are also 'graduates of a very good school' and do stupid things."

Uniquely Righteous and Often Wronged, Building Walls

In "Transparent Wall, Opaque Gates," written with Dr. Dalit Baum, Ruchama argues that there is an "imagined collective of Zionist Israelis."[11] This group is bound together by an over-riding and self-perpetuating experience of victimhood that demands a vigorous army which is purely self-defensive in nature (the Israeli *Defense* Force), and inherently moral in attitude and behavior. Wrapped in the long shadow of the Holocaust and the ongoing Arab threat, whether in the form of invasion, demography, or suicide bombings, these Israelis share a "deterministic belief that 'the whole world is against us.' 'The Arabs' too become part of this ahistorical enemy entity, focused wholly on Jewish destruction, always intent on 'throwing us into the sea.'"[12] The other important principle necessary to maintain this single-minded conviction of a uniquely righteous and often wronged people is the belief that pre-1948 Palestine was an empty land, available for the taking, and rightfully due to the Jewish people.

Ruchama writes that this formulation worked relatively well until the First Intifada, when it became more difficult "not to see Palestinians."[13] Now, the rapidly growing separation wall that is snaking through the West Bank is not only a physical barrier that exists for "protection," but also a metaphorical blinder that acts to conceal the existence of Palestinians altogether. From a psychological viewpoint, making Palestinians invisible enables Jewish Israelis to forget the existence, suffering, and humanity of the people on the other side. Ruchama writes, "A useful way of understanding some of the psychological mechanisms involved in the Wall is the concept of splitting...It permits only two extremes: the whole world is split into 'good' and 'bad,' with nothing in between."[14] She explains that according to psychologist Melanie Klein, splitting is the most primitive defense mechanism created by high levels of anxiety and a need to compartmentalize intolerably strong positive and negative emotions. The irony is that this conceptualization requires continuous psychological energy and is not effective as a long-term solution because anxiety is blocked rather than explored, negotiated, and ultimately reduced.

Ruchama explains, by splitting the external as well as internal aspects of the good self from the bad self, it is psychologically possible to project the unwanted parts of the self to the "other," i.e. Palestinians. It is then possible to despise these projected parts and attributes that now become inherent in the "other." The separation wall in her analysis is perceived purely as an act of self-defense, a protection against that savage aggression associated with Palestinians. "The Wall allows the ZIC [Zionist Israeli Collective] self not to see itself as aggressive, violent, cruel, possessive, a violator of human rights, by projecting all these traits on the Palestinians beyond the Wall."[15]

In a land extolled for its stark and ancient beauty and the vibrant Mediterranean sunlight, the separation wall is paradoxically both opaque and ugly as it slashes across the landscape. It could be argued that it is an attempt to create a simple technological solution to a complex historical, political, and psychological morass, ostensibly separating civilized, modern Israeli democracy from savage Palestinian backwardness and violence. Ruchama writes,

It is opaque in order to prevent the sight of misery and suffering on the other side. If it were transparent, we could actually see the troubling suffering of the people on the other side.

It is ugly – because it serves the need to create the illusion of an evil, ugly monster on the other side, rather than ordinary people. The Palestinian existence within the wall is considered inferior, ugly, dirty, violent, and dangerous.[16]

Away from population centers where the separation wall is an undulating series of razor wire fences, rolls of barbed wire, trenches, and military roads, there are various surveillance techniques and sensors that enable the Israelis "to oversee them [the Palestinians]... with nonhuman sight, through a gun sight."[17] Thus in its most sinister aspects, the separation wall creates a reassuring physical deterrent for the troubled Israeli psyche, while treating all Palestinians as potential suicide bombers. This obstacle adds to the checkpoints, roadblocks, and closed military zones that constrict movement throughout the West Bank, providing a blunt physical barrier not only to feared future terrorism, but also to the possibility of empathy, recognition, and observation of human suffering.

Additionally an extensive permit system has been created by the Israeli authorities. This includes the requirement that Palestinians now living in the seam area, the land between the separation wall and the Green Line, must apply for permits to live in their own homes or to move in and out of the area in the course of their daily lives. This has resulted in a de facto "buffer zone, an added volume to the physical obstacle, a living Wall."[18] Ruchama postulates that from a psychological analysis, just as in an obsessive disorder, "The body's orifices are conceived as danger zones, through which hostile agents may penetrate, infect, and cause disease or death."[19] The Israeli military concept of establishing increasingly bureaucratic and arbitrary but strict control of all openings in the wall mirrors the obsessive's need to control all of the body's orifices, and is a ritualistic attempt to preserve oneself through increasingly illogical and complex behaviors as anxiety mounts.

A child will refuse food or stop defecating as a display of control in front of worried or angry parents. Opening and closing the sphincters at will, despite outside pressures (international critique, international law) as well as strong pressures from within (economic necessities, state laws), indicates a fear of powerlessness in front of big and powerful parents, and a need to display basic and crude control of the situation.[20]

The separation wall with all of its gates and metaphors serves not only as the flashpoint where the powerful occupying force uses its power to control the occupied civilian population, but also as a distressing measure of the occupiers' own fundamental assumptions and fears.

I think of the graffiti I have seen spray-painted on the Palestinian side of those imposing concrete slabs, an upsetting reminder of the impact of the wall on those who are walled in. Much of the graffiti expresses outrage and historical irony. My gaze is gripped by the large lettering in English, Hebrew, and Arabic: "From Warsaw Ghetto to Abu Dis Ghetto," a swastika with the word "copy" next to a Star of David with the word "original," "Berlin 1953," "Fuck Nazi Sharon," and "Death to Fascists." There are also brightly painted expressions of hope: "Peace no wall," and "This wall will fall." Lately a more whimsical, very realistically drawn, eye-catching wall art has emerged. A little girl floats up the wall grasping a cluster of helium balloons. An incredibly realistic ladder is painted leaning all the way to the top. Huge scissors cut along a large, rectangular dashed line. A gentle fold at the base of the wall is depicted as if the wall were made of paper, revealing a lush, leafy forest with ferns and a stream. Gigantically oversized stuffed chairs circle a table under a window that reveals a scenic view of distant mountains. Trying to understand the psychological implications of these drawings in the context of Ruchama's writings, I wonder if the graffiti are not only a form of resistance, but also an attempt to change the meaning of the wall itself through the eyes of the people now living within these modern ghettos.

Rising Levels of Violence within Israeli Society

What is the personal price of this situation for Israelis? PHR-I has documented a dramatic increase in aggression and violence within Israeli society in the last few years, particularly violence towards women in the form of murder and rape. Ruchama suggests that serving in the Israeli army results in not only a devaluation of Palestinian life, dignity, and property, but also an increased tolerance of unacceptable levels of violent behavior and aggressive solutions that easily spill into

Israeli civil society. This is complicated by the dissonant experience of believing that the aggressive use of power will assure Israeli safety and the experience that military assaults against Palestinians only produce more Palestinian resistance and violence. As Ruchama writes,

> The mechanism of cognitive dissonance demands dissonance-reducing behaviors. Israelis cannot give up the belief that force is essential: This might destroy Israel's military character and policies. On the other hand, Israelis cannot ignore the overwhelming reality of children, women and men torn apart by explosives detonated in buses and restaurants. They choose, therefore, to turn a blind eye to the causal connection between excessive Israeli military power and the Palestinians' violent actions. This dissonance-reducing solution leads to feelings of loss of control and helplessness. Despite all the power in their hands, Israelis feel frightened, threatened and unprotected.[21]

The Activities of Physicians for Human Rights-Israel

This brings us back to the afternoon in Ruchama's home, the question of public discourse and principled dissent, a militarily powerful but psychologically fragile and traumatized Israeli population, and the responsibility of physicians in a conflict area. In an article entitled "Doctors and the Duty of Intervention," Ruchama describes a significant difficulty.[22] She sees policy-makers and a public that unconsciously disregard or avoid reality coupled with a belief system in which they themselves are inherently incapable of wrong-doing. Ruchama admits that her early belief that an Israeli public exposed to the uncomfortable realities on the ground would be shocked and moved to rectify social injustice proved naïve. The activities of PHR-I, "have been looked upon with disdain, hatred and fear. People did not want to confront the facts. As chair of PHR, this rage was often directed against me. For several years, I received frequent phone calls threatening me and accusing me of being a traitor, and a self-hating Jew." At the same time, Ruchama finds that the humanitarian part of the work of PHR-I is sometimes used by the media to create a more altruistic and compassionate picture of Israelis as well as to subvert the political implications of PHR-I's activities.

> Instead of building a bridge between people [PHR-I is] portrayed as patronizing; instead of acting in solidarity, we are portrayed as condescending; instead of making a political protest, our activity is illustrated as a

non-political humanitarian mission. In such ways, Israeli society protects the basic assumptions of its consensual worldview while identifying itself with PHR or other groups that actually object to this worldview.

Despite these forces, Ruchama asserts that PHR-I must continue to bring uncomfortable truths to the public discourse and to demand the recognition of the intrinsic connections between health care, politics, and human rights.

The Love of a Granddaughter

With all the controversy and stress in her life, Ruchama admits that she is lucky to have a new passion, her granddaughter Naomi. "She is a kind of joy which I never experienced before, intelligent, pretty, the cutest I ever saw. The moment I saw her, three minutes old, immediately I fell in love. What is even more beautiful, it's mutual. She loves back in such an open, clear way." Ruchama reflects that she didn't have the privilege of that instant love affair with her own daughter and son. Life was too frantic, she was too tired, and her former husband was not child-focused or supportive. Now she is enjoying the benefits and sweetness of grandmotherhood. She laughs and says that when this lively two-year-old was younger, Ruchama would call her "joya" which is Italian for "bliss."

As the interview comes to a close, Ruchama leans forward with her usual sense of urgency and self-deprecating style, but a coy twinkle dances in her eyes. "Tell your people that when you saw me I was sick with flu, tired, and that will excuse some of my appearance and talking. Promise me." I do.

3
Gila Svirsky: Liberating Israel

I N MAY 2001 I FIRST met Gila Svirsky when she was speaking in Boston and then in 2005 I had the opportunity to interview her in Tel Aviv with other members of the medical delegation. Her story is one of a US-born woman struggling with the contradictions that she faced when she fell in love with Israel, made *aliyah*, and then was confronted with realities she could not in good conscience ignore. Her personal history helps us to understand how a young Jewish girl from America can undergo dramatic transformations in her life and the personal, religious, and political consequences of this passage. We listen to her as she moves from Jewish orthodoxy to a life in a different place on the socio-political spectrum, working for social justice and peace. Exploring the journey of her family, the early clash between a yearning for Zion and a desire to live in America, the pull of religious orthodoxy and the ultimate journey to Israel reveals a fragment in the puzzle that came together to create Israeli society.

New Jersey Roots

In 1937, Gila Svirsky's Lithuanian parents settled in the US on a chicken farm in Iselin, New Jersey, and moved to Elizabeth when their daughter was five years old, joining the growing Jewish population and taking advantage of its Orthodox Jewish school. Facing rising anti-Semitism in Europe, Gila's father, Walter Schwartz, initially left Lithuania in 1928 and followed his siblings to the US, opening a chicken farm and continuing his love of all things Yiddish. Her mother, Sylvia, was a staunch Zionist and follower of Jabotinsky, the right-wing militaristic voice of Revisionist Zionism during the British Mandate in Palestine. She left Europe in 1935 and moved to Jerusalem where she became a "roomer" with distant cousins. She scorned the Yiddish culture into which she had been born and insisted that Hebrew was her mother tongue. Walter came to visit his parents in Jerusalem, met his distant cousin Sarah (later Americanized to Sylvia), and took her back to America. It is hard to know why this 21-year-old passionate Zionist ideologue fell in love with a man eleven years her senior, worldly, intellectual, literary, but with no interest in staying in Jerusalem. For 20 years living in New Jersey, Sylvia struggled bitterly, yearning for the life she had abandoned in Palestine.

In 1946, into the push-pull of this family, sheltered in a virtual Jewish ghetto, Gila was born. Although her parents were not Orthodox, for a while Gila attended the Jewish Educational Center, a *yeshiva* or religious Jewish day school. The *yeshiva* boasted a renowned ultra-Orthodox rabbi, "the pope of *Yiddishkayt*," strongly anti-Zionist, and deeply committed to bringing the Jews of Russia to the US. He advocated a stern, rigid form of Judaism that did not appeal to Gila who became increasingly rebellious. Nonetheless, as a result of attending a variety of Zionist programs, she grew up feeling strongly rooted in the Jewish Orthodox Zionist community. She later attended Brandeis University in Waltham, Massachusetts, attracted at first to the kosher kitchen on campus. While in the Boston area, she became involved with a Hassidic community and immersed herself in a more joyful stream of Orthodoxy. Gila moved to Israel at the age of 19 following a junior year abroad at Hebrew University, returning briefly to the US to complete her degree in philosophy. While doing her Masters in Israel at the Hebrew University in Jerusalem, she joined the Orthodox religious scene, voting with the National Religious Party, which supported the merging of religion and state affairs and, in the 1970s, espoused the expansion of settlements into the Biblical Land of Israel.

Early Years in Israel

In March 2005 the medical project delegates interview Gila in her West Jerusalem home, a modest but comfortable apartment in the upscale neighborhood of Baka. Before 1948, many wealthy Palestinians had beautiful homes in Baka. In the 1960s the Israeli government built public housing in the area to cope with the influx of Jewish immigrants. With a unique blend of softness and intensity, Gila shares the heady excitement of that time.

> It was in 1965 that I came to Israel for my junior year and the Six Day War came a year later. It was a very exciting time for all of us. Those of us who didn't have people who died in the war were thrilled over the fact that we were plucked from the jaws of destruction. I think that turned so many of us into people who could not leave this country. Right after the Yom Kippur War in 1973, the settler movement began in earnest; people going into the territories, into Hebron, and all over. In the beginning it struck me as a very idealistic movement. I was very happy and proud of my friends who went to settlements. One day, I was still at the university. I picked up my toothbrush and I said, "I'm joining them." I went down to one of the settlements south of Jerusalem, I spent the weekend with my friends, and I said, "You know this is really exciting and I love it, but I have to go back and finish my degree and then afterwards I'll join you."

After completing her studies, Gila taught communications at Hebrew University and at the Lifta Experimental High School in Jerusalem. In 1972, she married Shimon, an Israeli who had grown up in Los Angeles, and became immersed in raising two daughters.

Despite her initial enthusiasm, Gila gradually became aware of a certain ambivalence over the values of her settler friends. "Things that were very troubling to me about the settlement movement were above all their triumphalism over Arab neighbors, their lording it over Arab neighbors, their brutal attitudes towards the surrounding Arabs. I am saying Arabs because in those years we didn't think of them as Palestinians, especially people with my politics." Gila recalls that the Yom Kippur War in 1973 was also the first time that many Israelis began to distrust their own government. She remembers watching Chaim Herzog, the authorized governmental spokesperson and future President of Israel, pointing to maps and troop positions and realizing that he might not be telling the truth. A general public sense of disillusionment and loss of faith set in during this period, a dramatic change from the solid collective national purpose that had characterized Israelis in the past.

Over the next decade, Gila began to think that there was something fundamentally wrong in the relationship between the Israelis building homes and towns in the West Bank and the Arabs who bore the brunt of these settlements. Her husband, a non-Orthodox man who was born in "red Haifa," believed in Labor Zionism or socialism as the correct approach to building the country. He was a strong supporter of the Labor Party and ultimately had a great influence on her own thinking. Slowly she began to vote Labor and to, "open my eyes and open my ears. I was not very active in anything or thinking much about anything. I was a young mother, raising two children, trying to make a living." However, she describes herself as someone who was always questioning, starting with, "Is there really a God?" and moving gradually into political issues. Judaism for her was defined by culture and family much more strongly than by religion.

The Beginnings of Disillusionment and Political Awareness

Gila and her husband had friends who were further left politically than they, belonging to the precursor of Meretz, a secular, left-of-center party formed in 1992. When the war in Lebanon broke out in 1982, Gila began having more qualms about the government's policies and she and her husband attended their first Peace Now demonstration. She remembers feeling ambivalent about sending a non-supportive message to the Israeli troops fighting in Lebanon and, at the same time, feeling a deep discomfort with the war itself. It was at this point, particularly with the bombing of Beirut after official reassurance that troops would not be deployed that deeply into Lebanon, that Gila began overtly distrusting the Israeli government. Adding to that growing sense of betrayal came news of the massacres in the Sabra and Shatilla Refugee Camps south of Beirut. Hundreds of Palestinian refugees were murdered by the Phalange, a Christian Maronite militia, as the Israeli military, under the leadership of Ariel Sharon, averted their eyes to the killings they could have prevented. This event shocked Gila as well as many Israelis, and was a critical turning point. She started attending more Peace Now rallies where she remembers an infectious sense of optimism. In 1982, Peace Now organized what is now called the 400,000 Rally, the largest rally ever held in Israel. They called for a commission of inquiry into the Sabra and Shatilla massacres and the commission subsequently recommended that Ariel Sharon be removed as Defense Minister. The dismissal was carried out, although he returned to power as Prime Minister in 2001.

In 1985 Gila was appointed director in Israel of the New Israel Fund, an international funding agency that supports groups working for civil and human rights, promoting tolerance and working on the reduction of socio-economic inequality in Israel. It was here that Gila had a more serious exposure to the host of inequalities that face Arab citizens of Israel, to the conceptual idea of feminism, and to the lack of religious pluralism and tolerance in Israel for non-Orthodox Jews. It was in this context that the young idealist who had arrived in Israel filled with an uncritical fervor and devotion began to face the serious contradictions now more blatantly apparent to her in Israeli society.

In 1987, after 15 years of marriage, Gila and her husband divorced, she took her mother's maiden name, and began to mix with feminists, anti-governmental activists, and environmental advocates. She started exploring the lesbian scene and fell in love with an Israeli woman, who was also a newcomer to lesbianism. Her new partner was a committed progressive and they discussed different left political platforms and explored issues related to the conflict and economics.

Meeting with the "Enemy"

The First Intifada broke out in December 1987 and Gila was confronted with so much death and rioting that she felt compelled to act, not out of any political analysis, but as she said, "Why can't everyone be nice to each other?" On the urging of her partner, she started by joining a vigil of Women in Black, which had formed in January 1988. Every Friday she gathered with a group of women standing on a street corner in Jerusalem. "I held a sign that said 'End to Violence' and everyone else held signs that said, 'Stop the Occupation.'" "I came to understand that politics was driving the conflict, not some inchoate inexplicable violence. I began to take responsibility for being an occupier, and therefore I began to take responsibility for ending it." She remembers these early vigils feeling very vulnerable as well as courageous in the face of hostile comments made by angry people passing by.

A few years later, as a member of Women in Black, Gila was invited to the home of an acquaintance, Judy Blanc, a longtime Communist activist, friendly with left-wing Palestinians. The friend was hosting a guest that she wanted Gila to meet.

I went and her guest was lovely, spoke English in a beautiful Oxford accent, and we spoke all evening about the great food and the great restaurants we had eaten in. At some point I said to her, "Rita, where are you from?" She said, "Ramallah." I said, "No, no, before Ramallah." She said, "No, I am born and brought up in Ramallah." I said, "No, you couldn't be from Ramallah. You're not Palestinian are you?" She said, "Yes I am Palestinian." She was Dr. Rita Giacaman [a prominent member of the Palestinian women's movement and now director of the Department of International Community Health at Birzeit University]. Well I was shocked. This was the first time that I had ever had a conversation with a Palestinian. I was 43 years old. I didn't know that Palestinians were like us. It sounds so stupid and so simple but Israelis and Palestinians never meet.

Gila found Rita to be both articulate and sensitive as she discussed the suffering her family experienced under occupation. She mentioned to Gila that the PLO, headed by Yasser Arafat, had recognized the State of Israel from his headquarters in Tunisia in 1988 at a meeting of the Palestinian National Council. When Gila expressed disbelief that she had never seen that stated in the Israeli press, Rita informed her that the Israeli Broadcasting Authority had refused to carry any reports on the activities of the PLO. Gila doubted that such censorship existed in *her* Israel, but when she investigated the topic further, she found that Rita was correct. Gila was able to find the reports that the PLO had met in Tunisia and accepted the existence of the State of Israel, and a two state solution to the conflict. This was an eye opening revelation.

The next critical experience occurred after Gila had been vigiling with Women in Black for several years and she was approached by In'am, a Palestinian woman from Gaza. In'am was visiting Jerusalem and accidentally came across the demonstration. The woman shared her excitement that there were Israelis who were working to end the occupation, as she had been unaware that a peace movement even existed within Israel. The two women exchanged pleasantries and phone numbers and promised to visit each other. Several weeks later, In'am called Gila desperately asking for help. Her 16-year-old son Osama had been arrested and she was trying to get him out of jail. Gila asked sceptically about the charges and learned that the teenager had been arrested by the Israeli army for writing political graffiti. "I thought, oh my goodness, what did he write? She said, he wrote, 'Two states for two nations'. This was illegal in Gaza in those years. He and eight other friends were all arrested." Gila agreed to help her find a lawyer and embarked on an eight month odyssey that opened her eyes in ways she could not have predicted. Laughing with the bemused amazement of hindsight, she admits,

> I visited her [In'am] in her beautiful home in Gaza. I didn't even know that Palestinians had bathrooms; this is how stereotyped I had Palestinians and how ignorant I was. There was a wonderful family; she taught English, he taught mechanics, all their five children today have gone through universities with flying colors, they have a beautiful home, they have bathrooms just like real people, and eight months it took me to learn that Palestinians are normal like us. So that was really my education.

After eight months in jail, the boys were found guilty as charged and sentenced to the eight months they had already served. Gila explains straightforwardly that this young man went on to graduate from a French university and he is now a water engineer. He initially returned to Gaza to work on water issues but after the Israeli army destroyed much of the water infrastructure, the young man returned to France where he how lives with his wife. His four siblings took degrees in surgery, computers, advertising, and diplomacy. The two women still call each other every few weeks and maintain an intimate, heartfelt relationship. One thing they always agree on is that all of the leaders are *"majnoon,"* which in Arabic means "crazy."

Challenging the Stereotypes

As Gila became more involved in anti-occupation causes, she began visiting the Occupied Territories and discovering the common human experiences that she shared with Palestinian families. In the territories, she worked with B'Tselem, an Israeli human rights organization formerly funded by the New Israel Fund. Gila's old friendships with members of the Orthodox community who were committed to the building of settlements changed as her political outlook evolved. She observes that a strong religious commitment is often a barrier to positive political growth.

> Today I do have Orthodox friends. I am no longer Orthodox but my Orthodox friends are people who share politics with me. I have to say my politics is not radical. I have never been one of those who consider themselves anti-Zionist or who want to see an end to the State of Israel. I am very much in favor of a two state solution. I very much consider myself

a Zionist and for me that is not about controlling land, that's about the character of the State of Israel, making it the kind of place we imagined would be here when we founded it.

When Gila left the New Israel Fund in 1991, she knew she wanted to work on issues related to women, human rights, and education. She joined the board of the Adam Institute for Peace and Democracy, a group that develops and implements educational projects aimed at breaking down stereotypes and teaching non-violent conflict resolution to Jews, Arabs, Israelis, Palestinians, and international students. She was also active in founding Kol Ha-Isha, the Woman's Voice. This is a grassroots feminist women's center in Jerusalem where women of all backgrounds and persuasions can meet, celebrate women's culture, and develop programs that empower and support each other while working on models for social change, peace, and tolerance. Her greatest involvement was with B'Tselem, literally in Hebrew, "in the image of," but synonymous with "human dignity." She was asked to chair the board, and thus became focused on documenting human rights violations in the Occupied Territories while working in an organization dedicated to changing Israeli governmental policy. While she is still active in B'Tselem, she was drawn to the power of women's peace-making and consequently accepted the position of director of Bat Shalom, an Israeli feminist organization of Jews and Arabs working both on a peaceful resolution to the conflict and on an equal voice for Jewish and Arab women who are citizens of Israel. When the Second Intifada broke out, she and her friend Hannah Safran, a Haifa activist, called for a meeting of the existing women's peace organizations, at which they all agreed to join together and form the Coalition of Women for Peace. They hoped to increase the power of their individual voices and bring a feminist approach to peace-making.

The Birth of Feminist Peace-making

In 2005, the medical delegates assemble in Gila's living room, several members sitting on a blue suede couch, scattered with decorative woven pillows with geometric patterns in orange and blue and tassels at the corners. A brightly colored picture hangs over the couch and the room is decorated with dried grasses and Bedouin art. Gila's gray-green eyes, magnified by her large glasses, sparkle with intensity and warmth and her manner expresses a sense that what she has to say is utterly reasonable if anyone will just listen carefully. She is eager to share her thoughts on the Israeli peace movement in general and the work of activist women in particular and to comment on a recent documentary video about the Coalition of Women for Peace. Her face framed by silver curls, she explains that in 1978, the first major mainstream Israeli peace movement was founded called Peace Now, during the Israeli-Egyptian peace talks. At a point where the talks appeared to be breaking down, reserve officers and combat soldiers from the Israeli army published an open letter to the Prime Minister. Tens of thousands of Israelis sent letters of support for the original statement.

> We are writing this with deep anxiety, as a government that prefers the existence of the State of Israel within the borders of "Greater Israel" to its existence in peace with good neighborliness, will be difficult for us to accept. A government that prefers existence of settlements beyond the Green Line to elimination of this historic conflict with creation of normalization of relationships in our region will evoke questions regarding the path we are taking. A government policy that will cause a continuation of control over millions of Arabs will hurt the Jewish-democratic character of the state, and will make it difficult for us to identify with the path of the State of Israel.[1]

Gila notes that Israel made peace with Egypt, but the Lebanon War then broke out in 1982. Peace Now started to agitate, demanding that Israel stop its incursions into Lebanon and opposing the bombing of Beirut. Peace Now continued to play a very important role through all of these years. In 1988 when the PLO accepted UN Resolution 242 and the principle of a two state solution, Peace Now led the demonstration that demanded the Israeli government negotiate with the PLO, the official negotiating body for the Palestinian people. However, Gila adds,

> Peace Now was rather quiescent any time Labor got into power, any time Meretz was in power, because it was hand-in-glove with those political parties and was reluctant to criticize those parties. There were times though when it did speak out, but Peace Now is very careful not to distance itself from consensus opinion. We were very glad when it spoke out, but there was a feeling all along throughout the history that there is room for a more outspoken party. So the progressive peace movement was established. The women's peace movement began in January 1988, one month after the First Intifada broke out which was early December 1987, and there has been no turning back ever since.

Let me explain why the women's peace movement has been so prominent and outspoken. When Peace Now was holding its rallies, to our chagrin, there were no women speakers on the stage at any time, except, of course, for the woman who sang "*Hatikva*" at the end. But throughout, there were no women. There were no Arab Israelis speaking. There were no *Mizrachi* Israelis; those are Israelis from northern Africa and Asia, the Arab countries. It all together looked to us like a white boys' game with no room for the rest of us. It was not at all surprising that when the Women in Black movement began, so many women said, "Ah, a place where a woman's voice can be heard."

Women in Black

At this point Duchess the cat saunters into the living room to investigate the gathering. Gila introduces her as my "Cat in Black" and with a touch of wit and humor clarifies that Duchess was born and raised in Philadelphia and is an *olah*, a recent immigrant, who made *aliyah* to Israel. It was a "spiritual uplifting immigration, she's a Zionist cat." Once the cat is settled, an obvious veteran of political discussions, Gila returns to more serious topics.

> Women in Black is a presence in Israel, it's a symbol in Israel. Women dressed in black standing there completely silently or holding a sign that says "End the Occupation" every single week for the last 17 years. You cannot do your shopping for the Sabbath without coming across them. It has become the conscience of Israel, we like to think. Even and perhaps especially for those who disapprove of us and our views. We have stood there through a great deal of violence against us, some of it verbal, a good deal of it physical, and we intend to continue to stand until there is an end to the occupation.

Women in Black also sponsors international conferences to discuss the prevention of war, violence, and oppression. As a movement, it has spread to all five continents; the women of Serbia who protested the actions of Slobodan Milosevic are probably the other most well-known group outside of Israel. In 2001, there were rallies throughout Europe, Asia, and North America where tens of thousands of women in 150 cities demonstrated in solidarity with over 5000 Israeli and Palestinian Women in Black and their male supporters. The Israeli group marched from Israel to Palestinian towns carrying banners that stated, "The Occupation Is Killing Us All" and "We Refuse to Be Enemies." The international movements as well as the Israeli group have received a number of peace awards, and the Israeli and Serbian groups were nominated for the Nobel Peace Prize in 2001.

Gila adds that she has seen a great deal of harassment, especially during the First Intifada. At that time they were attacked by followers of Rabbi Meyer Kahane. They are a violent, reactionary movement advocating a theocratic "Greater Israel" and the forcible deportation of all non-Jewish citizens. The group circulated a flyer that named six "black widows" in reference to six members of Women in Black, with their names and phone numbers. Gila remembers a phone call where a strange, ominous voice said, "'We know where your children go to school.' That scared me a lot, but very little happened. It was mostly harassment, not serious damage. There were some homes that had their doors set on fire."

Coalition of Women for Peace

In November 2000, six weeks after the start of the Second Intifada, Gila helped found the Coalition of Women for Peace, bringing together the voices of nine women's peace organizations composed of Jewish and Palestinian Israeli citizens. These women attend each other's actions, share resources, and do outreach to Russian-speaking women and teens. The Coalition sponsors "reality tours" for mainstream Israelis, taking them to the separation wall, Palestinian refugee camps, and Israeli checkpoints in the West Bank. She notes that half the Coalition members are in their twenties and many young activists demonstrate at nonviolent protests, such as in the West Bank town of Bil'in, against the building of the separation wall and the actions of the Israeli soldiers.

> Let me just mention some of the basic principles of the Coalition of Women for Peace; it includes sharing Jerusalem, ending the occupation, a two state solution, each state independent, viable, sovereign, addressing the refugee problem in a way that would be just and equitable and general equality and justice for all Israeli citizens including Arabs, Mizrachim, and of course women.

Gila clicks on a DVD, her TV lights up, and she begins to describe the mass actions that the Coalition has organized, beyond the regular vigils and demonstrations. She adds to the narration of the film as crowds, banners, and soldiers flash on the screen.

In May 2003, we had a die-in in Tel Aviv where 1000 women lay down on the street dressed in black with a sign that said, "The Occupation Is Killing Us All." We have marched through the streets of Jerusalem with Palestinian women under a sign that says, "We Refuse to Be Enemies." We think that says it all. We refuse to raise our children to be enemies of each other. We want to raise our children and create a world that is much better than the one the generals have.

She describes meeting with Palestinian women's groups from the Occupied Territories, providing emergency and school supplies to women and children. She shows us video clips of Palestinian and Israeli women picking olives in the West Bank at harvest time. We hear Palestinian women singing and see the signs, "The Occupation Is Killing Us All." Sometimes the women are allowed to demonstrate peacefully, sometimes they are attacked by Israeli soldiers, tear gassed, and beaten. There are actions against the separation wall, such as in Mas'ha, a small West Bank town that is bisected by the barrier. The women are sometimes joined by internationals and by Knesset (Israeli parliament) members.

At first, the activists felt safe because the protesters were all women, but over time, Israeli soldiers started to shoot directly at demonstrators, no matter if they were men or women. As a mark of protest, the demonstrators started wearing targets on their shirts as if to defy the soldiers. We continue watching footage as Gila comments. "Now we see Israeli women in September 2003, marching towards the separation wall in Tulkaram bringing desperately needed school supplies to Palestinian women waiting on the other side, despite an exploding tear gas bomb." In another video clip, Gila explains,

This was April 2002, it was a very tense event. We were marching to enter Ramallah, to bring food supplies and medical supplies. We were a couple of thousand women and some men and the soldiers were massed to prevent us from entering. All we were doing was singing, this is in Arabic, here is the group. I don't know if you have a sense seeing the expressions on the faces, of the fear that they were going to open fire on us. These are women, the leadership of the Coalition of Women for Peace, calling for peacefulness. We sent this woman ahead to negotiate with the soldiers to permit our crossing and to allow the food to cross. In the midst of her negotiation, here is a tear gas canister, suddenly boom, everything came out, tear gas and stun grenades and many women were injured, over 20 ended up in hospital. After this, still there was chanting, "Occupation no, peace yes." And this is the truck load of supplies they let through.

She talks us through a demonstration in Tel Aviv by a group called Black Laundry, lesbians and gay men against the occupation. They are demanding that Sharon leave Ramallah where Arafat has his battered headquarters, chanting that the occupation is impoverishing Israelis as well as Palestinians, that there is no money for food and education in Israel. The women chant that Sharon has blood on his hands, and their own hands are dramatically dripping with red paint. The last vignette is a group organized by Bat Shalom, a mix of 50 Palestinian, Israeli, and international women. The women are marching and singing together to protest the construction of the separation wall; the local villagers are watching cautiously. The closer the crowd gets to the wall, the more nervous the soldiers appear. Three women walk towards the soldiers, holding their hands open to show they are not armed. The soldiers retreat and the commander shouts at the crowd to back up, that this is an illegal demonstration. We can hear the woman's voice saying, "We Palestinian, Israeli, international women are here to prove solidarity for peace." Before another word is spoken, the stun grenades and tear gas are unleashed, the women are backing away from the smoke, and the soldiers charge on horseback, beating some of the women with batons, fracturing one woman's shoulder. Gila ends her narration with, "This is a Hebrew song for peace that they have translated into Arabic. So that I think kind of says it all."

As we discuss Gila's political work, she mentions a distressing irony that adds to the complexity of the whole endeavor.

> We noticed that at dialogue groups [between Israeli and Palestinian women] the Israeli women were coming in order to declare to the Palestinian women that it's not us who wants the occupation. It is somebody else voting for the generals and somebody else who is making all your trouble. So we just want you to know that we are on your side. At some point a Palestinian woman said to me, "These dialogue groups appear to be a case of the Israeli women who come so that they sleep better at night, assuage their conscience that they're not guilty of any wrongdoing, whereas the Palestinian women are coming to prevent the Israeli women from sleeping well at night. They want them to know how they are suffering." So that's what it has been like very often in the dialogue groups. It's been "I want to tell you how much I am suffering" on one side, and on the other side "I want to tell you that I didn't do it to you, it's somebody else."

Thoughts from her Neighbors

The delegates wonder how all this activist work has affected Gila's relationships with her friends and neighbors who may not share her passion or be sympathetic to her viewpoints. She admits, "I keep my politics to myself in my neighborhood. If people walk into my house, they don't notice that all this decoration is Bedouin stuff, but when they go into the next room they will see all the posters but they don't often go into my office space." In the early years of this decade, there was an article about the Coalition in a major Israeli newspaper, *Ma'ariv*, with a picture of ten women, each representing a different group in the Coalition, with their names, addresses, and personal interviews. Gila's picture was featured there, and later on, one of her neighbors stopped by the house to pay his apartment dues and said, "Oh Gila, we won't fight about the fact that you are a member of Peace Now." She laughs because he could not distinguish Peace Now from the more activist organizations. They are all the same in his analysis and he disapproves of the whole collection, but he is still happy to be her neighbor. The article was ominously called "The Pariahs." On the other hand, she feels compelled to be an extra good neighbor, in charge of apartment dues and maintaining the grounds, as if she has to prove that a left-wing activist can be a responsible citizen as well.

She finds the distance between her views and mainstream Israeli opinion is often painful and explains that she concentrates on articulating issues with English speakers, focusing on her deep concern for Israel and Zionism. Nonetheless, she receives angry letters accusing her of traitorous activities and undermining Israel in the eyes of the world. She finds these indictments agonizingly distressing and notes that there is a certain irony behind that hostility. She explains that once women became organized in the peace movement, their ideology tended to be ahead of what she refers to as the "mixed gender" movement. As examples, she claims that women were talking about a two state solution before Peace Now adopted that platform. Women were advocating sharing Jerusalem as a capital and it is now part of the Labor Party platform. Women have also been more outspoken and daring as activists. They were the first to lie down in front of the Defense Ministry to prevent access to its buildings, the first to march through a checkpoint disregarding the orders of the soldiers, the first

to attempt to dismantle a checkpoint. Now many people participate
in such actions. It is somewhat reassuring that she finds:

> Public opinion in Israel has shifted radically. It is not just over the past two
> years, but over the past 20 years you can see a dramatic shift in Israeli public
> opinion. First of all, right now 68 percent of Israelis say that they want to
> give back all of Gaza. A similar number say they want to give back all or
> some of the settlements in the context of a peace agreement. They don't like
> to use the word "occupation." Occupation to them sounds like we've done
> something wrong. They use "disputed territories." That's why sometimes
> we say "The occupation is killing us all." We think that is a message they
> can more likely hear, than "End the occupation." Nevertheless, people are
> willing already to get out of the West Bank, not only Gaza, and that's very
> welcome and a great relief to us.

Gila adds that Sharon took a major step by using the word
"occupation" and by clearly stating, "We cannot continue to occupy
three-and-a-half million Palestinians. It is not good for us economically
or in any other way." His tremendous popularity is based on his promise
to end the occupation and create peace and security. "Even people who
are troubled by his blood soaked career, say to themselves, if Sharon
says we can end the occupation then we should do it." She warns that
there is a discrepancy between Sharon's utterances and his behavior
and there is clear opposition between Sharon's game plan and the "left"
game plan. "Sharon is leaving Gaza in order to entrench himself more
deeply in the West Bank. We in the left are saying he is leaving Gaza,
let's use that as leverage to get him to leave other places as well. Once
he has established the principle that you can leave settlements, we can
apply that elsewhere."

Facing the Difficult Questions

Gila believes that moves towards disengagement will lead to a two state
solution to the conflict, but her views have some intriguing nuances.
When asked if she feels that an Israeli state must always maintain a
Jewish majority, she admits this is a difficult question. She explains
that Jews worldwide need to have a place where they can feel safe *as
Jews*, a place to turn to should something terrible happen like another
Holocaust. "So Israel would continue to provide that as part of the
law of return *to Jews who suffer from anti-Semitism*, not just Jews in

general." On the other hand, she does not feel that Jews must always maintain their majority status. "I would like nothing better if over the course of time the number of non-Jews increased in Israel and we had a non-Jewish President and Prime Minister. I would think that would be a great success for us. Israel for me has to be a completely democratic country with complete equality for all citizens of Israel on every matter." Her only exception is the limited asylum for Jews suffering at the hands of anti-Semitism.

Nonetheless, she feels that a one state solution encompassing Israel and the Occupied Territories is totally impractical because at this point in history Israeli Jews do not feel safe in a country where they are not a clear majority. Because the number of Jews and Palestinians in the combined area of Israel and the Occupied Territories is approximately equal, the Jews would quickly become a frightened and threatened minority given the higher Palestinian birthrate. On the other hand, if there was a stable two state solution and Jews were a majority for a long time, then at some point in history with gradual demographic changes and the opportunity to build trust and a sense of security, with the special Jewish asylum exception, Gila feels that the majority status would become a non-issue.

This conversation brings up the question of the Palestinian demand for their "right of return." Gila responds thoughtfully, clearly attempting to juggle the hot button emotional and human rights issues with a blend of humanism, tact, and realism. She reminds us that the nuance and complexity required of peace-making does not occur between "friends" or "partners," but rather between longtime "enemies."

I am grateful to the Palestinians because they have several times asserted formally that they consent that Israel can have the land and be sovereign in the area on the Israeli side of the Green Line. I am very grateful to them because I know that they have a historical right to this land as well. Based on that compromise, I think there should be no problem at all with establishing two states here. The refugees are a very difficult problem but not insoluble. It's my opinion that we can solve it on two levels. On one level the declaratory level, where Israel says we think that the law of return for Palestinians is legitimate and just. On the second level, the implementation level, it has to be implemented in a way that Israelis can live with. This formulation of the two levels, the declaratory and the implementation, is not original with me, it has been said many times by senior Palestinians and I see no reason why it cannot be enforced. Needless to say, we will require the cooperation of the surrounding Arab countries. They will have to absorb many of the Palestinians. They will have to be compensated for their absorption, the refugees themselves will receive reparations, some to-be-determined number will enter Israel, others will enter Palestine, and the rest will remain and be absorbed by the host countries. Palestinians too do not want several million refugees entering Palestine. Its economy could not cope with several million Palestinian refugees.

Acknowledgement and apology and maybe financial compensation are certainly well within what they deserve and their right. Israel should give them an apology and Israel should say *mea culpa* for what was done to them and should compensate them financially. Whether or not they would want to return, nobody really knows. I think we have to base it on the viability of Israel and Palestine and not necessarily on ultimate justice.

Our delegation presses her on the issue of the level of mutual violence and distrust that exists, and she replies that both sides have perpetuated terrible violence, but that the end to violence is predicated on a workable, mutually viable agreement. At that point, if both sides can live in relative peace, can improve their economies and the quality of life in their societies, then they will have invested in suppressing the extremist forces within their own societies. "That to me is the insurance policy against further outbreaks of violence. So it is not that terrorism has to stop first."

When we ask about Palestinian extremist groups, she reminds us that in some sense it is best to think of them as historically parallel to Jewish groups at the time of the founding of the State of Israel. From Jewish terrorist groups such as the Irgun and the Stern Gang came two Israeli Prime Ministers, Menachem Begin and Yitzhak Shamir. Ironically at the beginning of statehood, Ben Gurion had to forcibly disarm his own extremists; now they are thought of as national heroes who fought for Jewish liberation. She predicts that the same pattern will occur among Palestinians although Israeli military actions have disrupted much of the Palestinian security apparatus. Gila admits that extremists on both sides will never be satisfied, but when there is a growing investment and acceptance in the building of two separate states, then extremism will be less appealing as a solution.

The next obvious question involves the Jewish settlements in the West Bank that are thought to be a major obstacle to peace and a two state solution. To some in our group, Gila is strangely optimistic.

If you look at the numbers, what you see is 400,000 settlers. Of the 400,000, half of them are in the immediate vicinity of the Jerusalem area. Now I am assuming what the Geneva Accords assumed that most of the settlers in the immediate vicinity of Jerusalem and near the Green Line will be annexed to Israel, there will be a land swap, so that the Palestinians will receive for Palestine, territories that were formerly in Israel.

She further clarifies that she sees Jerusalem as the heart of both countries and the gateway between them, that sharing Jerusalem is key. She says that a deep investment in peace will decrease the fear of terrorist cells in either nation. "You already have heard Palestinians condemn terrorism; Palestinians on the street, not just the leadership and Israelis would also not stand for extremist Israelis who are upsetting a solution. So I think that having a peace will be enough insurance against terrorism on both sides."

Gila presents her ideas with a calm conviction that sounds so rational, so obviously reasonable in its simplicity, yet neglects the political, emotional, and financial minefields that underlie this conversation.

Now if we annex a good many of those settlers, what we are now looking at is many fewer settlers. A survey was conducted in the territories by Peace Now about whether or not settlers would leave their homes. Eighty percent of the settlers said that they would leave in exchange for financial compensation. If the state paid the settler for a home and for property, the settler would move back into Israel. Now what is left is 20 percent of the settlers and of those, according to this survey, some 17 to 18 percent would argue and use all legal means at their disposal, but not be violent to remain in their homes. So we are left now with the violent ones. The violent ones constitute something like 2 to 3 percent of the population of settlers. Now let's take the worst case scenario. Three percent of the settlers who want to be violent times 200,000 settlers who have to be moved, we are talking about 6000 individuals who say they would be violent. Now half of those individuals are children. So now we are left with 3000. Three thousand is manageable in military terms, in strategic terms. You can send in an army to move and to defeat militarily 3000 people in a way that is much more doable than thinking about them as a huge mass of 400,000 people.

Gila actually feels that these 3000 far right settlers are more than a symbolic threat; they actually deny the legitimacy of the State of Israel. She describes these settlers as the "disloyal opposition," because they believe that God wants the State of Israel to be a theocratic messianic state, rather than the democracy, however flawed, that it is striving to be. She notes that the extremist settlers actually would like to dissociate themselves from the laws of the land, they are "trouble-makers," "secessionists," "the legitimate enemy" of the Israeli state. She sees that Israelis are unhappy with the settlers' militant behavior and their willingness to put their children in harm's way in order to prevent evacuation. This has consequently delegitimized the cause of the right wing. She cites a court case against settler parents for bringing their children to a very violent event that placed the children in danger. She does admit that there is very little Israeli public awareness about the violence that these same settlers commit against Palestinians, harassing and shooting at them, destroying age-old olive groves, seizing land, and so forth, so there is much public education to be done.

Balancing Risk while Building Bridges

Despite her optimism and her belief in the possibility for peace, like all Israelis, Gila worries about terrorism. Similar to many people we interviewed, she has developed a special awareness and set of behaviors that she feels will reduce her risk of becoming a victim of a suicide bombing. In times of increased worry, she does her food shopping late in the evening in an effort to avoid crowded markets. She refuses to take buses and takes a taxi if she needs transportation. She doesn't frequent crowded restaurants or cafes, but rather prefers empty public places. She notes that most Israelis have restricted their lives in some way in an effort to increase their chances of survival.

Ultimately, though, she feels compelled to address the issues underlying the conflict as a more fundamental approach to decreasing her own risk, as well as to minimize the suffering and losses of her Palestinian counterparts. She also believes that there is a unique place in this struggle for the voices of women. She finds that Israeli and Palestinian women are more easily able to acknowledge their common suffering, their common concern for human life above all other values, to move beyond legalistic language and address the emotional needs of their two tormented peoples.

> I have one more thing to say because I have been thinking all the time about your question of what do you say to Americans or American Jews. I think what you have to say to them is ending the occupation is ultimately the liberation of Israel, not just of Palestine. The liberation of Israel, to be the kind of country that we had always wanted it to be when it was first founded. That's why we have to get out of there. Not just on behalf of the Palestinians.

4

Listening to the Israeli Street: We Are Surrounded by Enemies

R UCHAMA MARTON AND GILA SVIRSKY represent two fragments in the vast mosaic of Israeli opinion, but there are many divergent voices in this conversation. I find that it is sometimes possible to explore the larger mythos of history and culture by focusing on the intimacy of a moment, by capturing a dialogue that churns with the assumptions, reactions, and attitudes embedded in its marrow. Israel has been described as a victim and a conqueror, as a home for a vast melting pot of visionaries and a resting place for the deeply wounded, as pious and condescending, socially conscious and racially insensitive. The complexities and contradictions of the early Zionist vision have been interwoven with the personal horrors and world guilt over the Holocaust. Additionally, the desperation and arrogance of imposing a little piece of Eastern Europe on the shifting sands of the end of the Ottoman Empire and the refusal to return that precious fragment of land conquered in the Six Day War of 1967 have left an intricate and convoluted legacy that is echoed in the daily bustle and banter of the living. I hope to explore this puzzle by attending to personal bits and pieces of human interaction as I talk with people ranging from physicians to taxi drivers and to share my own reactions and insights. I want to examine the palpable cultural, scientific, academic, and social muscle of this society, along with the contradictions and the blindness, to understand how victim and victimizer, dreamer and destroyer can coexist unfazed, often simultaneously within each person, yearning for safety and wholeness.

Visiting Shaare Zedek Medical Center, Jerusalem

It seems reasonable for me to start this somewhat daunting effort on a drizzly, chilled January in 2004, in a major hospital in Jerusalem. From my early childhood, the building and sustaining of Hadassah Hospital has had a magical aura, the embodiment of every Jewish mother's dream for a doctor in the family. This effort represented a potent mix of Jewish intelligence, caring, and commitment to the highest principles. Over and over again, the Diaspora gave its collective sigh of relief, held another Hadassah fundraiser, and in that solid and ephemeral way we were all part of the dream, sharing the anxiety as well as the pride in this prodigious Jewish undertaking. As a Jewish physician on a medical delegation, it is only natural for me to make a pilgrimage to the impressive medical facilities that have blossomed from all of these varied efforts.

After visiting staff at the Mount Scopus and Ein Kerem campuses of the Hadassah Medical Center, the delegates find ourselves crowded around a conference room table at Shaare Zedek, a major Orthodox hospital. It was first constructed in 1902 and now houses almost 600 inpatient beds. The hospital is famous for its sophisticated emergency room and trauma facilities. One-third of the patients are Israeli Arabs, and Jewish and Arab staff and patients mix openly in the churning process of providing and receiving medical care. We hear from the Jewish staff of the ironies that this creates; an Israeli Arab cleaning the exam room floor that is wet with the blood of a Jewish victim, a perpetrator of violence lying in a bed next to a victim, Jewish and Arab staff caring for each of them. An emergency room doctor describes an episode where an eight-year-old child was crying in pain while a Jewish orthopedist was setting his leg. The child was reprimanded by his mother in Arabic, "Don't show weakness. You will grow up and kill these dirty Jews." Some of the staff understood her words and were understandably outraged. On *Shabbat*, the elevators are programmed to stop on all floors so that Orthodox Jewish staff and patients can visit the hospital without violating religious injunctions. Similarly, on *Shabbat*, when the medical staff make rounds, Arab staff write the notes, again so religious Jews are not to forced to break the prohibition against writing on their day of rest. The ancient and the modern have somehow made a convoluted truce on this medical turf.

Meeting with Staff

In this tiny conference room, there are shelves of medical texts and journals jostled together on two walls with a large plastic model of the inner ear perched as if listening on the edge of a shelf. A clock with the word, "Effexor," a well-known antidepressant, ironically hangs on the wall, its hands circling purposefully. Dr. Judith Guedalia, a vivacious neuropsychologist and trauma expert who left the US for Israel 34 years ago mentions that many of the staff are Jewish settlers living in the West Bank. She assures us confidently that everyone leaves their "political persona" at the door, describing the hospital as "an oasis of humanity." Dr. Guedalia radiates competence and that sense of a woman on a mission who will never be deterred. She worries, "If you watch TV, you would think we are only about death." She feels that people develop "the bullet-has-my-name-on-it mentality" and finds that there is increasingly reckless behavior and car accidents. "I don't want us to be the country of death." She is eager to share examples of Jewish–Arab cooperation within the hospital and speaks fluent Hebrew and enough Arabic to be useful.

Wearing his *yarmulke*, with a serious and intent demeanor, Dr. Sol Jaworowski, a psychiatrist originally from Australia, discusses the wide variety of patients he sees, from ultra-Orthodox Jews to Israeli Arabs living in Jerusalem. He adds that security issues affect mental health. People have to adapt to the "situation" and he sees a general rising level of tension. His first weekend on-call involved caring for victims of a suicide bombing at a crowded restaurant and this was a real "trial by fire" for him. We learn that there are complex, sophisticated, state-of-the art preparations and protocols at the hospital for terror attacks as well as other disasters, with careful attention paid to both the medical and emotional aspects of trauma. With all of these contradictions and stressors, living and working in Jerusalem, Dr. Jaworowski notes, has come to feel normal. He only senses the tension when he leaves and then returns, but is restored by "the spiritual beauty of the place." He loves the intensity of interpersonal relationships and the need to be mutually supportive that is strong in this kind of environment.

Interface with the Occupied Territories

As the discussion proceeds, Dr. Itay Friedman, a slightly more sceptical psychiatry resident, talks about the poor quality of health care in the Occupied Territories. He asserts that Israel is still responsible for the health of Palestinians until they have the resources to care for themselves. The other health care providers do not agree and we watch what we have come to see as a common occurrence, Israelis arguing passionately with each other about politics. Dr. Jaworowski notes that there is a chronic shortage of funding for mental health as well as all health care in general and the issue of payment is critical. Nonetheless, he asserts that no one gets turned away. I suspect that "no one" for him means only citizens of Israel, and wonder what he thinks of the thousands of migrant workers from all over the world who live in the shadows of Israeli social supports or the Palestinians in the Occupied Territories who rarely get permits to obtain first-world health care. The general hospitals, Hadassah and Shaare Zedek, are private hospitals with some funding from the Israeli sick funds, but most funding is through outside support, much of it from the US. Dr. Jaworowski concludes without irony, "Israel survives on the basis of charity."

Dr. Friedman, also wearing a *yarmulke*, explains earnestly that in his three years of army service he was mostly in the Negev and now, like most Israeli men, he is in the reserves. He recalls five years ago at a checkpoint near Ramallah, he watched an 18-year-old soldier stop a well-dressed Arab man in his fifties and start laughing at him. Dr. Friedman asked the soldier how he could treat this older man with such disrespect. The soldier explained that his friend had recently been killed; the anxiety of daily work was taking its toll. In fact, Dr. Friedman notes increasing numbers of young people are finding ways not to serve in the army. As national service is mandatory, women often do alternative nonmilitary service and are critical to the staffing of the hospital. With the reports of an increase in the number of nervous breakdowns among Israeli soldiers, Dr. Friedman remarks that since schizophrenia often emerges between the ages of 16 and 20, such findings are not surprising.

Dr. Freidman then reflects on how, because Israel is a small country, soldiers frequently come home while serving in combat units and, as Dr. Guedalia adds, "The edge is never far away." To illustrate their point, the physicians discuss the recent suicide bomber at the Erez crossing in Gaza. An Israeli soldier was told by a Palestinian woman that she had a metal plate in her leg due to a medical problem, she was allowed to cross, and then blew herself up, killing a number of Israeli soldiers. The doctors say that there is always this "Catch 22," and add, "Israel is losing the propaganda war." I can feel their sense of weakness and victimization in the court of world opinion as well as their unquestioning belief in the historical rightness of their cause.

The Cost of the Occupation for Israelis

Later, I sit in the office of Dr. Cornelius Gropp. Thoughtful and more laid back than the other clinicians we met earlier, he originally came from Germany and attended medical school in Israel. During his 18 years as a psychiatrist at Shaare Zedek, he finds increasingly that young people are less motivated to conform to expectations regarding army service, and he notes an increase in drug abuse, open marital strife, divorce, family violence, and incest. He has treated Arabic patients for years and feels that they are becoming more open; the men are more empathetic and concerned regarding their wives. In all families, he sees less of the macho culture and an increased willingness to use antidepressants. Similar to physicians in the US, he bemoans the increasing costs, shorter visits, the trend towards medicating psychiatric patients, and the increasing malpractice suits. Happily, he remarks, "In this political context, being a doctor gives you space not to talk about political issues, you can interact with all walks of life."

He leans back in his chair, his long fingers clasped pensively in front of his face, and reflects on the soldiers who complete their three years of army service and increasingly travel to India, East Asia, and South America, trying every drug on the market. "They start talking and ask, what is this crap I did in the army? We send our young people, 18 to 22 years old to the army; in normal countries they are in university or travels. Army service is very difficult. There are moral dilemmas, the more sensitive the soldier, the harder. There is a big sense of duty, many volunteer for combat units. The soldier at the checkpoint is often a confused adolescent. He wants to survive; he wants to defend his country." He reiterates that being a soldier is part of Israeli life, but it is a very complex experience. "Very few go from the army indifferent to what happens. The army will make their opinions more extreme, black and white, patriotic." Now he sees more people trying to get out of both combat service and reserves, the decades-long army obligation for men after three years of active service. They often use a mental problem as the excuse, although in the past this would have been unthinkable. Overall, he feels, "The consensus is, this conflict is bad for young people, but we have to deal with it. People like myself, completely opposed to settlements and occupation, have not an easy time in the army."

Dr. Gropp concludes that physicians are exposed to the inherent violence in the overall society. "They see people are brutalized, more extreme, more desperate, and easily aggressive. We as physicians are in the firing line of this aggression. We can't afford this conflict. I don't believe in all this politics, I am too busy being a doctor, trying to do decent medicine." To stay balanced, he runs long distance and enjoys reading philosophy. "I am trying to be a normal person. I have to stay even, not looking any further." He states, "I am not embarrassed to be a lefty," but adds, "Someone else can do it."

Losing a Son to a Suicide Bomber

Dr. Eli Picard comes quietly into the conference room. He sits before our video camera and tells us he is a pediatric pulmonologist. He emigrated from France 23 years ago, is married to an obstetrician-gynecologist at Hadassah Hospital, and is the father of four children. We look into his sweet, sensitive face, the friendly twinkle of his eyes framed by wire rimmed glasses. He sits almost serenely before us, leaning into the table, wearing green scrubs, a stethoscope hung around his neck. A shadow of sadness passes across his face as he begins to speak. Last year he was working at Shaare Zedek with a Palestinian child transferred from Hebron,

> from West Bank, or Judea and Samaria as we prefer to call these places. A pretty Arab boy, eight years old, he was transferred and we cared for him and God bless him, he is feeling better now. But this night that I was in charge, as I told you before, I had four children. My second child was 18 and he was learning in a college near the Gaza Strip. At midnight, a terrorist entered in his college during bible lesson. This terrorist from Gaza killed him with four of his friends. Fortunately the other children, even if he threw a bomb into the room where the children were learning, fortunately the other children were alive. It was a night that was terrible.

We are sitting quietly, inhaling his grief, struggling to bridge the abyss of his private loss. His sorrow feels merged with a deep sense of personal outrage at this unbearable injustice and violation of human decency.

Despite my personal situation I didn't change my behavior and I continued to work in my hospital. I think this is what my son would want. He was a smiley, very nice guy. I teach him to love all kinds of people, without difference of races or ethnicity. I think even when you have political problems, medicine has to be out of politics. So I know even my deep sadness, even though I didn't show it towards the people because it is my personal problem, I continue to work here in our hospital. I continue to care for Arab children, or from Israel. You have to know 20 percent of our population is Arab, so when you enter the emergency room or my pulmonary clinic, I didn't ask him, OK you are an Arab? OK. You will not receive safe treatment. All children in our establishment receive the same treatment, the same approach. Sometimes we received children from the West Bank or from Gaza Strip. One month ago, we received a child from Gaza with a very difficult problem of kidneys, and our colleagues phoned us and without hesitation we received him and we are taking care of this child.

There is a long pause in his narrative and I sense he is struggling with what he is about to share. His eyes betray a pained bewilderment.

I saw the terrorist's mother on a film and she said that she is very proud that her son has killed five Israelis. I don't understand such behavior. My son was not a terrorist, was not a soldier. He was supposed to be a soldier as we have to, because it is a law in Israel anytime, it is not a voluntary military service, but I cannot understand this behavior, to send, to be proud of a son that kill five innocent boys only because we are Israeli. I hope that in the future, such disaster will not happen and as we used to say in the Jewish tradition, God gives us strength to overcome our sadness. So I pray that God will give me strength to overcome my tragedy and that my child in the sky will be proud of his father.

He glances up at the ceiling and smiles. We sit in a silent circle of tears and even Dr. Guedalia, who has undoubtedly heard this story many times, is dabbing at her mascara, trying to rearrange her professional detachment.

My Unanswered Questions

Since that afternoon, I have listened to this interview dozens of times with the open heart of a parent trying to fathom the bottomless loss of one's child and the extraordinary summoning of strength to continue living and working without apparent bitterness. Standing before this man's grief and resilience, I wonder about so many of the details and of the future now lost in that bloody moment. I wonder for every child from Gaza that this generous doctor cares for so willingly and decently, what would need to happen for him to worry about the thousands of children who may not get permits, or cannot afford the trip, or are trapped in the bureaucratic tangles of Palestinian and Israeli authorities? I wonder if he really believes that Judea and Samaria belong to the Jewish people or if he is willing to grapple with sharing the land? He used the expression, "Arab children or from Israel". Does he mean that real Israelis are solely Jews? By using the term Arab, does he recognize the identity of Palestinians? Are his other children filled with despair and ready to hate? Can they, the next generation, manage forgiveness and compromise in the face of their immense personal sorrow? I wonder what kind of soldier his lovely son would have become. Would he have stood easily at checkpoints, automatic weapon in hand, controlling the lives of thousands of Palestinian civilians trying to get to work or school or the market? Would he have commanded tanks, enforced curfews, or been assigned to a more bureaucratic military task? Would he have refused to go at all, this smiley innocent boy? And what of the Arab mother? In the privacy of her kitchen, what tears does she shed? Did she send her young man of a son to the ignominious task or was he unemployed, hopeless, uncontrollable, and easily recruited for *jihad* by men more militant and less impotent than he? What wounds, humiliations, and loss provided the fertile soil for revenge? Was her son hunted as well; found, and killed by Israeli soldiers? Would she have preferred the living flesh of his body to martyrdom, his face now plastered on the faded, pock marked walls of a forgotten refugee camp? There is so much pain and loss in this story and so much left unanswered.

A Taxi in Tel Aviv

A year later, the delegation is back in Israel and we have just spent the afternoon with Adam Keller and Beate Zilversmidt, two articulate leaders of Gush Shalom, the peace bloc in Israel. Founded in 1993, Gush Shalom actively opposes the Israeli occupation of the West Bank and Gaza, consistently builds bridges with Palestinian counterparts, and provides political in-depth analysis. Adam and Beate's completely cluttered Tel Aviv apartment is wallpapered with slogans, cartoons, and a history of almost all of the movements around the world that have ever attempted to accomplish left-wing social change. Adam is a wealth of information and wisdom, writes prolifically, and has spent time in prison for acting on his views. Beate frequently corrects and interrupts him with her own brainy versions and interpretations and clearly could have done the interview by herself. We are having the classic experience of putting two Israelis in a room and getting ten opinions, all fascinating and provocative. We are intrigued by this intellectual duet and comfortable with their historical and political analyses.

After the visit, when we get into the taxi, the driver questions us, "You a friend of Adam?" We ask him what he thinks about Adam's views and he says that he is "on the other side" and proceeds to give us a sharp dose of street reality. He says that he believes that the settlements should end and that the Jews should be completely separate from the Arabs. I have heard this opinion many times in Israel, a desire to end the occupation in the name of security, and then to obtain a permanent separation. There is for me an odd lack of concern for the viability and stability of such a future Palestinian state, let alone the implications of such a divorce for the 20 percent of the Israeli population that are Arab. Does this cab driver want these Palestinians in segregated ghettos too? He notes unapologetically that Arabs have too many children, don't educate them, the children play in the street and throw stones. We sit quietly astonished through this vitriol of racist, derogatory commentary, a shocking contrast to our afternoon with Adam and Beate. The taxi driver explains that just like a parent protects his children, that, "we, the Israelis, are Sharon's children and he protects us." I start thinking about what are the risks of treating leaders in a passive, trusting manner. What happens when the citizenry are obedient children?

The taxi driver takes us to a Tel Aviv restaurant and I notice again that in Israel whenever you go into a public place there's a burly guard at the door. These men tend to be big guys with metal detectors and they go through your back pack and sometimes scan your body. I wonder if these guards really provide for that national yearning for *security* or do they just make people *feel* more secure? I note that they usually do not thoroughly search everything, but their presence does create the feeling of living in a country under siege, every café experience a potential terrorist bombing. This is the cultural message, loaded with well-earned fear, irony, and blindness. The irony I confront at these moments is extraordinary. While Israel is a country that is one of the major military powers in the world, controlling the lives of 3.5 million Palestinians, ignoring UN and international law, expanding settlements, building more bypass roads, concrete checkpoints, and barriers, the security guard standing at the door is a living symbol of the country's vulnerable underbelly. All that military hardware and poured concrete cannot ultimately protect against angry young men, hopelessness, religious fervor, and suicide bombings. Having the security guard there gives us the illusion of protection and makes us feel safer, but just what are the limits of this strategy and how can this possibly be the solution as long as injustice and discord continue their unrelenting march? When, I wonder, does the fortress really become a prison?

Meeting Soldiers at the Erez Checkpoint, Gaza

I want to talk with soldiers and it turns out that a checkpoint can sometimes be the ideal place for conversation. The Gaza Strip is slightly over twice the size of Washington, DC, wedged between southwest Israel, the Mediterranean, and the Egyptian border. The Erez checkpoint, the main entry/exit point for visitors, is located on its northern aspect. With the help of PHR-I we file for the permits months in advance and, through some unexplainable quirk of fate, we learn that the Israeli authorities have granted us entry permits. That is why I am getting out of a cab on a dreary March morning in 2005 with four other colleagues and dragging my suitcase towards something that looks for all the world like a dusty tollbooth. Trepidation and curiosity are vying for my attention as I hand my passport to two smiling Israeli soldiers, a young man just old enough to shave and an apparently recently pubescent young woman, who ask if we have permits, check our papers and a computer screen, and send us towards the next hurdle.

This is a larger building with a number of rooms, soldiers working behind counters, Israeli rock music blasting, and a general sense of bustling activity. At our station three women soldiers sit behind a desk at their computer screens. The woman who interviews me is very beautiful with a mane of lovely, curly hair and delicately manicured nails. I force my sweetest smile, explain that we are visiting Gaza as if that is the most normal travel destination in the world, engage in mindless chatter, and wait. She mentions that the Erez checkpoint is a very good placement for a soldier because it's not dangerous, but it is very boring. She takes all of our passports and focuses intently on her computer screen. I ask her where she is from and she replies, "Hebron." I remember in a disquieting emotional lurch that the Jews in Hebron are the most right-wing, violent settlers and try to match that image with this attractive young woman who is immersed in her computer, pouring over who-knows-what information the Israelis have about me.

A friendly soldier in his early thirties comes over to us and explains that he is in charge of NGOs and foreigners. Using our developing checkpoint skills, we start a conversation and he says that he grew up in a small town near Tel Aviv and is a career army man. The soldier talks earnestly about how much the people of Gaza need assistance, the importance of NGOs, and how improving the situation there is not Israel's responsibility. I wish I felt comfortable asking him how he frames the legal and social ramifications of 38 years of occupation, the conscious neglect of infrastructure, targeted assassinations, and the deliberate policy of economic de-development by Israeli forces in the Gaza Strip. We survey the huge amount of construction in progress, the large concrete slabs and a big open building with multiple chutes for funneling people under a large peaked blue roof. He explains, "They are building this as part of the plan with Abbas." He adds that with the removal of the Jewish settlers from Gaza, the Palestinians from Gaza will once again be allowed to return to work in Israel.

I point to the chutes and ask, "What are these?" The soldier replies without hesitance or ambivalence, "They are building the special holding pens for the workers." He explains that once this is all completed, approximately 1000 Palestinian workers per day will go through the checkpoint between 3 and 5 am. The men will get up very early, go to the checkpoint, wait in line, get their papers checked (the same papers they had yesterday and the day before and the day after), then go through the checkpoint to the waiting transport vehicles. They are taken to Israeli work sites, usually in construction, agricultural labor, or some kind of physical work. At the end of the day, the Gazans return to the checkpoint, go back into these pens and channels, get rechecked, and return to their homes and families. The men have dinner and go to bed because they need to get up very early to start the process all over again. I remind myself that these workers are the lucky ones, they are employed. At the same time, I am gripped by my awareness of the obvious grinding hardship of such a life, not only for these workers but also for their wives and children. I speculate privately, would this lovely soldier find these conditions acceptable if the laborer were his own father or brother? Does he actually see these Palestinians as fellow human beings or are they merely invisible or part of a faceless, nameless, terrorist other?

Everybody Hates Us, We Are Surrounded by Enemies

The conversation turns to the need for Jewish safety. This same soldier has a large automatic weapon slung casually over his shoulder, as comfortably as if it were a natural body part. He is clearly totally at ease in his role and is talking about how Israel is the only place in the world where Jews can possibly be safe. I wonder how he might comprehend my sense of safety living in a suburb of Boston where I personally know many Jews and not a single gun owner. Perhaps he sees people in the Diaspora as blindly delusional, another Holocaust always lurking in the future. He talks openly about how he can feel anti-Semitism in Europe, how Jews have to have their own state, and this military response is necessary. He exudes no sense of bitterness, resentment, no sense of irony or concern about the impact or consequences of imprisoning an entire population or why that population might object to the terms of the arrangement. He tells us about the horrific suicide bomb attack that we heard about a year earlier at Shaare Zedek. "So, we don't have any choice, this is what we have to do. We are surrounded by enemies." I find this is a common theme in Israel; an unambiguous sense of the state as a little beleaguered nation in a world of adversaries. "Everybody hates us, so Jews have to be tough."

Finally we are given stamped orange permits and we start walking through the area of construction. On our right are all the long, concrete holding pens for the future laborers. The chutes end in revolving turnstiles so that only one person can go through at a time. We see tons of concrete blocks, walls, barbed wire; everything looks very prison-like. We wander through endless structures, bleak and grey, soldiers and construction workers everywhere, a dusty dirt floor. I imagine what this would be like for a Palestinian child going for medical care in Israel or a sick cancer patient in a wheelchair trying to negotiate chemotherapy across the border. I wonder what this is like for my friend who is an obstetrician-gynecologist living in the Jabalya Refugee Camp in Gaza and working in Soroka Hospital in Be'ersheva, Israel. I imagine him with his grey suit and dark tie, briefcase in hand, negotiating this dusty concrete prison, trying to hold on to some sense of professional dignity and purpose. He has told me his stories of humiliation and frustration. A cluster of Palestinian laborers waiting in some line reminds me of the faces I have seen of Mexicans who have scrambled across the border into the US and are hoping with quiet desperation for work, any work. Crossing lines, I fear, always involves the risk of this kind of double vision.

Meeting the Palestinian Authority

After a lengthy trek through the austere and imposing construction, the delegates arrive at a very long, covered walkway with concrete walls, curls of barbed wire, birds flitting in and out. At the end we see a concrete block and three men casually sitting at a table. As we walk past them, one calls out in a thickly accented voice, "Whoa, whoa. You've got to show your passports here." At this point, my frustration boils over and I lose my careful composure. Another time? I mean they've taken my passport, they have checked me on the computer twice, they've given me a special permit, they've collected the permit at another point, they have interviewed me, they've let me in, I have dragged my suitcase for at least a mile, and now some other guy is demanding something else? Suddenly we realize that these men are Palestinians from the Palestinian Authority and they want to check us into Gaza. After our embarrassment, I notice their military uniforms as well as the dramatic change in mood at this end of the checkpoint. They are laughing with amusement because we have not understood who they are. Then one of the soldiers gives me this look and I see beyond his laughing face, his very dark, black eyes, brimming with sadness. He speaks quietly, "Like Dachau, yes?" For a stunning moment, I cannot breathe. The thought of last year's suicide bomber's fragmented flesh, her blood splattered and drying in a contorted fusion with that of her Israeli victims, the feeling of being herded like human chattel, the dusty prison walls, the curling barbed wire, and the inevitable sense of impending disaster sweep through me like an icy wind. And I think, welcome to Gaza.

The Making of a Soldier

Several days later, after we have completed our visit to Gaza, I continue my search for conversations with soldiers. On the advice of a contact in the Israeli Refuser movement, I travel to Be'ersheva, Israel, to interview a reservist and helicopter pilot now studying medicine. He explains gently that the interview cannot be taped and I cannot use his name. He does not feel comfortable being a public person. Few people here know who he is and what he has done. I am allowed to take notes, given permission to tell his story, and at the end of the discussion, take a quick photo to remember his face, thick straight hair, dark eyes smiling in the bright Israeli sun. We are sitting in a cafeteria which could be in any major first-world hospital with the general hustle, beepers pinging through the low-level din, a stream of scrub suits and white coats. This 30-year-old reservist sitting intently across the table after a night on-call is not just any medical student. He is one of the original Israeli pilots who signed "The Combatants' Letter" which began the Courage to Refuse Movement in 2002 and abruptly changed the tone and content of Israeli public discourse.[1]

Through our conversation, I discover that he did not start life as a man destined for what many now see as a moment of courageous dissent initiated by a group of elite soldiers in the Israeli military. Like most Israeli children, he tells us he grew up learning about the early days of Zionism, the brave heroes and exhilarating military battles. As in many countries intent on building a national identity, he explains that the indoctrination starts very young. He remembers stories from kindergarten about the early Israeli settlements in the 1900s in Galilee, near Lebanon. It was here, he claims, the new, militant, powerful Jew was born, leaving behind the stereotype of the submissive, pale, Torah scholar living in a *shtetl* in Eastern Europe. He remembers from his childhood the heroic stories of the Jabotinsky group, a right-wing military force during the British Mandate in Palestine. The student heard legendary accounts of the War of Liberation in 1948, the formation of the Israeli Defense Force from the Haganah, which had protected early Jewish settlements and fought the British Mandate. The student explains Israeli children grow up with this bedrock of stories about military conflict with potent reoccurring themes; we are the few who fight the many, we are victorious, everyone always wants to destroy us.

He goes on to describe how the schools feed directly into army service and sometimes the teachers themselves are actually soldiers who are placed in classrooms, acting as role models for their aspiring students. The medical student comments that in the last year of high school, preparing for army service is a hot and all encompassing topic. In addition, everyone has brothers, fathers, and uncles, who are in the reserves until their fifties, so military service is a significant and interwoven part of the context of every child's life. Because the experience of military service is so universal, he explains that the country tends to have a military perspective on many issues and to draw its political leadership from the military elite.

Becoming a "Refuser"

I wonder how this young man reached a point of refusal when pro-military societal forces are so pervasive. He explains he moved up through the ranks, training as an elite helicopter pilot. He is still proud that the army "is a very moral army; soldiers talk about moral questions and issues. They learn to appreciate values, but something happened." With the Second Intifada in 2000, he began to feel that many Israelis saw all Palestinians as terrorists, that Israelis could not see Palestinian lives as having any value. For him in particular, there were a series of incidents that became increasingly troubling until he could not tolerate serving and felt he had to refuse to fight in the Occupied Territories, despite the huge personal price. He came to a point where he found that his military activities did not correlate with the grounding in moral behavior that he had developed during military training.

He describes a particularly troublesome operation called Wall Defense. After the suicide bombing in Netanya during a Passover Seder where 29 people were killed, the Israeli forces carried out a retaliatory operation with a large number of Palestinian civilian casualties. In

another operation, he talks about the Israeli incursion into Jenin
in the West Bank. He doubts the Palestinian claim that there was a
blind massacre of civilians, but was nonetheless disturbed by the large
number of civilians killed. He said he was also aware that Palestinians
were used as human shields and that there had been home demolitions
of innocent Palestinians.

Another turning point occurred as a result of Israeli press reports of
a driver of a Caterpillar bulldozer used to destroy Palestinian homes.
The man was publicly considered a great hero and described himself
as being very proud of his work. The medical student explains that this
man boasted that he would destroy the homes before the residents could
leave so he would actually knock down the houses with the people in
them, killing the inhabitants, often large multi-generational families.
The driver's justification was that the Palestinians were all terrorists.
The medical student said he wasn't sure whether they were or not, but
that this was inexcusable behavior. To add further insult, this man was
drinking alcohol while operating his bulldozer. The medical student
was very troubled as a soldier that there was no retaliation from the
army, no punishment for this behavior.

The next event that contributed to the student's alienation was the
killing of Sheik Salah Shehadeh whom he described as a dangerous
Palestinian terrorist. A one ton bomb was dropped on his house in a
crowded residential area, which resulted in the deaths of 14 innocent
Palestinian civilians. The student's disaffection with the army grew.
He describes an incident in which Jewish settlers near Nablus went
into a Palestinian olive grove and hacked down the ancient trees that
were critical to the Palestinian farmers who owned the groves. Again
there was no punishment for the settlers; they had free rein when it
came to targeting their Palestinian neighbors. As his service continued,
he describes seeing more and more cases either where Israeli soldiers
killed Palestinian civilians in what he felt was a criminal manner or
where Jewish settlers harmed Palestinians without any reaction from
the army. Over time, this really started to bother him and he says, "It
made me feel that there had to be something done to open the eyes of
the Israelis." At the same time he was aware that there was tremendous
suffering in the families of Israelis because of the suicide attacks. These
contradictions and paradoxes were costing everyone and he felt he had
a responsibility to act as an Israeli and as a soldier, to refuse to fight in

the Occupied Territories. He worried that with all of these incidents, "Our eyes and hearts had become blind to our neighbors."

A Crisis of Identity

This young man describes an interesting contradiction: in matters of defense, Israel feels very nationally secure; it is clear that Israel is a major military power. Nevertheless, on a personal level, riding on a bus, sitting in a café, walking down the street, Israelis are very insecure. I ask him if he has ever met a Palestinian in a nonmilitary situation. Ironically he replies that no, in fact the only time he even stepped foot in the Occupied Territories was in 1993. He served in Gaza as a regular soldier, before the Oslo Accords, and even there he never had a face-to-face meeting with a Palestinian! He says that just being in Gaza gave him a much better impression about Palestinian life and he found it very difficult to see 5000 Israeli settlers living on 25 percent of the land, "having normal lives." Living next to them were hundreds and hundreds of thousands of Palestinians experiencing tremendous poverty and suffering. He explains that most Israelis don't understand or question the brutalizing impact of settlements, bypass roads, and checkpoints and that usually the lives of Jewish Israelis and Arab Israelis are also completely separate.

Our discussion turns to the issue of checkpoints manned by Israeli soldiers in the Occupied Territories. He reports that soldiers are dealing with unarmed civilians, standing for hours, bored, tense, and constantly worrying about who is going to present a threat. Thus, the student understands that in this context, people easily lose their human sensibility. He explains that the Erez checkpoint in Gaza is such a militarized area because of the suicide bombing last year. Thus he feels that checkpoints are really an insoluble problem for soldiers and there has to be another solution which is political. He explains that if Palestinians "took the methods of Gandhi," they would already have a state. I am fascinated that he doesn't seem to make a connection between the behavior of the Israeli government and soldiers in the Occupied Territories and the continued Palestinian resistance. I wish I had asked him whether he would he expect the Israelis to give up targeted assassinations, home demolitions, collective punishment, and to also use "the methods of Gandhi" to achieve peace.

During his military service in Gaza, he admits that he wasn't really surprised to see the level of suffering in the Palestinian population. I am puzzled and wonder aloud, what do Israelis choose to know and what can they not bear to know? He explains that there is a difference between "knowing" and "seeing and understanding" and what most Israelis say is that the Palestinians are the "bad guys" in the territories. "All they want to do is to kill us." So, he clarifies, the typical Israeli doesn't feel much pity for Palestinians because, "Palestinians don't have faces." Many Israelis feel that the Palestinians have brought their troubles on themselves. He finds this analysis much too black and white and says that he sees "all the grey" in everything. At the same time he says that Israelis have let a group of extremists lead the way for their own country so they are culpable as well.

I want to understand better why he made his particular decision while other soldiers continue to serve without questioning. In a quiet but forthright manner he explains that what happened to him was that he succeeded in feeling and seeing "the other side." He adds that he wouldn't really call this feeling *sympathy*, but rather, *empathy*. He does not identify with Palestinians, but as a fellow human being, he can feel their suffering. He also observes that today attitudes are changing; there is more controversy over the purpose of having the Israeli army in the Occupied Territories. People are thinking more about themselves, about developing their own lives, and are feeling less threatened by the Arab world.

A Small Zionist Country with Powerful Friends

The student ends the interview by talking about the importance of Jewish immigration to Israel, the Arab "demographic threat," and the importance of maintaining a Jewish majority. He thinks that it is very difficult for Americans to understand how small an area of the world Israel comprises. Without any sense of the unusual, he then compares the distance across Israel to two nondescript places near Dallas. As I register my astonishment, he clarifies that he did military training in Texas. In fact, several times during his military education for the IDF he trained on simulators for Bell Helicopters in Dallas. I wonder why a US military group in Texas is training an Israeli soldier. The medical student says that there are numerous relationships between the US and

Israeli military and that he is aware of combined trainings with the US and Israeli armies in the Mediterranean. Additionally, during the Gulf War he reports that American soldiers came to Israel to operate the anti-missile missiles. As far back as 1973, in the Yom Kippur War, he says planes from the US brought crucial military supplies to the Israelis and he saw a television report about Israeli army forces training US forces in Iraq. The military and political implications of this intimate relationship give new meaning to the US–Israeli friendship. I wonder, does the behavior of our troops at Iraqi checkpoints and in Iraqi prisons actually reflect the Israeli experience in dealing with Palestinians? He goes on to say he initially resisted the war in Iraq, but now he wonders if it might not make for positive change and might actually be good for Israel in the long run.

As we talk further, I marvel at this student's amazing blend of loyalty to the Israeli Zionist national vision which stands proudly beside his powerful sense of ethical dissent and his absolute refusal to commit what he sees as "immoral acts." I wonder how he will sustain a sense of wholeness as he evolves in his blossoming life and how he will reconcile the palpable contradictions between righteous victim and brutal occupier.

5

Returning to Jerusalem:
The Taxi Driver and the Rabbi

A S I TRY TO DIGEST this medical student's complicated observations and paradoxical personal story, I realize that it is time for him to go home to his family and it is time for me to get to my next destination, Jerusalem. Despite promises to my own family back home, I decide to take a bus from Be'ersheva to Jerusalem. Before this trip, one of my deals with my husband was that I would not take buses in Israel. Like many Israelis, it was my way of having some control over my anxiety about being blown up. When I reflect on this decision honestly, I realize that it involves some magical thinking; an injury can just as easily occur in a car driving next to a bus or sitting in a café. There is no reality-based protective shield created by avoiding buses, but I had decided that this was my limit. Sitting with this young medical student, I feel compelled to walk in his shoes a step further and explore a bit of his daily life experience on a more personal, emotional level; thus, soon I find myself queuing up at the bus stop with Israeli passengers.

Becoming Paranoid

After the student leaves the bus stop, the crowd slowly gathers. Although I have been told that my greatest risk is actually from crazy Israeli drivers, I can feel my anxiety rising as I wait. I think of all the Israelis I have talked with who do not let their children take buses, who do not let themselves take buses. Apparently many people in this country share my fantasy. As we stand at the stop and I become increasingly aware of this rumbling fear in my gut, a wave of hyper-vigilance sweeps over me. I begin looking carefully at the prospective travelers: this one bearded with a tall hat, that one young and Semitic looking (Arab? Jewish? Who can tell?), this one clearly of Ethiopian descent. I am engaging in my own curious and embarrassing ethnic/political profiling. I wonder about a suspicious bulge in a backpack, an odd shaped briefcase. My paranoia is blossoming.

Once the bus comes, the passengers board and over the rumble of the engine, I immediately notice that although the bus is very crowded, it is also very quiet, a remarkable observation given the loquacious, argumentative reputation of Jews in general and Israelis in particular. I stand in the aisle, my strained hand hanging onto the overhead bar. Try as I might, I cannot read the social cues. I don't know whether the silence is a normal cultural phenomenon or whether there is some kind of bus tension in Israel, everybody dealing with a low-level anxiety that spikes to a higher pitch in this setting. As I stare into my fellow travelers' faces looking for clues, it is really striking to me that perhaps half of the bus riders are soldiers, late teens, early twenties, men and women in military uniform with their automatic rifles leaning between their legs, or lying haphazardly across their laps, chatting, dozing, staring vacantly out the window. I have never been this close to so many weapons in my life.

Unlike the US, because the military service is not separate from civilian life, there is not a particular military look. Like many of her peers, one of the women soldiers is wearing faultless makeup. She sports lovely, dangling earrings, her eyebrows are perfectly tweezed in a high arch that looks like a cross between permanent disdain and astonishment, and she has a huge gun cradled in her manicured hands. I keep reminding myself that in this country, this is *normal*. Soon I realize that I really don't know what to be afraid of any more; a bus full of heavily armed teenagers or a single suicide bomber. What if one of these kids has a bad dream and wakes suddenly, finger on the trigger? The possibilities are endless in my fertile imagination. To add to my disconnection, wedged in between the soldiers are Orthodox men with high, wide-brimmed black hats, huge beards, and long, black coats. Their wives sit with heads discretely covered like escapees from an eighteenth-century Russian village, elbow to elbow with teenyboppers who could have walked out of any mall in the US.

I struggle to breathe slowly, adjusting my grip on the overhead bar, staring at each passenger, trying to imagine a mundane human moment in their ordinary days. As we roll through farms, and miles of highway, the music on the bus catches my attention. It is a popular Israeli singer, crooning in Hebrew, some kind of rock and roll with an Arabic lilt to it. I do not know whether it is the minor key or if she is accompanied by Arabic instruments, but I can hear a clear Middle Eastern influence. I've heard people say that this is a positive sign, that the music is showing the blending of these two cultures, of these two peoples. My anxiety is calmed by this reassuring thought.

A State of Disequilibrium

Finally after 45 minutes a seat becomes available and I sit down and immediately fall asleep, exhausted from the tiresome, humiliating morning checkpoint experience leaving Gaza, the interview with the medical student, and the anxiety and intensity of living in between and within two contradictory worlds. I feel like my left foot is in Palestine and my right foot is in Israel and I am stumbling along the borders between these worlds in a state of utter disequilibrium. I think about this elite officer in the Israeli army, the pride of his country, patriotic, Zionist, yet willing to risk his future for the sake of saving his soul. I think about the Palestinians he does not know or understand yet refuses to destroy. I marvel at the separation wall he supports, worry about the humanitarian and economic consequences of unilateral solutions, and the price of seizing land while imprisoning an entire population. I understand that Israelis have a right to be fearful and their neighbors have a right to be angry. I am trying to capture my appreciation for the enormous imbalance in military power between Israelis and Palestinians. The Israeli sense of rightful ownership of this promised land and the powerful will to survive is fused with a belief in permanent Jewish victimization and an inherently undemocratic, militarily arrogant stance that is often blind to the suffering of Palestinians. Then there is the sense of the Palestinians I have met, wronged in 1948 and once again in 1967, victimized by years of Israeli aggression, Palestinian governmental corruption, and international abandonment, claiming resistance as their birthright and only chance for survival and dignity. As we approach Jerusalem, our arrival is heralded by a massive traffic jam and the macho drivers who combine utter chutzpah and a crazy, suicidal sense of entitlement. We have arrived in one piece, in the city that is claimed by all the wounded players in this fractured and troubled conflict.

The Libyan/Romanian Taxi Driver, a Mixed Marriage

On my way to interview Gila earlier in the delegation, I took a different drive to Jerusalem from Tel Aviv. On that leg of the journey, I have the opportunity to speak with a lively cab driver named Mordecai who fortunately likes to talk. He explains that his father is from Romania and came here in 1948 and is an *Ashkenazi* Jew. His mother is from Libya and immigrated in 1949. He was born in Israel in 1950 so he is a *Sabra*, but his wife is from Syria. These are called "mixed marriages" in Israel, *Ashkenazic* and *Sephardic*; Eastern European and Arabic, North African, Oriental. As he drives, I watch his sun-wrinkled face and twinkly eyes, and relax in the aura of his happy, sweet disposition. Unlike many Israelis, he graciously does not smoke because we are not smokers. He tells us that he married at the age of 19 and was in the IDF. He has two children and four grandchildren, his daughters are both teachers, and his wife is at home. He speaks fluent Hebrew, English, and Arabic. I am trying to understand his concept of identity; in my eyes he is Jewish and Arab. I ask him if he or his wife is Arab and he responds immediately, "Oh no. We are Israelis." I reframe my question, "You speak Arabic, one of your parents is from an Arab country, your wife is Arab, so ... are you Jewish Arabs?" This leads us into a fascinating discussion that reflects the complexity of this society where both Palestinians and Jews may share an Arab background, where Arab-speaking people may be Christian, Muslim, or Jewish, and where Jews and Palestinians share Israeli citizenship. Mordecai speaks fluent Arabic because he was taught by his Libyan grandmother and I find it amazing to see the varieties of identity contained within this one family.

Yearning for Peace, Preparing for War

With a sense of yearning and optimism, Mordecai goes on to talk about his tremendous hopes for peace. He says that the Israelis should return the Occupied Territories and East Jerusalem. He reflects back to when he was in the army; he was in Gaza in 1968. The soldiers used to eat at restaurants and there was a lot of commercial activity between the Gazans and the Israelis. Since then, one of his daughters served in the air force and one daughter was in a security command. He is relieved that neither was involved in any active fighting. This leads into his memories of the Yom Kippur War in 1973. He remembers that he was in synagogue and that the army sent out a message through loudspeakers as it did then in times of crisis. He says he went directly from the synagogue to report for the reserves and was gone for four months, which he assures us is not unusual for an Israeli reservist. He explains that he was a truck driver who drove bombs to Egypt and he is very proud because he crossed the Suez Canal with Sharon. I ask him what he thinks of Sharon and he replies, "He's a fighter. He's smart and strong." I ask what he feels about the Gaza disengagement plan and he is supportive. "Who needs all this fighting?" He reiterates that he is done with fighting. He claims the real problem in Israel is the religious people, both Jewish and Arab, and the power they have. "You know what we call the religious Jews in Israel? We call them the Jewish mafia."

He is quite knowledgeable about Israeli politics and explains to us why the religious have so much power although they are only 15 percent of the population. In the Israeli Knesset, to have majority power, the larger parties must make coalitions with smaller parties. The small religious parties are the ones who make coalitions and thus they have a disproportionate impact on policy. We drift into a conversation about the US and he says, "Bush is good for Israel." I retort, "Why is he good for Israel?" and he says, "Bush has Sharon's brain." Then we start joking around about whether Sharon is thinking Bush's thoughts or Bush is thinking Sharon's thoughts; it is a friendly banter but laden with hidden truth. When I inevitably mention the war in Iraq, he responds, "The war in Iraq is good for Israel. The Iraqis were a threat." He laughs and says, "You know, Israel is the 51st state of America." To add to the irony, we pass numerous American brand stores and American hotels, and a big Office Depot truck hurtles by, the website address gleaming on its side. For a dissociated moment, I cannot place exactly where I am. I point out the Office Depot truck and Mordecai notes, "You know, if not for America, Israel would be nothing. All the world would eat us. America is the big uncle, Uncle Sam."

In and Out of the West Bank

To add to my confusion, the taxi passes a large Jewish settlement and Mordecai starts talking about how he thinks the settlements are bad and should be dismantled. We drive through checkpoints and pass army outposts draped with brown camouflage netting. I am perplexed and ask why we are seeing all these army installations? Mordecai explains, "We are in the Occupied Territories." This feels so bizarre because we left Tel Aviv on a superhighway and now somehow we are in the Occupied Territories and there was no obvious boundary. I get this feeling that Jews and Palestinians are not living side by side; it is more like they are two hands wrapped around each other, sometimes in a handshake and more often in a death grip. As we zoom through another military checkpoint I ask, "Why are we able to drive through so easily?" He replies, "The soldiers are just looking." Bewildered, I ask, "What are they looking for?" He says, "They look at your face," and I reply, "What do you mean?" He answers, "They are looking for Arab faces." Incredulous, I question, "Wait a minute. You told me that sometimes people think you are Arab because you look Arab and you speak fluent Arabic. I've seen Palestinians who are blond and blue eyed. What do you mean they are looking for Arab faces?" Unabashed, he answers, "They know when they see an Arab face. Then they also check the license plate. But they know. They're looking for the Arab faces." I can only manage a quiet *oy vey.*

As we pass another Jewish settlement Mordecai admits that he feels the discrimination against Jews from Arab countries has diminished because Israeli society is so blended. He confesses, however, that he sometimes has trouble at Ben Gurion airport because he's mistaken for an Arab. He has been stopped and quizzed by Israeli soldiers. He says what the soldiers are doing is listening for the accents, that is how they can tell who is a "real Arab."

Mordecai tells me he has traveled to America, loves America, and particularly likes New York City because it is big, filled with people, and busy. He explains Manhattan is his favorite but he also loves San Francisco. To my amazement, he adds, "At night, I love Las Vegas!" and then he starts laughing and he chuckles, "I love Disneyland too."

As we approach Jerusalem, Mordecai's thoughts turn back to Israel and he mentions that he thinks the big problem is really with the recent

Russian immigrants. This is a complaint that I have heard frequently. He says the Russians are poor, they maintain a separate social scene, and they make people nervous. "They're just not good people." I can only marvel at the tumble of prejudices, racism, demonization, and confusion that spills over this country of immigrants and discordant socio-economic and cultural waves. I am trying to understand the frequently voiced desire to get out of the settlements along with the strong support for Sharon, the belligerent warrior architect of the settlement project itself. The political, military, and economic blending of US and Israeli interests is also obviously woven into this friendly banter. Combining all of this with the deep disconnection between Israelis and Arabs and the complex and often hostile relationship between *Ashkenazic* and *Sephardic* Jews just adds another disconcerting element to this contradictory country.

Visiting the Rabbi and his Wife

Thanks to a recommendation by a colleague in Boston, I had the pleasure of visiting with Rabbi Levi Weiman-Kelman and his wife Paula on the medical delegation trip in 2004. We return in 2005 to visit them in Jerusalem after our afternoon with Gila. With my secular Jewish identifications, I am eager and curious to talk with Israelis who are strongly shaped by their religious conviction. After graduating from the New York Jewish Theological Seminary, Levi moved to Israel, lived on a kibbutz, spent a year at West London Synagogue and, like Gila, finally settled in the Baka neighborhood.

In the spring of 1984, a group started meeting in his home and began to develop a community that was spiritually oriented and focused on social justice. Bearded, balding, with playful eyes highlighted by intense eyebrows, the rabbi describes how this small group of worshipers grew into Kehillat Kol HaNeshama, now a nearly 400 member synagogue and an influential leader in the Israeli Movement for Progressive Judaism, also known as Reform Judaism. Offering an alternative vision to the right-wing, Orthodox, nationalistic Judaism that is a dominant force in Israel, this charismatic rabbi is known for developing a unique style of prayer. He borrows from the counterculture and yoga, but is rooted in a spirituality grounded in traditional Judaism. Dedicated to pluralism, social justice, and equality, at the end of every service his congregation recites a prayer for peace, *shalom-salaam*, in Hebrew and Arabic.

The delegates are sipping coffee and sitting around a table on Rabbi Levi's patio, which was recently completed, he notes, by local Palestinian laborers. The wood is nicely crafted with artistically placed mosaic tiles. A statue from Thailand of a female Buddhist monk graces the garden with a touch of Asia that reflects the rabbi's year-long sabbatical in Hong Kong. We are talking with the rabbi and his wife Paula, a documentary film-maker and videographer. Philadelphia born, Paula has traveled extensively, made films ranging from a documentary about a Seder in Dharmsala, India, to the first Bar Mitzvah in Beijing, and co-taught a documentary film course bringing together Israeli and Palestinian women through video production.

Children, Out of the "Bubble" into the Military

Levi is describing the experience of his son, Benjamin, who is currently training to be a paramedic in the army, living closely with a cross-section of Israelis that he has previously never encountered "in the little bubble we created in Jerusalem. So he's living with settlers who live in Gush Katif [in Gaza] and he's very pessimistic." The son is learning how committed these settlers are to paralyzing the upcoming Gaza disengagement; they are willing to do "everything it takes." The "bubble" Levi is referring to is the community of families he has built with his synagogue, a mix of people from English-speaking countries and native-born Israelis who are part of that congregation, "very much left-of-center, very intellectually oriented, very idealistic, very much committed to coexistence and a two state solution." I wonder aloud what happens to children who grow up in a liberal-minded family and then at the moment in life when they are at the edge of adulthood, self-discovery, and self-definition, find themselves in the Israeli military with all of the contradictory attitudes that abound there. Levi responds, "So far I've had two kids in the army and both of them handled it very differently and both of them were obviously raised with the same values and the same environments with the same brainwashing."

As Paula faced her son's upcoming military service last year, she told me that she had said to him, "I will support you if you are a refuser." He replied, "If I don't do it, only the thugs will go." At that time she feared that, like his older sister Zoë, he would be unable to cope with the moral contradictions presented by military service. Now Paula explains that Zoë, her oldest daughter, was drafted before the Second Intifada, during a time of optimism. "She went into the army in August 2000, and she worked as a liaison to the UN. She was going to bring peace. One of her first jobs was in Rafah, Gaza, and she would take the newspapers to the Egyptians and pick up their newspapers, so that we could read each other's newspapers, and then the Intifada started and ..." Levi chimes in and explains that all Zoë's hopes and dreams fell apart and instead of participating in a mission working with the UN and Israel, between Egypt and Israel, suddenly their daughter found herself in the midst of a war.

> After a little less than a year, she left the army because she was so unable to cope with that reality and that was a big crisis in the family. Our son who has similar left-of-center politics, but a very strong sense of duty and obligation, felt very strongly about serving in the army and he's made a big commitment to be in the army for extra time. He's going to be in the army for at least a whole extra year because of the medical training that he's getting. So on the one hand, very committed to being in the army, on the other hand for him it is very important to be in a medical unit so that he could be involved in saving lives and not taking lives. It's certainly one of the big challenges when you raise kids here, what are the values you want to give your kids and how you find the right balance between them, sharing all of your criticisms and patriotism at the same time. It's hard to get right. It's a real tough one.

Firmly in the Zionist Camp

The Weiman-Kelman's two older children have friends who are in full battle units, others who joined the refusers, fought political battles and went to jail, and others who have avoided army duty by being designated as "unsuited" for a variety of reasons. Paula adds that she and Levi support men and women who do not serve in the army on an individual basis, but not as a policy, because they see refusing as part of the problem, rather than as part of the solution. Levi has debated these complicated ethical issues within his own organization, Rabbis for Human Rights (RHR). RHR is the only Israeli rabbinic organization comprised of Reform, Orthodox, Conservative, and Reconstructionist rabbis and students. It was founded in 1988 in response to serious human rights violations by the Israeli military in the suppression of Intifada-related violence. He explains that RHR made a conscious policy not to be involved in supporting the movement of soldiers refusing to serve in the West Bank, but there is a variety of opinion within the group about this issue. Almost all members of RHR serve in the army and in the reserves and "we see ourselves firmly in the Zionist camp and that part of the obligation of being a citizen of this country is serving in the army. Now you actually have the phenomenon of older people like myself volunteering to go back to the army to help evacuate settlements to make up for the soldiers who aren't going." He assures us with a weary laugh that he has not volunteered; "I did enough army thank you."

My experience is that "Zionist" is a term with a multitude of connotations and I am curious how Levi defines the word. With total assurance he explains, "There is only one definition of Zionism that I know, the national right of the Jewish people to have a national homeland in the Land of Israel. I can't think of any other definition." He admits that this can get qualified and explains that he sees himself as, "a religious Zionist, so my Zionism is very much influenced and tempered by a religious vision, influenced by the prophets of Israel, a just society." He expands the definition, adding that Zionism is also, "a national movement of the Jewish people to re-establish a Jewish homeland after 2000 years of homelessness, in the Land of Israel."

Marginalization of the Left

The delegates wonder if he can reflect further on the state of the Israeli left and Levi remarks that he sees a steady continuation of deterioration and disintegration. He feels that Arafat's death seems to have proven that the right was correct about what an obstacle Arafat was to peace-making and that it now appears that the right wing was correct in refusing to deal with him.

> On the one hand, people on the left feel very marginalized because the right is implementing our plan. If Sharon and the Likud are implementing the political platform of the left-wing parties, then on the one hand we feel irrelevant, on the other hand, someone's implementing it so, but people don't know exactly how to digest it. So that's also why the right wing is traumatized, completely disoriented. How is it possible that the guy who

was the father of the settlement movement is now implementing the left-wing peace plan?

So there is a lot of confusion which is probably not bad in terms of things being very shook up, a feeling of ideologically everything is being thrown in a blender and nobody can really pretend to have clear answers. But, there is a sense of deep unease, both right and left, what on earth is going on here? The happy people are the people right in the middle, I would say, people who didn't trust the left but want peace. They wouldn't vote for the left because they didn't think the left was committed enough to Israeli security but they were disappointed that the right wing wasn't able to push any kind of peace plan forward. Now you have a right-wing party pushing a peace plan that pretty much speaks to the needs of the big center in Israel.

I ask if he really believes that the disengagement of Gaza is equivalent to the position of the political left. My understanding is that at the same time as the settlers in Gaza are being removed, Sharon is consolidating the settlements in the West Bank and building the separation wall at a furious pace. Levi explains that the first stage of any peace plan involves disengaging from Gaza. He readily admits that Sharon's long-term plans are not identical with the left in Israel. "I think the fantasy in the left is that there'll be a sort of inexorable dynamic with the beginning of this process and that the Palestinians will respond in fact, also with moderation, and then there will be so much pressure on Israel that if Sharon can't keep it moving forward, there will be elections and who knows?" He shrugs, confessing that it is impossible to know. Although Sharon's Kadima party had not yet emerged, Levi proposes with amazing premonition that some kind of center party will emerge and that there will be a realignment of the whole political spectrum.

But I say there is also a deep sense of anxiety because so much can go wrong. It can go wrong on so many levels that just as much as people are cautiously optimistic, people are deeply anxious that it won't take much for everything to grind to a halt and then to deteriorate further, so people are very confused and ambivalent. It's hard to know what's going to happen.

Sense of Confusion in the Community

Levi sees this duality in his own community, what his children call "the bubble." In this progressively oriented congregation, there is a deep sense of confusion regarding Sharon, an undermining sense of insecurity even going downtown or to a movie, and much anxiety over the economic situation. Reminding us of the economic crisis facing Israel, he estimates that approximately 25 percent of his congregation is unemployed and adds that the phrase he hears all the time is, "waiting for the shoe to drop. People are just waiting to hear the bad news. That's not a good place for people to be at." He describes how he can feel this tension, particularly at the regular weekly *Shabbat* services where he includes prayers for peace. "You can feel the intensity when we do those prayers. When things look good and we feel a little better then you can feel the hope in people's voices as we pray those prayers. When things are not so good you can hear the anxiety and despair in people's voices. Prayer is a good indicator of where people are at."

Just having returned from the West Bank, I wonder if the members of his congregation are aware of the separation wall. In his unpretentious, gentle but straightforward manner, Levi responds,

> People are really confused and ambivalent about the wall. On the one hand, nobody I know can possibly imagine that the wall is a good thing. Just aesthetically, it is so ugly, demographically it's so stupid, but it makes people feel safer. There's no doubt, since the wall's been going up, there's been less bombings, so people are deeply ambivalent. I'd say that we all deeply know that the wall is not a long-term solution, but there is nothing wrong with feeling better. People feel better, people feel safer.

Levi explains that the separation wall is a ten minute walk from his temple, so most of the members of his synagogue have seen the wall, feel badly about the suffering of Palestinians, and feel strongly that the wall should be built in such a way as to minimize this suffering.

> But I would say most people, and I would have to include at least myself, given the choice that it takes a kid two hours instead of a half hour to get to school, versus a bomber getting in easily or not easily, it's very inconvenient, I feel bad for the kid, but I'd rather not get blown up. I think that reflects how people feel; people don't want to get blown up. Again, I don't think anybody believes that the wall's a long-term solution to that. Terrorists are always just going to find new ways of overcoming obstacles. People like me believe that the only solution is a political solution and not a military solution.

Personal Insecurity

Levi's comments lead us into a conversation about the sense of deep personal insecurity that infects Israelis. He describes the experience of having guards at every public space. He cannot go into a supermarket or a restaurant without the ritual checking of bags. On the one hand, this feels like an endless waste of time and on the other hand he is grateful that the guards are checking.

> I know for me there was a pivotal moment. There's an electronics store that we take our things to get repaired right in our neighborhood. I remember the owner of the store who you just know from the neighborhood. We are not talking about someone deeply involved in politics or not a professor at a university. He described how one day he was just standing in the doorway of the store. He was just looking at the street and he saw a Palestinian approaching the entrance to a restaurant. He saw what looked to him from afar that the guard was roughing up the Palestinian and pushing him out. He was someone who is vaguely left-of-center, every fiber in his being protested and he started walking over to tell the guard to stop it. It turned out the guy was wired with a bomb and it was only a miracle that the bomb didn't go off.
>
> He described in very simple terms how his whole moral universe was collapsed at that moment because every fiber in his being was worried about this poor Palestinian who was being mistreated by an Israeli guard. If the guard hadn't done that, who knows how many people would have been killed in a restaurant where at any given moment there are five members of my synagogue. I think that is sort of a snapshot of how we on the one hand feel very distressed at Palestinian suffering but have a strong sense of self-preservation and there are people out there who are trying to kill us. To find a policy that both helps to preserve life and doesn't cause more suffering which will in turn create more terrorists is a lot easier to criticize than it is to implement.

With her dark penetrating brown eyes, earrings dangling on her delicate face, Paula goes on to explain the daily reality of risk. The other day there were road blocks on the way to French Hill after a "hot warning," which implies that the authorities have information that there is an imminent bomb threat. She says that the authorities eavesdrop on phones and have an incredible system of listening to cell phone conversations. For an entire day police and army were everywhere and it was impossible to move about the city. But they found the assailant. Levi adds, "He was Islamic Jihad," and Paula says that they traced him back to Syria. With a shrug, Levi says everyone wants to blame Syria now, so who knows the full story. Levi adds that there can be road blocks in the city three days in a row and then nothing for three weeks. Living with this constant anxiety and uncertainty has made Israelis emotionally fragile. They are smoking more, losing their tempers in pubs, people out walking their dogs end up shooting each other over some trivial altercation.

> That's why it's hard not to be cautiously optimistic at the same time we are deeply anxious. Part of that is the pernicious effect that the occupation has had. There is no way you can act in a certain way when you're in the army and then come home and think it's not going to affect the way you treat the people you deal with. So one of the dangers of the occupation is that you end up treating people like objects and not like human beings. That definitely spills into real life.
>
> It spills into your personal relationships and into your professional life. So if you're spending a month in reserve duty working at a roadblock or in a unit in Jenin [West Bank], there's no way you can't bring the occupation home with you into your life within the Green Line, which is why it would be good for Israel and Palestine for the occupation to end.

The Role of the International Community

The conversation drifts into a discussion about the role of international pressure on the conflict. Levi insists that American pressure is especially important and that,

> Israelis rightfully are very suspicious of Europe and are reluctant to relate to European criticism of Israeli policies, to take that seriously, because the perception in Israel is that Europe is so pro-Palestinian, so quick to criticize Israel. There is more of a sense that America does have Israel's best interests at heart. On the one hand there is not much we can do facing American pressure. We are so dependent on America.

He adds that people on the left are disoriented because,

> It seems like Bush's policies are having a very positive effect on this region of the world. There is no doubt that Bush's policies in general, including the war in Iraq and his very stubborn stance demanding democracy, look like a positive effect on our part of the world. There is no doubt in my mind that a lot of the movement towards democracy in the Palestinian camp is a combination of Arafat's death and very clear American pressure.

He argues that although none of us wants to say anything nice about Bush, his current policies are supporting "the winds of democracy blowing through the Middle East in a way they never were before." With Levi's underlying optimism he feels that in times like these where there is great confusion, there is also the possibility of the emergence of new leadership and new ideas although there is always the danger of "the crazies" grabbing power.

Israeli Political Movements

When looking at the left-wing movements in Israel, Levi notes that in his congregation there are monthly meetings of both Peace Now and Meretz, the dovish civil rights party of Israel. Levi at 51 is part of the "youth delegation" and he states there has been little success in attracting the younger generation. He finds that his own three children are very idealistic, but fairly cynical about movements and politics in general. We ask about other Israeli peace and coexistence groups and Levi reiterates that they are all very marginal, even Rabbis for Human Rights, "not even remotely mainstream." To make his point further, he explains that if he goes to a peace rally, most of the demonstrators are in their fifties and sixties. On the other hand, the right-wing settler movement is dominated by teenagers and twenty-somethings who have tremendous youthful energy and passion, "Obviously totally misdirected and perverted, but very real and that's certainly part of their appeal." He finds that the secular world is, "pretty much directed towards all the worst excesses of American culture that have seeped into Israel, consumerism and partying."

Levi believes that the great failure of the Israeli left has been to focus only on peace issues and thus they have not garnered grassroots support among lower-class *Sephardim* or Russians. He claims that no one on the left has really addressed their social issues. He also notes,

> The left's inability to talk in religious terms is also poison to mainstream Israelis who don't see themselves as Orthodox but see themselves as traditional and are very put off by people who talk in non- or anti-religious terms which the left has sadly traditionally done here. Part of the great appeal of the right wing is that they know how to manipulate religious language and the left seems to be tone deaf and completely inarticulate. This is tragic because all our values are found in religious texts, part of our Jewish tradition. It's a huge failure of the left and the peace camp to talk in that language.

On to the Next Meeting

We leave this warm gathering with all of its thoughtfulness and paradoxes, washed in a bitter-sweet feeling. On the one hand, Levi and Paula are part of a vibrant, progressive, growing community; the idiosyncratic and eclectic rabbi is now a mature and respected religious leader with a devoted and international following. On the other hand, his sober assessment of the emotional pain, economic distress, and rightward political swings in Israel and his generosity towards Bush's policies are enormously worrisome. Levi remarks that he never imagined that he would be involved in an organization like RHR, where he is fighting for tolerance and basic human rights in a society that has come to feel that a Jewish life is of greater value than a non-Jewish life. I wonder if that belief has not actually been true since the inception of the state and is one of the underlying weaknesses in this struggling and contradictory, blundering democracy.

But there is no time for further conversation today. Levi, the son of a leading American Conservative rabbi, a lover of Star Trek, and a deep believer in the spiritual power of breathing while praying, straps on his bicycle helmet, grabs his bike, kisses his wife, and cycles off to his next engagement. We hail a cab and begin to engage our next unsuspecting driver. "We want to go to a supermarket in the shopping center in French Hill ... So where are you from?"

Part Two
Palestinian Trauma, Resilience
and Resistance

6
Checkpoints: Crossing the Line

L OOKING BACK AT THE EARLIER chapters, much of this story is about finding my voice as a Diaspora Jew, grounded in mutual sympathy and history with my Israeli cousins as well as a refusal to demonize Palestinians. An important part of my education has involved crossing lines, traveling, working, and listening in Israel and then crossing over to the West Bank and Gaza and experiencing daily life as faced by my Palestinian colleagues. I am not speaking of metaphorical lines in the sand, but rather jagged, dangerous lines of raw emotion and sharp-edged barbed wire. I am repeatedly struck by how Israelis and Palestinians suffer from fear of the other's violence. Working with Israeli and Palestinian health and human rights groups, my understanding of the painful human price of war and occupation, of two peoples inextricably bound by land, hope, and mutual distrust, has gradually crystallized. This chapter is thus about my own transformations, crossing traditional lines, looking for the human faces that personify these difficult issues. I have learned that each society has a long history of trauma at the hands of the so-called "enemy," yet the current balance of power is hardly equal, the suffering hardly the same.

The Fear of Suicide Bombings

I remember the moment at the beginning of the Second Intifada when Paula and I had to go pick somebody up downtown. We get in the car and Paula said, "Maybe we shouldn't both go. If something happens and we both get killed, then what will happen to the kids? Maybe just one of us should go and do this errand?" What does it mean to have that kind of a conversation when you are just going to pick somebody up in an office downtown? I think that even though you go outside and see people and everybody seems to be functioning, people are really just barely keeping it together. This has been four-and-a-half years of living with incredible anxiety, living with real fear, unbelievable uncertainty. It's a lot to live with. I think it's amazing that we cope as well as we do on some level and that for everything, I think one of the things that characterizes Israeli society which you are only beginning to see in Palestinian society, is [that it is] remarkably self-critical. Every day there are articles in the newspapers describing Palestinian suffering. I think though people don't know what the solutions are; people are very committed to looking at what's wrong with Israeli society. Sadly all my 20 years of very intense dialogue with Palestinians, [I think that] what Palestinians and Israelis share is an ability to be critical of Israel. (Rabbi Levi Weiman-Kelman, Jerusalem)

The Tanks Were in Front of my House

One night about 11:30, the Israel troops get to our area. First, there are two helicopters shooting around me. So we found the safest place in my home to stay. After a while, the tanks come into my area and in front of my house and went to a neighbor's house. One big tank was standing all of the time in front of my house so we were not able to move. They start to phone that building for the people to leave it because they want to destroy it. It's a four-story building with at least 40 people living there. After half an hour, I was watching from the window and the people left and the tank started, the soldiers started taking bags and [then there was] a very huge explosion. So I got my children in the middle of the house and I brought cotton to put into their ears and blankets to cover them, many blankets [so] that they won't be injured by any pieces of damage, whether from my house or coming in. What I saw is a very big flame getting in from the window, breaking all the windows, and getting in the window in the middle of the house. Flame with a very dark smoke was getting in front of me and many things around me start to get broken. I lie over my kids to see if they start shouting after this explosion though we were telling them stories, trying to comfort them because they don't recognize what might happen. I saw a lot of the glass around the house, the windows were broken. I went running to see what has happened to that building, the whole building was down and the neighborhood that was beside it exactly one meter, two meters beside it, also were damaged severely. (Safwat Diab, project manager, Human Rights Project and the Children's Project, Gaza Community Mental Health Program, Gaza City)

In the Name of Security

In my conversation with the Israeli medical student, he explained the contradiction that while Israel is a major military power backed by the world's superpower, individual Israelis feel personally insecure, although they are mostly able to live their daily lives in a predictable fashion. In contrast, Palestinians living under occupation face a total disruption of daily life as well as economic and social development. Many Israelis feel that their needs for better security mandate the creation of multiple checkpoints in the West Bank and Gaza, as well as the growing separation wall. Palestinians, on the other hand, universally find the checkpoints and the separation wall brutal and humiliating, and assert that they have little relationship to Israel's security needs. The checkpoints and wall are chiefly designed to disrupt and destroy Palestinian civil and economic society and any hope for a viable future. Ironically, mental health providers often point to the fact that a predominantly young, poor, angry population is at great risk of turning to violent resistance when faced with daily humiliation and restrictions. I was surprised to learn that most Jewish Israelis have little or no contact with Palestinians and no experience in the Occupied Territories except possibly in the army. Given this massive disconnection, I think it is important to examine what actually happens at checkpoints, which are rapidly becoming the last intimate places where the average Israeli may meet the average Palestinian.

A Network of Obstructions

According to a number of Israeli and Palestinian sources, there are many barriers between Israel and the Occupied Territories and even more within the West Bank and Gaza.[1] These create a network of obstructions that the Israeli government has stated are necessary for security; dissenting Jews, Christians, and Palestinians strongly disagree. In November 2004, the UN Office for the Coordination of Human Affairs (OCHA) estimated the total comes to 719 physical barriers or obstructions of some sort, ranging from highly militarized terminals and guard towers to piles of dirt and trenches across roads.[2] In addition, there are 41 roads and sections of roads, often major arteries, covering over 700 kilometers, where Palestinian travel is restricted or forbidden.[3] Since the Gaza disengagement, the IDF's ability to close down all movement of goods and people to and from Gaza has repeatedly led analysts to call this area "the world's largest prison."[4]

While I cannot truly know what is happening in the mind of an Israeli soldier or a Palestinian student, mother, laborer, or professor waiting at a checkpoint, I would like to share a number of experiences from my 2005 trip to Israel and the Occupied Territories. These descriptions will give an intimate glimpse into the imbalanced and mutually destructive relationship between the controller and the controlled.

Seema Jilani at the Al-Aqsa Mosque, March 6, 2005

Seema Jilani is a lively and engaging medical student from Baylor College of Medicine in Houston. Though born in Louisiana, because of her father's work with international corporations such as Halliburton, she has lived all over the world. Her parents are originally from Pakistan and she has felt varying levels of attachment and adherence to her Islamic faith as she has evolved into adulthood. She was interested in exploring the Israeli/Palestinian conflict with a group of Jewish medical activists. While in Jerusalem, she went to pray with a medical student, ST (she declined to be named), at the Al-Aqsa Mosque, the third holiest site for Muslims.

On returning, she tearfully recounted her experience.

First, to get into the mosque, we had to pass a checkpoint and they [Israeli police] didn't believe that I was Muslim, and they made me show my passport and then I had to do *wudu*, the cleansing ritual that you should do before you enter the mosque or before you pray. The Israeli soldiers watched me walk in, with my headscarf. They didn't say anything, and as I walked out from the cleansing ritual, I didn't even realize I am so used to walking into my mosque so freely, they stopped us and they shouted at us and they said, "No, no, wait, stop," When they stopped me, they said, "Why are you here ? Give me your passport."

I was made to recite verses from the Koran that they don't know. They didn't even pronounce it right when they asked me to recite it. I was very surprised and then in the middle of the verse, they said, "Stop it. I don't want to hear it anymore." Then I said no, I won't stop it. I have to continue and I have to finish it because you don't just stop a prayer in the middle. He wouldn't give me my passport until I said the Koran verses and then as I said them with each intonation, he would shake the passport and they were laughing, when I did it. With each verse that I said, he would shake the passport right in my face about two millimeters from my nose. When I said, "Amen," he said, "Here, now you can have your passport."

We were so taken aback, [ST] just said that they're assholes and she wasn't shocked so I assume this has happened before. I've always been the type of person that's been nonconfrontational with soldiers and I don't take too many risks, but at this time I've never felt so strongly that I really would like to finish. You can't turn me on and off like I am a puppet. This was only about control. You ask me to say the prayer, now let me finish it. You can't turn me off and then wave my passport in my face as I am saying the holiest verses of my religion. I'm not even that religious but it should mean something you know?

I really felt like, not even hitting him, I just wanted to spit in his face. Then the amazing thing is, you walk into Aqsa and it's the most beautiful mosque I have ever set foot in. It's the most beautiful building. It's more beautiful than Mecca or Medina by far, which I found astonishing because I thought I would never feel that. I've never felt so much happiness and so much sadness in one second.

Although there are good reasons to have soldiers guarding an important mosque in Jerusalem, I cannot understand how intimidating and humiliating a Muslim from the US improves Israeli security. Seema also found the experience excruciatingly painful. "I don't know how people do it here every day, I don't understand. I'm a wreck. I'm crying. I was praying in a mosque." It is interesting to me how quickly after an episode of intense humiliation, Seema felt provoked to a more aggressive response, spitting in the soldier's face. I can only shudder thinking what would have happened if she had not restrained herself. Later she remarked that the Israeli guards made her feel less than human, "like a savage or an animal." This is a complaint I frequently heard from Palestinians who often stand for hours at unpredictable checkpoints, awaiting the decisions of young Israeli soldiers.

An Afternoon with Machsom Watch, Sawahira Checkpoint, March 6, 2005

Machsom Watch, an organization of close to 500 Israeli women, was founded in 2001.[5] Its members are dedicated to daily monitoring of checkpoints in the West Bank and Jerusalem, and thus the delegates were curious to join two of these women on one of their shifts as we struggle to understand the role and impact of checkpoints on Israeli and Palestinian society. Ronnie Perlman came from Czechoslovakia at the age of 25 after her family perished in the Holocaust; her children are officers in the Israeli army. Ofra Bernarcy grew up in Israel and like Ronnie is a psychotherapist as well as a peace activist. Both of these women work with Machsom Watch, documenting the conduct of soldiers and Palestinians and attempting to intervene when they see violations of human rights, intimidation, and severe restrictions of movement. They explain that the checkpoints are mostly staffed by young Israeli recruits, usually men, 18 to 22 years of age. The group also submits regular reports on their website and files written complaints to the responsible Israeli agencies.[6]

Leaving the German Colony, a former Arab neighborhood in southwest Jerusalem, now trendy and gentrified, our delegation climbs into two small cars and heads out to the hills of East Jerusalem. Near the checkpoint we pass a cluster of Arab homes and a group of donkeys. Ofra explains straightforwardly that the families are not allowed to travel to their homes in cars and are forced to use donkeys to transport all of their belongings. We park and walk towards a sophisticated concrete block and barbed wire checkpoint, Sawahira, with headquarters that include a computer system and concrete enclosure. It is placed between rocky rolling hills, goats and sheep grazing, little Arab villages tucked in the folds of landscape, a Jewish settlement perched across the crest, a string of orange rooftops. The sky is a stunning Mediterranean blue that belies the human drama below. There is a concrete divide and a long line of traffic stretching away from us. To our right, Palestinian laborers who are leaving work in Israel stand in line waiting to return to their homes in the West Bank. The checkpoint is manned by several Israeli soldiers carrying automatic weapons, looking at permits, and waving people through one by one.

At the concrete barrier we see an elegantly dressed woman in a dark pants suit, high heels, stylish hairdo, pleading with the soldiers. To her left, a nicely dressed Arab man is pacing and chain smoking. Beyond the headquarters is a young man in his twenties who is handcuffed behind his back, sitting dejectedly in a roofed pen, apparently detained. As the afternoon unfolds, we learn that the older man is a 36-year-old nurse from Jenin who is going to his sister's wedding in Bethlehem with a female relative and her son, Pascal, who live in East Jerusalem. Shortly before we arrived, an Israeli soldier had an interaction with Pascal, refusing to let them pass. The young man reportedly raised his arms in anger and frustration.

Ofra explains that there is an arbitrariness to the soldiers' decisions and the "rules" are constantly changing. During the Second Intifada,

Palestinians living in East Jerusalem were fortunate in that they could travel easily into the West Bank to visit friends and family. Now East Jerusalem residents are facing greater obstacles and there are even plans to require special permits for them to enter the West Bank at all. The actual decision, however, is often left to the individual soldier.

The soldiers immediately restrained and handcuffed Pascal and now he is being charged with attacking a soldier. The mother is desperately appealing to the soldiers to let her son go but they have already called the police and he is to be taken to a police station for interrogation. Ronnie comments, "She's trying, she's trying, and that's what very often works at the checkpoint. Because there are no rules, you know. It's ridiculous, stupid, irrational rules, so she's trying to convince the soldiers to let him go. But I think it is too late, I think they already called the [police]."

Ronnie and Ofra begin a cautious dance, letting the soldiers know they are here, bearing witness to every move, offering advice and legal assistance to the Palestinian woman who is not sure these outspoken Jewish women will improve her case or doom her to failure. Ofra explains,

> This is just a family on the way [to a wedding] and you can see how nicely they are dressed, and in this sense they are very resilient in the sense that they keep their life, they keep their dignity. This is something that is very astonishing, despite the difficulties and the humiliation. On the other hand, Amira Hass [a Jewish Israeli journalist who lives in Ramallah] said sometimes the checkpoints are going very smoothly and one of the explanations is that because people, if they don't need to go, they don't go. So they are tamed already, because they don't want to go through all this. So next time they will think many times before trying to go to Bethlehem. My point of view, this is a policy, somebody up there knows exactly what he is doing. He knows that in this way you will train the people not to go, not to cross, and so many families maybe will say, "OK, we give up."

Interestingly, the older man is eager to talk with us and angry that Pascal has not behaved appropriately at the checkpoint. Ronnie remarks, "He's furious because they are late for the wedding, he says, [Pascal] did it wrong because you have to be obsequious, that's the rule of the game. The more obsequious you are, the better chance you have of getting things done. When you show any pride, it's an 18-year-old against another, you know." Commenting on the dynamics with the soldier, who like many has immigrated from the former Soviet Union,

Ronnie adds, "He's Russian and of course that's the most annoying thing because whenever you talk to them, they [behave] as if the Palestinians are naughty children, [who] don't know how to behave." But the dynamic is even more complex. "He's Russian, so Russian means, he hates me. He hates me for what I stand for, a successful Israeli who has time to play here at the [checkpoint]. He's not doing it because he is a Zionist; he's doing it for money." Ronnie observes that in addition to their political differences, there are underlying conflicts related to education, class, and racism towards Arabs.

Ultimately Ronnie is able to convince the commander at the checkpoint who is *Druze* (a distinct Arab community that serves in the Israeli army), and "a nice guy," to admit that Pascal did not physically attack the soldier, but raised his arms in anger. The commander transmits this information to a higher-level military authority by cell phone, and Ronnie obtains a lawyer for the family. I watch Ronnie use a combination of sheer chutzpah, patience, caution, and her ability to speak Russian with the soldiers. At times, the Russian soldiers yell or laugh at her, but she never loses her composure. We leave before there is any resolution, hoping that the soldiers may be more willing to compromise if we are not present and watching. Of course, the family misses the wedding. Bethlehem is all of 15 minutes away by the most direct route.

In "A Counterview, Checkpoints 2004," the Machsom Watch website annual report eloquently states:

> After four years at the checkpoints, day after day, we can state with a certainty we did not have at the start, that there are two separate groups at the checkpoints. One group, holding the gun, has all the power and is corrupted by it. The other group is oppressed and humiliated but definitely not defeated. Each functions alongside the other, linked by lunatic and tragic ties of humiliators and humiliated, controllers and controlled – soldiers and Palestinians, Palestinians and soldiers. When we watch the soldiers, as women peace-activists, we consider them as agents of the occupation. When we watch them as if they were our sons – flesh, bone of our bones, the next generation of our shared society – we are appalled by the intolerable experiences they undergo and the moral values they crush underfoot.[7]

Dr. Allam Jarrar, Nablus, March 4, 2005

Our medical delegation attempted to visit the city of Nablus in 2003, 2004, and 2005, working with members of PMRS. Sometimes we passed through the checkpoints with a minimum of interrogation, sometimes we waited for hours without success, sometimes within hours one checkpoint was closed to us when a nearby one was open. There were never any explanations. In March, 2005, our taxi drops us off at the Beit Iba checkpoint where we are greeted by imposing guard towers on an overlooking hill, clusters of tanks, well-armed Israeli soldiers, and concrete chutes to funnel the human traffic. After a series of fairly brisk, hostile interchanges with a young recruit, clutching our letter of invitation and our growing sense of indignation, we are allowed to pass, only to be approached by a small crowd of cab drivers, each vying for our business. We are taken to the Al Yasmeen Hotel in the old city of Nablus, unpack in charming rooms draped with plastic ivy vines, and gather to meet Dr. Allam Jarrar.

We sit around a long conference table in the hotel, surrounded by graceful archways, a stained glass window pock-marked with bullet holes, and endless cups of thick Turkish coffee. Allam, a savvy, well-traveled physician with a twinkly sense of humor, is speaking on a wide range of topics as we pepper him with questions. Born in Nablus in 1954, educated in the USSR and at Boston University, he has worked as a medical officer with UNRWA, and since 1981 helped found and manage PMRS, one of the largest NGOs providing health services in the Occupied Territories. His focus has been on community-based rehabilitation. He has had an active role in the Palestinian NGO Network[8] since 1993 and more recently the Democratic Alliance movement.

We soon fall upon the issue of his inability to move freely within the West Bank. His face becomes intense as he explains,

> I live in Nablus. I work in Ramallah. It's difficult for me now to cross almost everyday this Huwwara checkpoint. The checkpoint is not a means of security. Let's be very clear with that. It's a means of repression, it's a means of intimidation, and it's a means of punishment for civilians, because, if they want to keep the security of Israel, well they can have these checkpoints on the entrances of Israel, not between Nablus and the surrounding villages. Why put the checkpoint up outside Nablus? Just for humiliation purposes, just to show the people that you are under control, we're controlling your life, and if you don't behave, we will make your life impossible. This is exactly the aim of the Israelis to disintegrate the Palestinian society, to effect disintegration within Palestine and to deal with Palestinians as clusters – Jenin, Nablus, Tulkaram, Ramallah, Hebron, Bethlehem – and not to deal with it as a whole community, a whole society,

a whole integrity. This is a kind of result that has happened. A process of disintegration is taking place.

As the conversation unfolds, Allam describes an incident that occurred during a recent election when he was traveling with one of the presidential candidates, Mustafa Barghouthi.

We were after a campaign in Jenin area and it was night and usually you don't drive at night because it's so dangerous. We drove and it was a checkpoint and I remember there were three cars [in our group], one of them is a Palestinian car that we drove in and the other one with a Jerusalem plate, it's a yellow plate car, but they passed because it's a yellow plate [identifying the vehicle as registered in Israel]. We were stopped of course, and I just went out of the car and tried to talk to the officer there. I said, "Good evening. We're in a campaign and this is Mustafa Barghouthi the presidential candidate," and the Israeli soldier just laughed. "As you say, and so what?" I said, "What do you mean, so what? I'm telling you this is a presidential candidate and you should respect this because your government is engaged also in this." And he said, "Fuck," sorry, "Fuck you and fuck Mustafa Barghouthi!"

Then Mustafa came out of the car and [the soldier] tried to beat me, and Mustafa tried to protect me, and then the other guys who are with us, they tried to engage in a fight with the soldiers. When the officer realized that there is a fight, this is unacceptable, where people can fight just by hand with the army, so he shouted out to the other soldiers. They started to put the guns ready for shooting, then they started to beat up me, Mustafa, and the rest of the group, put us on the ground and put the guns here [to my neck]. Then there was a kind of talk between us, we said something about, you will be sorry for that, you will pay for this.

They started to say something like, "Fuck all Barghouthi, fuck all Palestinians, you're, what did you say, presidential candidate?" Or something like this. In their minds, I think as kids, it was a cultural shock for them that Palestinians can get up to this level of being democratic and launching a kind of campaign and being involved in a presidential election. This guy wants to be president of these stupid Palestinians? They are trying to make a president? This was kind of intimidating for them; the retaliation was very violent.

So, the other car with the other guys started to make contacts [by cell phone]. Ruchama [Marton of PHR-I] with our friends in Israel, and international representatives, and there was a kind of interference through the military liaison offices there, and after one hour, they came to us and said, "You'd have been allowed to pass in a peaceful manner without any kind of interference from our side if you behaved" not in a "submissive" [way] ... but "if you behaved," as he said, "in accordance with the procedures."

We said, "Fuck you and fuck your government! We'll show you." Then we went to the hospital and made a press conference and made a big noise out of it.

But I mean, I just want to describe my feelings while sitting there with the gun put here [at my neck] and the soldiers, we're thinking what stupid thing we are doing, presidential elections? Under occupation? With these circumstances? It's just ridiculous. Maybe we should stop that. But after moving from this side, we said, OK maybe this is good. Maybe to have elections and do things like this is also good. I'm not sure but, I mean in such an incident, inside you there are like two things. One is a peaceful guy that is looking forward with hope and with determination that things will change, and another guy that wants to fuck up everything.

I struggle to understand what provoked the soldiers, what had Drs. Jarrar and Barghouthi done? Allam is all of 5'5," clearly in his fifties, slightly overweight, and not at all physically threatening. As the conversation unfolds, Allam explains that his crime had probably been one of attitude. He agrees that when it's a little tense, if a Palestinian wants to get through a checkpoint he approaches very quietly, holds his hands in front, and never looks in the eye of the soldiers. "Never look into the eyes of the soldiers. This is the 'procedure.' The 'procedure' is to be submissive, to be inferior and to obey as a slave. This is the 'procedure,' and of course we violated the procedures!"

For me, several important themes emerge from this interaction that can also be seen as a metaphor for the Israel/Palestine conflict as a whole. Allam admits that his refusal to behave as a submissive person living under occupation, driving at night in the Jenin area and looking the soldier in the eye, is both an act of foolishness and an act of resistance. He starts the conversation with the soldiers in a dignified manner and is met by rude and arrogant young men who he understands are threatened by the concept of an educated Palestinian working on a democratic election. The soldiers respond with a physical attack, the frequent language of the occupier, and the Palestinians fight back despite their lack of weapons, reminiscent of Palestinian youth throwing stones at oncoming tanks. I wonder what is happening in the minds of young soldiers who are able to behave in this arrogant, disrespectful, and physically threatening manner when approached by an articulate, middle-aged, professionally dressed Palestinian physician. Was it difficult to dehumanize him and thus necessary to provoke and shame him when he acted too "uppity," to use a term from our own racial struggles? This incident also provokes in Allam a moment of self-doubt, followed by a desire for revenge, and then what I would call a "civilized revenge," the press conference. When not under physical attack, Allam's resistance is all nonviolent and verbal, but he is very angry nonetheless and refuses to be humiliated. Thus he is able to keep his self-respect in a potentially dangerous situation and able to end on a note of defiance. It should also be noted that he needed pressure from other Israeli and international forces to resolve this dispute without serious injury, suggesting that outside influences may be necessary to disengage these enmeshed players.

Dr. Majed Dweik, Hizma Checkpoint, March 1, 2004

Several of the medical delegates are scheduled to give a series of academic lectures at a hospital in Hebron. First, we must travel from Ramallah where we are staying at the City Inn Palace Hotel, meet up with our medical student guide in East Jerusalem, and then set off to the hospital in Hebron. In the hotel lobby, clusters of men smoke cigarettes, there are large, inviting leather couches, an impressive fountain, and huge, ornate vases filled with bright orange, yellow, and red plastic flowers. *Al Jazeera* blasts from the TV and there is an intermittent hum from the coffee shop where the aroma of freshly made Arabic coffee drifts into the smoke.

We are awaiting the arrival of Dr. Majed Dweik, Dean of Students at Al Quds Medical School and radiologist at Augusta Victoria Hospital in East Jerusalem. He plans to take us to the hospital where we will meet the medical student and then travel on to Hebron to the Al Ahli Hospital. The evening before, he mentioned, "I'll pick you up at the hotel at 7 am." We assume that he will come in a car but when he arrives, he explains that he can't drive to East Jerusalem because he has the wrong colored license plates on his car and thus his driving is restricted to the West Bank. He hails a cab and we drive to the checkpoint.

When we pull up, there is a churning mass of people, mostly children on their way to school and adults on their way to work, all attempting to get into single lines, much like herded cattle. We find the chute designated for women, people over 50, children, and doctors. At the actual checkpoint there are two Israeli soldiers, probably in their twenties, a woman and a man. The woman's face is almost blank. She does not make eye contact. Her voice is gruff and she yells repeatedly. There is a flood of little school children, five or six years old, cute little kids, the girls with their hair in quirky pony tails. They each wear a backpack. The soldier yells at each one and makes them stop and opens the backpack and feels inside. I look at the faces of these children staring fearfully at her, aware of her power over them. If one of them gets ahead she makes them come back. During this interaction, there is a brutality in her face that is very frightening. I keep thinking, she's wondering, which one of these kids is carrying an explosive. When I look at the faces of these children, they look like innocent children caught in an ugly, complex interface that is probably beyond their comprehension.

Next to the female soldier is a slightly older male who is smiling, much more friendly and engaging. We are standing behind the Dean of the medical school and he takes out his five ID cards and permits. We watch this lovely, dignified man with his briefcase, in his suit, looking very professional, standing in line, and realize he has to do this every time he wants to go from home to work and from work to home.

The cabbie that drives us to Augusta Victoria Hospital has to go through a special checkpoint where he has to have a permit not only for himself, but also for his cab. At the side of the checkpoint there is a widened area where the taxi parks. The soldier takes the cabbie's papers and as we wait, I watch the face of the cab driver. At first he has this look of resignation, and then he starts to look really annoyed. He and Majed start talking animatedly in Arabic and we wait and then we wait even more. We are wondering what is going on and finally the cab driver has reached his limit. He gets out of the cab, walks over to the place where the soldiers are sitting and storms back with his permit.

I ask Majed what has happened and he explains that when the cab driver went over to the soldiers, the soldiers just looked up and said, "Oh we were just bringing you your permit," when clearly they were not just bringing his permit. They were just making him wait. I suspect this kind of incident happens to this man hundreds and hundreds of times a year.

As I reflect on this experience it seems clear to me that Majed both needed to maintain his sense of dignity and professionalism in the face of a humiliating situation and also experienced the checkpoint as such a normal situation that he didn't feel a need to explain until we were in the middle of the encounter. It was apparent to us that the complicated permit system, the detailed level of control over daily movement, the level of aggravation and harassment obviously produces a disruption and unpredictability over life's most ordinary tasks. It was painfully obvious that Majed can never predict if he will get to work and how long it may take him and that these questions are answered by soldiers young enough to be his children. Walking in the shoes of a Palestinian, it feels like this system of control is primarily designed to make the civilian Palestinians miserable, but it also makes them angry. Ultimately that cannot be in Israel's interest. In my view, for the young Israeli soldiers this appears to be an impossible, dehumanizing task; a heavily armed military controlling a civilian population where every ordinary Palestinian is viewed as a potential terrorist. Experiencing this as an outsider, I was struck that this dynamic is now part of "normal," yet it is, for both peoples, detrimental to hope, to understanding the "other," and to feeling that life could ever be better. I wonder what it would be like to grow up and never meet a Jewish Israeli who had a decent thing to say to you. I wonder what happens to young Israelis who only meet Palestinians at the opposite ends of a gun, who fear every child is a potential suicide bomber, who mourn the loss of friends from Netanya or Tel Aviv.

A Taste of Palestine, Ben Gurion Airport, March 12, 2005

I understand that it is never possible to truly know another person's experience but my turn to walk in the shoes of what Israeli security views as the "enemy" comes early one morning at Ben Gurion Airport. We are leaving Israel. The medical delegation arrives bleary-eyed and anxious at 4:30 am and strolls through the newly rebuilt, modern entry. Once in line to check in, we are immediately accosted by a woman and her persistent questions. "What were you doing in Israel? Where did you go? Are you alone? Are you with a group?" She is very interested that we traveled as a group and wants details as to our relationships, our purpose, and our destinations. While I understand the need for airport security, the barrage of questions keeps coming over and over again and she is soon joined by four more airport interrogators. They are particularly curious about our Muslim medical student and they want to know the origin of her name. After some dancing around, Seema replies, "My mother and father," which clearly annoys the security officials. The cat and mouse game has begun in earnest. Finally after multiple questions, Seema states that she is of Pakistani origin and then they want to know when she last visited Pakistan, who she had visited, and so forth, although her passport clearly states she was born in Louisiana and her accent is distinctively Texan.

The swarm of officialdom continues with questions repeated over and over and our repeated answers. "What did you do in Israel? Why are you here?" I notice that different color security stickers are being affixed to different passports and that Seema and I are different from the rest of the group. When I ask one of the women about this, she replies hostilely, "Oh, it's security."

I want to be clear that in addition to this all happening pre-coffee and at an incredibly early hour, I am not particularly threatening in appearance. I am a 56-year-old Jewish physician, mother of two. I wear a wedding band. My features mirror my Russian and Polish grandparents and I have the kind of face that usually provokes strangers to share their most intimate secrets with me in public places like airports. I am not wearing any political buttons and carry no literature from any organization remotely Palestinian or peace-oriented. My crime may be that I am traveling with a medical delegation invited by PHR-I, my passport bears a stamp from Gaza, and one of my colleagues is Muslim. I do not think that we have been selected for extra security by accident. Last year the pediatrician in our delegation was singled out for especially intimidating airport treatment and barely made the plane flight home. Later he discovered that his Palm Pilot had been downloaded by airport security agents.

After the interrogation, they herd us over to an enormous x-ray machine where all of our possessions are x-rayed and then the airport officials pick the medical student and me for further security clearance. No explanations are given and we are escorted to another area of the airport by two unsmiling women. All of our belongings are searched, every suitcase, every backpack, everything is taken out and re-scanned and wiped with a black wand covered with white paper that I believe is sensitive to explosives. Despite this invasion into my personal belongings, I also feel a sense of safety because it is so public, despite the edge of humiliation and embarrassment, the underwear and socks strewn about. Everything is re-x-rayed, but there is particular interest in my mini-disc recorder. The mini-disc is taken away, further inspected, and creates some general commotion that is subsequently resolved.

The next thing that really bothers the inspectors is a box of halvah I had purchased for my husband. The box is sealed and they want me to open the halvah. Despite my understanding of the need for airport security, I am beginning to feel the utter absurdity of this whole experience. I bought this halvah in the supermarket. I do not want to open it and risk confiscation at US customs. After a few minutes of arguing, we come to a negotiated settlement which involves piercing the halvah with the inspector's name tag pin and then shaking the box and scanning whatever crumbs sprinkle out. All this time people keep prodding, why are you here, are you with friends, what did you do, how did you find Israel? I wonder if this is some kind of stress-inducing technique for the weary traveler who may blurt out some incriminating information.

At the table next to me I catch a glimpse of an unfortunate lady. She sounds British, probably in her sixties, tussled grey hair, and she is frantic. All of her luggage and piles of literature advocating Palestinian liberation theology is strewn over the metal table. I understand from the conversation that she has been working with SABEEL, a major Christian peace organization in Jerusalem. She is clearly upset and the officials are interrogating her. A wave of sadness sweeps over me; working for peace or coexistence seems to be considered a suspicious activity.

Next a brief command informs me that I am going to another security area. This time I am a bit unnerved as I am escorted through doors that require special cards and I am no longer in a public space. I stare intently at the security guard. She has a big lumbering body, looks young and pregnant, her nametag sounds Polish. I ask her where she is from, she replies, from Poland via Argentina. I am able to get a little conversation going, but she is not going to make small talk with me. This general hostility seems to be part of the job description.

The first thing I am instructed to do is take off my coat and my jacket and she pats down every inch of my body, running her fingers intrusively inside my clothes, after the odd comment, "I'm just giving you a massage." She also keeps the same questioning going: what are you doing here, what cities did you visit, over and over again, until she takes my shoes away. I sit alone in this tiny white cubicle staring at my socks, wondering what will happen next. In my sleepless state, I start to speculate whether they ever torture US citizens in the airport. She returns and removes my passport holder and all my identification. The strange part is that there is no explanation, no, "I'm sorry for the inconvenience," it just happens. This is the first time in two weeks that I have parted with my precious identification. I feel like I had better cooperate quietly or I may never get out of this airport. The thought occurs to me that maybe I am starting to feel Palestinian.

The guard returns with my identification papers, silently she escorts me back into the main area where I am reunited with my disarrayed luggage She takes me to the head of the line at British Airways, waits for me to get checked in, ticketed, and physically escorts me through the airport to the British Airways security check. She then takes me up to the next level of passport checking. I am beginning to feel too dangerous to be let loose in a public space.

At the end of this early morning ordeal, she turns to me and says, "How did you find Israel?" and I say cautiously, "It's pretty amazing." She replies, "I only wish that everyone who lived here could see that." It was an odd comment because I couldn't tell what she was implying. I felt this little glimmer that made me think, I wonder what she's thinking about her job and what's going on in this airport. Before my thoughts could wrap around her remark, I get to passport control where again I am asked why I came to Israel, what cities I went to, what I visited, if I work here. Since there's a Gaza stamp on my passport, I explain that I went to Gaza and this provokes even more interest. By this point, I am seriously questioning, what is the purpose of all of this. My mind is racing with a quirky gallows humor mixed with real fear and exasperated annoyance.

With the welcomed smack of a stamp, suddenly I enter the international area and I am finally a free woman. I sit down in a big open space, totally exhausted, and check my watch; this interrogation took one hour and 35 minutes. I wonder what is in my profile that triggered this security response. The message clearly is that people like me, despite my Jewish credentials, are not particularly welcome here. This confirmed other reports that people who cross lines, people who refuse to be enemies with Palestinians or with Jews who work with groups from both sides of the Green Line, are in some way considered a threat. As I drape myself over the row of airport chairs, I remember a recurring dream I had while traveling here. I am interviewing a Palestinian who is recounting a painful story of loss and humiliation when suddenly, as we lean towards each other, the microphone blows up, shattering our faces. Perhaps the guards in the airport are right. Perhaps speaking the painful truth, listening with close attention to the voices of the victimized and traumatized is a powerful and dangerous form of resistance. I consider this part of my Jewish heritage and a key to a Jewish survival that makes me proud and unashamed. Perhaps they should be more careful next time.

7

Visiting the Mythaloon Maternity Home: Like Women Everywhere

A S I PURPOSEFULLY SEARCH OUT the unheard voices in this conflict, I become particularly interested in women living in the Occupied Territories. The newspaper clips I see usually focus on militant young men, older male politicians, or bearded religious leaders. An occasional woman stricken with grief is photographed weeping over her dead son or picking through the rubble of her recently demolished home. On the radio, I have heard the cultured, articulate voice of Dr. Hanan Ashwari, a Palestinian academic and political leader, describing the suffering and aspirations of her people with a powerful blend of nationalism, intelligence, and urgency. I have seen commentators accusing Palestinian mothers of sending their children on suicide missions or condemning them for expressing pride in their martyred sons. I was once told by an Israeli pediatrician that, "Palestinian mothers do not love their children," as an explanation for the young boys who throw stones at Israeli tanks. Implicit in the statement is that the boys are encouraged to be in harm's way by their uncaring mothers who are violent and less human by nature.

As a physician, I remember evaluating female patients in 2004 in the village of Seilat El Harthiya near Jenin, West Bank. The women came to see me with familiar concerns: pregnancy, contraception, irregular bleeding, infertility, breast lumps, loss of libido. I could never predict what I would find under each woman's modest, long grey coat; a discreet cotton dress, sexy, black lace underwear, or the tattered, grey, multilayered undergarments of poverty. At the Al Ahli

Hospital in Hebron, some of the women medical students draped themselves entirely in white with only their eyes visible, while at Mokassed Hospital in East Jerusalem, the student dress ranged from heads covered with the traditional *hijab* to tight jeans, low-cut blouses, and fashionable spiked heels. As I interview patients and health care providers, I begin to suspect that Palestinian women stand in the cross hairs of multiple cultures and catastrophes, stretching from religious traditions to nationalist politics. I find that they are often both invisible and at the same time central to life in the Occupied Territories and that their voices are rarely homogenous, clearly heard, or understood.

Meeting with Two Women Doctors

Statistics are more powerful when translated to the human level of individual experience. In March 2005, I spend an afternoon with two women doctors who work at a maternity home southeast of Jenin in the West Bank. Dr. Muntaha Hamarsheh explains apologetically, "I am not strong." Her gentle face and dark eyes are framed by a white headscarf, her body draped in a long-sleeved pink sweater and floor length black skirt. I look at her incredulously and remind her that she is the director of the Mythaloon Maternity Home and mother of six. She faces the daily risks of checkpoints, heavily armed Israeli soldiers, and has come for this interview six weeks into her maternity leave.

We are sipping strong, sweet Arabic coffee and talking in a new, white stone clinic, along with Dr. Khadeja Jarrar, head of women's health care for PMRS. Khadeja's nicely cut black hair is uncovered, she is dressed in a black suit and brightly patterned red blouse and is quick to laugh and interject her comments. We are talking like women everywhere about our lives, our work, and our families. "I don't have the strength to stand with the problems. I try all the time to save tears for my home." I push Muntaha further and she confesses that she is worried that she is too emotional. Khadeja suggests that being emotional may be a form of strength. I marvel at how these two very different Palestinian women negotiate family and work in a patriarchal society dominated by the daily brutality of the Israeli occupation and the legacy that unfolded with the establishment of the State of Israel in 1948.

Soon we are exploring the details of Muntaha's life, her degree from Jordan University, her training in obstetrics and gynecology at Mokassed

Hospital in East Jerusalem. Like many middle-class Palestinian women, she is highly educated and active in the workforce. One year ago, she became director of this newly built maternity home, supported by PMRS as part of a project funded by the US Agency for International Development. The maternity home has back up from Al-Amal Hospital (Patients Friends Society Hospital) in Jenin and affiliations with three primary village health care centers. Additionally, there is cooperation with the village council and local Mythaloon society in running and managing the maternity home.

Mythaloon Maternity Home

Muntaha works with nurses, midwives who have been trained solely to provide obstetrical care, and health workers who focus on patient education. The clinic sees 200 pregnant women per month with a catchment area of about 25,000 people, an estimated 6000 women in the reproductive age group. Sixty deliveries are expected per month and the clinic charges 250 shekels (approximately $55) for a normal delivery. Most of the people she sees have what she calls "intifada insurance." The Palestinian Ministry of Health waived all fees for a hospital delivery with Al-Aqsa Insurance after the beginning of the Second Intifada. Besides the antenatal clinic, there is general gynecologic and menopausal care. She explains that the maternity home offers no pain relief during labor, but the women are encouraged to move, shower, and are given massages and comfort from the staff and family, usually the mother and mother-in-law. With reference to the fathers, "Because of our culture, they don't like to attend deliveries, but if they like, no problem, we ask them." Most of the women use intrauterine devices (IUDs) to space their pregnancies. As for the option of permanent sterilization, Muntaha herself has an IUD and does not plan any more pregnancies, but with a familiar acceptance touched with irony she explains, "It's enough. If God wants to give me more and more on top of IUD, no problem. But me, I am not planning for another baby. All my spacing was by IUD. I started once combined pills and it makes a lot of problems for me, headache, nausea, vomiting for a month, and so I stop that and go to IUD. Thank God there is IUD."

A Typical Day

Muntaha is 40 years old, "I am just a baby," she laughs, and lives in the town of Ya'bad 20 kilometers from Mythaloon with her husband, who is also a physician. She awakens at 6 am, helps her four daughters get ready for school, takes the fifth to kindergarten and the baby boy to the home of her sister-in-law. She drives her car to work, which usually takes 45 minutes, but can take up to three hours if there are active checkpoints. Her workday is six hours long and then she returns to her home. She confesses that she is too frightened to bring her infant to work because she is worried about the potential dangers on the road. After this full day, she cooks dinner, does house work, and cares for the children. "I haven't a maid!" she exclaims laughing. We are soon comparing notes on our working husbands. Muntaha's husband sometimes cooks "quick meals" or cleans, but he reaches his limit on the issue of laundry. Khadeja laughs and says, "Because he doesn't want the neighbors to see, that's it, that's the only cause. He can do many things inside the home, but outside no." Muntaha argues, "My husband asked for things inside the home because really he wants to help me, but I don't ask him to help in things that are refused by our culture. I respect him. He wants to help, and I respect this idea." She also reports that he takes an active role with the childcare and notes this is unusual among Palestinian men. On the issue of laundry, Khadeja's doctor husband is just the opposite, "Allam the opposite is going! He doesn't do anything inside the house but if I want him to hang the laundry, he goes outside. He wants to be an example for the neighbors, that he is doing the housework and he is helping his wife."

Muntaha smiles and says she is very lucky, "I have a very nice man." She explains they first met "through our families. I knew him through his family and he knew me. When we speak with each other, we like each other and we accept each other first. Now we fall in love. The start, it was accepting and respecting each other, then it became love and life." She then returns to her emotionality and says she wants her children to be like her, but "more tough and strong." She admits that it is the dangers of the occupation in Palestine that make her so worried, but since the last baby, "I have my son, no problem now."

Birthing Homes and Checkpoints

The Mythaloon Maternity Home reminds me of freestanding birth centers in the US that started in the early 1970s. It is clean and cheerful, family-friendly, geared towards extensive patient education, low-risk obstetrics with carefully arranged back up facilities, natural childbirth and breastfeeding support, and postpartum home visits. The centers in the US came out of the feminist and natural childbirth movements, promoting women- and family-oriented care, and focused on the celebration of childbirth as a natural empowering moment in women's lives. A very different political reality propelled the need for this center in Palestine: the problems of checkpoints, closures, curfews, and the subsequent lack of access to safe health care and childbirth. As Muntaha explains:

> You know about closure, checkpoints, this was something very difficult for pregnant women to reach the hospitals in Jenin. They tend to go to midwives at homes and deliver there. By this way, we got many problems, cases of postpartum hemorrhage, cases of problems for the babies. The concept came from these needs, that we need safe delivery for the mother and the baby, this is our mission. To do this, we developed the idea about establishing a maternity home and working in a way that we only accept low-risk pregnancies to deliver here.
>
> We have been working about one year and more and we haven't any problems. The midwives have done about 400 deliveries. We referred about twelve cases perinatally. We accepted them as low risk but during labor they developed some hypertension, one postpartum hemorrhage, one no progress of labor, and so on. We telephoned for the ambulance, they came and we send the patient with her midwife with a delivery kit. They all reached the hospital and delivered with no problems later. The women went mostly to governmental hospitals [rather than private hospitals] because there is no payment for delivery. We also have referred about 100 women who came to deliver here but we found that they were high risk. That's all our problems.

This story is not just about medical care. Mustafa Hassan, mayor of Mythaloon, wrote about the center:

> Having a maternity home in our community is preserving the dignity of our women. No longer will a father have to worry that his daughter will be forced to give birth in a taxi or at the side of the road at a checkpoint. Our wives and daughters now have a safe and comfortable place in which to give birth. One that is nearby and accessible. One they can get to without

crossing checkpoints. The peace of mind that having this facility gives to us is priceless.[1]

There are currently four such maternity homes in the Occupied Territories: in Beirzeit, a large village near Ramallah; Aqraba south of Nablus; Balsam in the town of Al-Nada, northern Gaza Strip; as well as Mythaloon.[2]

Consequences of Lack of Medical Access

The tragic lack of access to medical care is well documented by Israeli and Palestinian groups. PHR-I reports:

> One of the groups most significantly impacted by these limits on movement is pregnant women. Numerous cases have been documented of women giving birth at checkpoints because they were banned from passing while on their way to hospital. The difficulties involved in going to the hospital has [sic] resulted in a decline in the number of women giving birth in hospitals, and an increase in the number of women giving birth at home. Furthermore, because many women give birth at home due to the challenges involved in accessing hospitals and prenatal services, there has been a sharp increase in stillbirths in rural areas of the West Bank.[3]

I think back to March 2005, when Palestinian colleagues told me of a pregnant woman in labor in the West Bank who was denied passage at a checkpoint and delivered premature twins. They died shortly thereafter.

PMRS and the Palestinian Red Crescent Society have also documented multiple instances of denial of ambulance access to patients, restrictions and delays in ambulance movement. They have reported restrictions and attacks on medical personnel, attacks on health care facilities, suspension of services, acute blood shortages, and so forth. In addition, they note that restrictions of access due to the stopping of patients at checkpoints have prevented Palestinians in need of medical care from accessing services.[4] They estimate that over 70 percent of the Palestinian population lives in rural areas that do not have hospital services. Thus for a majority of the population, there are severe restrictions to obtaining care at higher-level health care facilities and these constraints have also severely impacted the manufacturing and distribution of pharmaceuticals and medical supplies such as delivery kits.[5]

It has been estimated that the growing separation wall being built by the Israeli government will ultimately affect 750,000 Palestinians in nearly 40 percent of Palestinian communities. According to PMRS, the health delivery system developed according to models proposed by the World Health Organization in which village, town, and city clinics provide different levels of care and are supported by a carefully planned referral network to higher levels of care and specialty clinics. This referral system has been almost completely disrupted by the separation wall and other obstructions that have broken down the coherence of the Palestinian health system.[6]

Reality on the Ground

While traveling with Khadeja in an ambulance from Nablus to Mythaloon, and then on to Jenin, these "facts on the ground" acquire a painful and urgent reality. Maybe it was the multiple checkpoints where the ambulance was stopped and inspected. Maybe it was the contrast between the terraced olive groves with their silvery green leaves and the raw waste that the nearby Jewish settlement of Homesh was discharging into a nearby Palestinian village. Khadeja comments,

> This land on your left is my friend's land and we used to come during summer and spring. My children used to play here, but now since the Intifada, we are not allowed to come here. We are in prison since the Intifada. We can't freely go to our trees and to our olive trees and our mountains, enjoy the nature. When I pass through to Ramallah or to Jenin, I see the flowers and I see the green everywhere and I feel sad our children are not enjoying it. Children from Nablus don't feel the change in the seasons. They don't notice the spring at all and the most beautiful season in our society is the spring when you see all kinds of flowers. They put all the "Palestinian animals" in cages and they [Jewish settlers and soldiers] are walking around freely.

Much of the time the ambulance is traveling on deeply rutted roads, a harsh record of Israeli tank activity in the area and the absence of a functional civil infrastructure to repair the damage. We pass a small village, a mosque with a bright turquoise dome, men and women in traditional dress, babies bundled in blankets, and donkeys vying with yellow cabs for a piece of the road. The potholes could easily do major damage to everyone. Khadeja and I are talking about the development of the women's movement in Palestine in the 1950s. "The first movement in the Arab world towards taking off the scarf took place in Egypt and Palestine, and the first place in Palestine to go to this direction was Nablus. The women's movement in Nablus was the most active one and they were the initiators of the women's movement in Palestine." She tells me about her son and daughter who are studying at a university in Jordan, about her teenage daughter who loves her new cell phone as well as traditional Palestinian dancing.

At one point, the road becomes even worse and Khadeja explains that we are on an agricultural road because Palestinians are not allowed on the well-paved main road. While rattling and bumping along, we talk about the large Ministry of Health hospital in Jenin which does 500 deliveries a month and often runs at twice capacity. We had just toured the hospital and were told that women are discharged two hours after delivery with no home visit. After visiting the wards crowded with tired looking women and their families and now riding this rutted road, the brutality of the political and medical reality is suddenly revealed to me with a glaring new clarity. I ask,

> A woman is at the maternity center. She is low risk. She develops high blood pressure. She has to be transferred in a rush to the hospital. She has to be taken on this gutted, bumpy, irregular, ridiculous road to get to the hospital while she is having a contraction every three minutes and seizing or whatever horrible thing is happening. This is the reality, right?

Khadeja responds patiently, "Yes, of course."

If the woman delivers at the Ministry of Health hospital, she is discharged two hours later, "How does she get home?" I ask again. Khadeja responds, "In the usual times they take the taxi and they go, if their village is not blocked. If not, they have to reach the blockage and then they have to walk." I think I am starting to understand. "So you could be three hours postpartum with fresh sutures and your breasts are full and you're exhausted and you are anemic and you have a brand new baby who is screaming and you could be waiting at a checkpoint and walking hundreds of meters between checkpoints?" Khadeja nods emphatically,

> That's right. This is the reality. You have to walk through the checkpoints. Sometimes you have to walk maybe 500 meters or more. If there is not a checkpoint and the road is closed, so you have to climb on the artificial mountain, which was made by the soldier, and to walk through it. I know a woman from Ramallah who gave birth for a premature baby and they

didn't allow her to stay with the baby at the hospital. She stayed for two days, the baby had to stay more in the incubator and they sent her home. Then she wanted to come to pick up the baby after one week of delivery, she has to wait, it was winter. She has to wait on the checkpoints for three hours, and when she reached the hospital, she sat on the chair and they found her dead on the chair.

I wonder aloud if she died of infection, high blood pressure, anemia, or maybe just plain heartbreak. Khadeja responds, "It doesn't matter, it was because of the Israeli actions. Whether it was whatever, she died because of the situation. Poor woman, she couldn't complain and even if she complained, so who would listen to her?"

When we arrive in Jenin, there is an open marketplace, wall-to-wall stalls, taxicabs, and people. Despite traveling by ambulance, we are late as usual and caught in the frustration of trying to wend our way between the huge piles of fruits and vegetables, red strawberries and bananas, people hawking their wares, mountains of potatoes and parsley. Racks of cheap brightly colored clothes made in China hang from storefronts amidst the baby toys and plastic guns. Schoolchildren with colorful backpacks and bundled babies are everywhere as tens of people crowd in front of the ambulance blocking our way. The walls are plastered with posters from the recent presidential election, posters of serious-faced young martyrs, Coca-Cola signs, large Arabic lettering. The traffic here is an intense dare devil game, with donkeys and vehicles inches from each other.

From Traditional Clans to Modern History

Khadeja's comment about the Palestinian women's movement makes me curious about the history of women in Palestine. I learn that for many generations, Palestinian families lived in traditional rural societies, often dominated by powerful, patriarchal tribal clans. This way of life began to collapse during the nineteenth century, starting with the armies of Napoleon, followed by the Ottomans, the World Wars, the British colonial efforts, and the influx of Zionist immigration leading to the establishment of the State of Israel. During the various hostilities and political upheavals, poverty, disease, and social disruption deeply affected all aspects of women's roles.[7] Rural women were often responsible for much of the agricultural work, selling produce as well as maintaining the home and raising children. The urban women had a better chance to obtain an education and to participate in teaching and charitable organizations. During the British Mandate, they organized petitions to the British parliament and held a mass demonstration in 1920 and in 1929, the first Palestine Arab Women's Congress convened, urging women to support their men in the national struggle.[8] After 1948, with many families living in refugee camps, men often emigrated to other countries in the Arabian Gulf, leaving their women back home with major responsibilities, and further destroying the traditional clan as a viable social, political, and economic force.[9]

Because of these changes, in 1948, a professional and well-organized Palestinian women's movement was established in the West Bank and Gaza Strip.[10] By the 1970s, women activists had founded a number of committees and movements involving university women, village and refugee women, as well as the urban poor.[11] In the 1980s they protested against the Hamas-led effort to mandate wearing of the *hijab*, supporting a woman's right to choose whether to cover her head for political or religious reasons. While women became more prominent in the national struggle and gender issues, they still remained subservient to the patriarchal society and were poorly represented in high political offices and the legislative council. In an effort to strengthen their efforts, by the late 1980s, Palestinian and Israeli women's peace organizations began to dialogue and work towards their common goal of a just peace for both peoples.[12]

Double Jeopardy: Patriarchy and Occupation

In 1987 in the First Intifada, Palestinian women were active in the political arena, leading the indigenous 1987 boycott campaign against products made in Israel.[13] The women experienced imprisonment, torture, and death like their male counterparts, accounting for one-third of all casualties during the Intifada.[14] Israeli army searches and house demolitions also destroyed the home, a time-honored place of seclusion and safety for women and their children. Female sexuality, traditionally sacred to the honor of the Arab family and the clan, was jeopardized by sexual harassment and intimidation by Israeli soldiers in the home, on the street, as well as in the prisons.[15] During times of prolonged curfew, when families were unable to leave their homes for days or months, the women played critical roles and bore responsibilities that contributed to everyone's survival. Their resourcefulness was stretched by the large number of men who were imprisoned, killed, injured, or expelled and thus absent from home life. Women taught the children when schools were closed, protected the teenagers from Israeli soldiers by forming human shields between the youths and the soldiers, learned first aid, developed home-based industries, and planted community gardens. This was a creative, mostly nonviolent resistance based on the needs of the local society.[16] In addition, women often became the primary care givers for the tens of thousands of traumatized children and injured family members, attending last to their own medical or nutritional needs.[17]

While women gained self-confidence and a new respect during the Intifada, they did not necessarily make strides towards social freedom or political equality. During the Second Intifada starting in 2000, although women continued to be well represented in the universities, political participation by Palestinian women markedly decreased and the women's rights movement took several steps backwards.[18] The 1993 Oslo Accords, which resulted in the creation of the Palestinian Authority, concentrated on the occupation as the only political issue of significance and resulted in a massive energizing of international NGO activity focusing on the humanitarian needs of the population. International women's NGOs, however, supported women's rights and gender equality without linking these issues to the relationship between Palestinian patriarchy and the Israeli occupation.[19] This made it more difficult to unite feminist and nationalist struggles, to understand that resistance to occupation and the creation of an independent state are intrinsically linked to furthering the status of women within their own society.[20] Many Palestinian women activists worry about the lessons they learned from the Algerian struggle where women played a significant role in resisting French colonialism, but failed to secure their own rights in the future state. In Algeria, the vision of the women's movement was deferred and ultimately trumped by nationalist consciousness. After victory, women were forced to return to their pre-liberation status of subjugation.[21]

Lack of Gender Equality

The current legal system in the Occupied Territories involves an amalgamation of outdated and archaic components of the Ottoman Empire, the British Mandate in Palestine, Jordanian law in the West Bank, and Egyptian law in Gaza, all in force alongside Israeli military law.[22] The Palestinian Authority, established in 1994, has done little to address women's issues, although efforts have been made in the area of improving health access. Additionally, some aspects of Ottoman law predate the secular movements within the Occupied Territories and are consequently based on overtly discriminatory religious directives. Thus, "personal status law," which covers marriage, divorce, child custody, inheritance, and domestic violence, is often deeply entrenched in gender bias.[23] The extent of oppression from a patriarchal society deepens with the level of oppression from the Israeli occupation, and is seen more prominently in Gaza than the West Bank.[24] Many human rights organizations have argued that until Palestine is an independent state, Israel as the occupying power bears ultimate responsibility for protecting the rights of women in the territories, but the Israeli government does not recognize that claim.[25] Nonetheless, the Israelis did grant Palestinian women the right to vote and run for office for municipal posts in 1967. On the other hand, discriminatory Israeli laws, such as the 2003 legislation that bans an Israeli citizen married to a Palestinian from the Occupied Territories from having family unification within Israel, have a detrimental effect on women.[26]

Because of the destruction of much of the Palestinian civil infrastructure by widespread Israeli incursions, Palestinians, male and female, focus primarily on issues of daily survival.[27] This societal crisis has coalesced with the lack of functional institutional protection as well a pervasive distrust in the legal system to produce a general state of lawlessness. The reduction of serious work on long-term legal and social reforms by women's groups in the face of external Israeli aggression has also resulted in the society turning inward to more conservative and religious Islamic values and interpretations.[28] Women who lose their husbands or sons to "martyrdom" are expected to suppress their shock and grief and to celebrate the nobility of the loss as a means of survival and coping. This cultural expectation obfuscates the psychological trauma and suffering that is so pervasive but less publicly expressed.[29] Mediation and settlement of disputes more often occurs through a growing number of armed groups or traditional and tribal organizations that further promote gender inequality.[30]

A young Palestinian woman returning from school, delayed for hours at a checkpoint, may face not only the harassment of Israeli soldiers or hostile Jewish settlers, but also the disapproval of her family.[31] When a husband and wife are from different towns, the woman traditionally joins her husband's family and with the increased occupation related restrictions of movement, she is more likely to suffer from isolation and lack of social supports. This only worsens when there is discord in the marriage that places the wife at greater risk of domestic abuse.[32] The increasing level of homelessness and destitution after Israeli incursions, compounded by curfews and closures, only adds to the constraints placed on women by a traditional Palestinian patriarchal culture.[33] In these dire situations, the women often bear the brunt of both the increased demands for care in the home and the rage and frustration of their male relatives humiliated by their inability to fulfill their expected roles to provide for and protect their families. Women are also at arbitrary and unpredictable risk of harassment, death, or home demolition because of suspected affiliations with men wanted by Israeli soldiers. They are thus targeted in their personal as well as public lives.[34] There is minimal documentation on the actual rate of domestic violence in the Occupied Territories, but researchers have noted an increasing incidence in both Israeli and Palestinian societies and a direct correlation between exposure to politically based aggression and violence within the family, including honor killings.[35]

Impact on Reproductive Health

Since the 1994 International Conference on Population and Development in Cairo, numerous international conventions have recognized women's health as a basic human right and as a key to the development of an overall society.[36] Reproductive health is a part of the larger human rights agenda and the higher-than-expected infant and maternal mortality rates in the West Bank and Gaza are a reflection of poor nutrition and lack of access to clean water and to quality health care. The reports by the UN and other agencies of an increase in stillbirths, a large rise in unplanned home births, and women delivering at checkpoints, often with disastrous outcomes for mother and baby, are examples of this intersection between politics and health.[37] I have come to appreciate the growing fear and anxiety that every pregnant Palestinian woman experiences as her pregnancy progresses; the physical and psychological stress produced by curfews and closures and the well-documented humiliation and brutal ordeals that may occur at checkpoints while the woman is in labor. The problem is common enough that PMRS, a major NGO providing health care in the Occupied Territories, has produced a patient education pamphlet with advice for pregnant women trapped at checkpoints.

Pregnancy is a critical part of female life in the Occupied Territories where over 3.7 million people live, with a birth rate of almost six children per woman and a projected doubling of the total population within the next generation.[38] Interestingly, there is a high level of knowledge regarding contraception, used primarily for spacing pregnancies, and the more educated the mother, the fewer children per family. Nonetheless, there is a general preference for large families and given the median age for marriage is 18, there is a long childbearing period.[39]

Straddling the Divide

I think back to Muntaha as she straddles the divide between traditional and modern women's roles, confronts checkpoints between home and work, provides medical care for women in the chaos and dysfunction of the Palestinian health care system and a fractured civil and economic society. At this point, I can only marvel at her quiet strength and unflagging perseverance. Like uncelebrated women over much of the world, it takes a special resilience to live the most usual and decent of lives in such a difficult and heartbreaking place. It is also apparent to me that women's liberation in all its varied forms is interwoven with the Palestinian national movement, opposing the Israeli occupation, and building a functional civil society. In a world where brutality and injustice have acquired an air of normality, Palestinian women having babies, raising and often supporting their families, and taking care of each other, are engaged in daily acts of unseen and uncelebrated heroism.

In July 2005, Nurit Peled-Elhanan, daughter of an Israeli Major General, whose 13-year-old child, Smadari, was killed by a suicide bomber in 1997, spoke at International Women's Day in Strasbourg at the European Parliament. Her comments strike a powerful chord in this complicated discussion, reminding me of my own reference points as well as our underlying commonalities.

> Living in the world I live in, in the state I live in, in the regime I live in, I don't dare to offer Muslim women any ideas how to change their lives. I don't want them to take off their scarves, or educate their children differently, and I will not urge them to constitute Democracies in the image of Western democracies that despise them and their kind. I just want to ask them humbly to be my sisters, to express my admiration for their perseverance and for their courage to carry on, to have children and to maintain a dignified family life in spite of the impossible conditions my world is putting them in. I want to tell them we are all bonded by the same pain, we are all the victims of the same sort of violence even though they suffer much more, for they are the ones who are mistreated by my government and its army, sponsored by my taxes.[40]

8

A Day in Nablus with Dr. Allam Jarrar: We Will Have Just Fun!

A S I MENTIONED IN THE chapter on checkpoints, our medical delegation was able to visit Nablus after negotiating the Beit Iba checkpoint just outside the city. This was a point in the trip when my aggravation and annoyance began to outweigh my fear. This heavily militarized checkpoint feels intimidating and supports the reputation of Nablus, with its long history of violence and militant resistance to occupation, as one of the most sealed off cities in the West Bank. We anxiously queue in line and when we reach the interrogating soldier, he questions us more intensively and repetitively than usual. My response to this scene surprises even me. Instead of being afraid, I feel more outraged that he is grilling us aggressively and that this bit of harassment is considered acceptable behavior. After all, we have our letters of invitation, our US passports, and even a letter of support from Senator Kennedy. Except for one student, we are all middle-aged Jewish professionals and we are being interrogated by Jewish soldiers who are easily the same age as our children. As I stare at one young soldier, I suddenly realize that I am feeling pushy rather than silenced. I am surprised. I tend to get quiet around hostile men with guns; now I feel provoked and annoyed, insisting that we have a meeting with Dr. Allam Jarrar and PMRS officially invited us. How dangerous can we be? We are determined to enter the city and despite the unpredictable vagaries of this system, to our relief and surprise, we finally do. After the icy verbal jostling, we are funneled through the concrete chutes to the other end of the checkpoint, accosted by bantering cab drivers, and taken to the Al Yasmeen Hotel.

A Meeting at the Al Yasmeen

Tucked at the end of a cul-de-sac adjacent to the *souq* in the old city, the hotel has an old world charm with its cream-colored stone façade and graceful archways. There are bullet holes in the entry and a scarred stained glass window, stark reminders of battles juxtaposed against gracious conference rooms and solid old furniture. As we check in, one of the hotel staff brings us ice-cold orange soda, so we are immediately welcomed with something to eat in true Arab fashion.

Our friend, Dr. Allam Jarrar, who is one of our key contacts and a leader in PMRS, comes over quickly. He lives in Nablus with his wife, Khadeja (the physician from the Mythaloon Maternity Home) and their daughter, and we know him from past experiences as an urbane, educated, funny man. After smiles, hugs, and an affectionate ritual of kissing everyone on both cheeks, we join him around a large oval table and endless cups of thick Turkish coffee. He explains that, "Today we will have just fun." He has planned a brief discussion about the city followed by a tour of the old *casba*, and then a traditional Palestinian lunch at his home. After a relaxing afternoon, he has invited several people from the city, university lecturers, and women activists, "just to have direct genuine talk about how we feel about the situation. Not to talk politics."

There is such a warmth and poignancy about the afternoon. Here is a man who knows his history and wants to share the stories of his city with us, his guests. He has spent his life in the service of his people. He's been beaten and had Israeli guns poked at his neck as he lay in the dust at a checkpoint. Despite everything, he keeps his sense of humor and, more strikingly, his sense of hope and commitment to democracy. Listening to him talk, it is wonderful to hear his pride in the 2005 election. He feels that the Palestinian people have shown that they can have a democratic election like normal people, despite the abnormal situation.

Nablus, the City of Fighters, the City of Sacrifice

After reviewing the plans for the day, he mentions that Nablus at night is a dead city because the area is sealed off by the Israeli army, with only two official entrances, Huwarra and Beit Iba. There are 17 locations where the Israeli army controls movement in and out of the city with multiple fortresses overlooking areas that make it impossible to cross. Allam estimates that in the past three years, the severe restrictions of movement have destroyed the economy and social structure of Nablus. According to some estimates, such as that of the World Bank, Nablus has lost 60 percent of its economic potential. Nablus was also formerly the center of social and economic interactions for 100,000 people in surrounding villages and towns, and now due to the economic collapse, this focus has largely shifted to Ramallah.

As the *muezzin* calls in the background, Allam describes the northern and southern mountains on which Nablus is built, the rich religious and cultural history that stems from the centuries of interactions between Romans, Greeks, Jews, Arabs, Muslims, and people from central Asia. We learn that Nablus now is one of the biggest towns in Palestine and is considered the capital of the north. There are approximately 160,000 people living inside the town, including in four refugee camps, the most well known being the Balata Refugee Camp. Allam explains that the inhabitants in these camps have refugee status, which means that they are refugees or descendents of refugees from the 1948 and 1967 Wars. The UNRWA is the relief and human development organization responsible for education, health care, social services, and emergency aid to these and other refugees living in the Gaza Strip, the West Bank, Jordan, Lebanon, and Syria.[1]

> The rest [of the inhabitants] are Nabluses and these are people of the mountain. They are mountainous people, in terms of culture, in terms of stubbornness, maybe, and in a way, generous, and what else? In a way violent. I mean, tough, because of the nature, there are what we call dignitary families, or noble families in Nablus. These families used to exercise the authority of the Sultan [from Istanbul or Constantinople] in Nablus and the northern part.

As if to emphasize his point, we hear a scattering of gunfire in the background. We learn that the old city of Nablus is a densely populated area with 20,000 to 30,000 people, and inside the old city of Nablus, there are many armed groups who consider themselves "the fighters." The hotel is located on the edge of this old city. The rest of the city was built 60 to 70 years ago stretching up into the surrounding mountains.

We probe further into the reasons behind the resistance and militancy of the Nablus population. Is it religious, political, economic?

[It is] more kind of tough in terms of culture, not only because of the mountains, it's because of the political activities that are taking place in Nablus. The people of Nablus consider themselves as the avant-garde for Palestinians. The First Intifada was started here, in Nablus, in Balata Refugee Camp, in 1987, and in the Second Intifada, in the first two years, if you look at the figures, maybe 30 percent of those who were killed and injured were from Nablus, the city of martyrs, the city of sacrifice, the city of fighters, and I believe it's because of its history through maybe 600 years.

As if trying to maintain his promise of a day without political talk, Allam describes some of the proud traditions of Nablus, in particular the production of traditional sweets and olive oil soap. I feel Allam's profound attachment to the city in which he was born and raised his family. Despite his devotion, he also mentions a deep frustration with his growing difficulties and delays crossing the Huwarra checkpoint on the way to his office in Ramallah.

Hearing the Palestinian Narrative

Because politics is deeply woven into the fabric of daily life, Allam feels compelled to explore a painful fundamental contradiction. He says that for Israel to live as a Jewish state there is a basic triangle that consists of democracy, Jewishness, and peace. However, this requires the acceptance of another idea.

There is another people, which is the Palestinian people, who live here in parts of historical Palestine, and the only way is to have two states, based on equality and mutuality and what we call reciprocity, in terms of culture, economy, and human interaction. This is the only visible and possible and dignified way of solving the problem.

Unfortunately, I know that in Israel, maybe there are more than 50 percent of the population, they believe in this two state solution, but they tend to bargain on how much for the Palestinians and how much for the Israelis. On our side, after the Oslo experience, we believe that this will never happen, because of the experience that we have been living through during the last ten years. And the idea here is please, take this, it's very genuine from me, I thought the ultimate goal will be the implementation of [United Nations resolutions] 242 and 338 and there will be a kind of environment that we can have two states. But instead of that during the last ten years instead of making peaceful bridges with Palestinians, the Israeli government started to expand settlements, to build more settlements, and to create obstacles on the ground and now, we are facing those obstacles. So who created those obstacles during the last ten years instead of making peace and then asking Palestinians, please solve this problem, the settlement problems?

We wonder if Allam finds allies in Israel with whom he can negotiate. With an edge of weariness, he replies, "Of course. On the other side, I see friends, I see good people, I see patriotism, I see human rights activists, I see partners, of course. Unfortunately, the political power is not there yet, but I hope this will come."

Allam mentions that many political circles in Israel believe that the West Bank is a contested rather than an occupied area, that Israel is actually liberating parts of "Greater Israel" through settlements and land acquisition. He disagrees with this formulation.

We must accept on principle that those areas are occupied and that East Jerusalem is part of those areas, and the solution for the conflict should be based on international legitimacy. The idea is how to implement those resolutions, not to negotiate on them. I mean without this, nothing will happen. When they [Israelis] talk about a Palestinian entity, they are talking about a Palestinian entity that is completely under control of Israel in terms of borders, not to leave Palestinians with free borders with other Arab countries.

We continue to discuss the UN resolutions and international laws that are the foundations of the Palestinian arguments for self determination. He explains that the Security Council resolution 242 (and subsequently 338) was the resolution after the 1967 War recognizing the inadmissibility of the conquest of territory by military means and the Security Council demand that Israel withdraw from the Occupied Territories. The whole international community, including the International Court of Justice, has recognized that the border of Israel is the Green Line and that the territories conquered in 1967 are occupied territories under the applicable international law. Many Israelis, however, believe that there are no borders to Israel, they are to be negotiated. "So this means when the Palestinians say they are willing to recognize Israel within the 1948 borders which is 78 percent of the Palestine Mandate, if they can keep the 22 percent, the Israeli response is often, yes, now we'll negotiate over who gets what of the remaining 22 percent."

Allam stresses the importance of a recent International Court of Justice decision which affirmed the territories captured in 1967 and East Jerusalem as occupied and in violation of the Geneva Convention. Additionally, the expanding Jewish settlement of the territories was considered illegal. He asserts, "I mean if you transfer 400,000 people from the area of the occupying power to the occupied areas this amounts to a war crime." The Court decision also stated that the separation wall is illegal and that Palestinians should be compensated for damages associated with its construction and land confiscation. The Court reiterated the applicability of international resolutions and the need to come to a political solution. He continues,

> This is an International Court of Justice with this very clear statement and nothing has happened. Israel continues to build the wall, in the southern and western sides of Palestine and there is more annexation of Palestinian land, there are more settlement activities, and there is no compensation for the Palestinians who lost their properties and lands. So if we talk international politics, the US administration and government is the major obstacle for implementing United Nations resolutions.

Possibilities for a Just Solution

I think about the meaning of resilience and resistance in the context of a long-standing, intractable conflict; of Allam's persistent belief that a just solution will be found and his ability to resist an oppressive situation through political work founded on international agreements. I think about my own government's unwillingness to use its power to be an even-handed broker in this conflict, about the huge construction projects, high-rise apartment buildings, and active settlement growth that we have just seen over much of the West Bank. Given the list of proposals and road maps that litter the landscape of this region, what possibilities are there for a positive future? Allam states it is important to acknowledge that Jewish settlement activities during the last 30 years are illegal and that negotiations and land tradeoffs are a possible negotiating position. "I mean if there is a will there is a way. Unfortunately, there are no means, politically speaking, there at the international level. There is no will."

Allam has been active in a group called the Democratic Alliance, *Al Mubadara*, working to build a sovereign, democratic Palestine. He stresses the importance of nonviolent resistance and describes activities that involve resisting the construction of the separation wall.

> First, we promoted the civil resistance against the Israeli soldiers that are protecting the wall, and involving hundreds and thousands of people. Second

is to try to coordinate with Israeli groups that are fighting against the wall, like Ta'ayush for instance, and there have been hundreds of activities in this respect which show the possibility of joint actions and joint resistance between Israelis and Palestinians that are reaching for human rights and reaching peaceful coexistence. Third, we also promoted the international dimension of the fight; that Palestine is not only a problem between Palestinians and Israelis. It's a case that the whole world should address because it represents the violations of rights, and a vigilant ignorance of self-determination for a people that are striving for this since tens of years.

Distant gunfire rattles in the background as Allam reminds us that, ironically, it is against the law for Palestinians to participate in demonstrations of any kind, including nonviolent ones. "Israel can do anything inside the Palestinian Authority areas, without asking the Palestinian Authority, without coordinating with it, and implementing Israeli laws on those areas," and this he says is a powerful disincentive to nonviolent protest.

Cultural Shifts

The conversation shifts to the impact and nuances of interaction on the younger generation, on the role of language, music and food, especially with the youth. Allam concurs,

> I like to talk about this because I think of course there are many changes in terms of culture, in terms of terminology of words, on both sides. For instance, on checkpoints, when we approach the soldier, we say, "*Shalom*," [Hello] and, of course the soldier will say, "*Shalom*," and then asks, "*Kaifa halak?*" [How are you?] in Arabic.
> We say, "*Kaifa halak?* How are you?" We say, "OK," in English. "That's fine." Then after the soldier finishes searching the ambulance, and intimidating us, he could say, "*Ala keefak, ya' ani*," "Everything is all right. You can go." "*Ala keefak*" is Arabic. If you go to Israel, you can hear "*Ala keefak*" everywhere, and if you say "Hello,", and the answer would be "*Ala keefak*" and "Hello." I mean this kind of new culture between the victim and the victimizer is kind of weird in a way, but very interesting. It's not healthy, but there is a kind of communication between Israelis and Palestinians.

Allam describes seeing Palestinian children playing and taking the parts of Israeli soldiers and Palestinian fighters. The children have learned the speech and body language of both of the players. At the same time he describes other Arabic phrases that are commonly heard in Israel. "*Ahlan, ahlan, keefak, keefil hal?*" [Welcome, how are you?] "*Yalla*" [Let's go]. "It's the effect not only of the Palestinians inside, it's the effect of the Palestinians here, in the Occupied Territories, it's the interaction between soldiers and residents."

I am starting to feel anxious about the periodic bursts of gunfire and inquire as to who is shooting. Allam explains that Palestinians like to shoot guns into the air, when they celebrate, when they go to a funeral, although he is not sure what is happening today. He returns again to the issue of the melding of cultures. This is particularly true with Israeli popular music that often has an Arabic-sounding melody or rhythm derived from Eastern culture. He finds the interaction unhealthy because it is not between equals.

We reflect on the fact that something like 40 percent of Israeli Jews are from Arab countries or from Eastern parts of this region and that also must have an impact on music. What does Allam mean by "unhealthy?" I finally grasp the concept when I think about how white America adopted much of African-American culture and music without changing the unequal power relationships between the two groups.

Trying to Tour the Ancient City

After this meandering discussion, Allam wants to give the delegation a tour of the old city because it is an ancient area where there are many important religious sites. We start meandering through the old stone streets. Again, we hear gunfire and it sounds close, Allam estimates 200 meters. First, it is sporadic and then it is much louder. Then it is much more continuous and then it is really close and continuous. I don't know why but I do not feel afraid. We are with Allam and he knows what he is doing, but we are also fully aware that apparently there are people fighting with each other, close to where we are, and that a stray bullet could ricochet our way.

I watch Allam go from jovial and talkative, to hyper-vigilant and cautious; ultimately he decides we need to leave, so we wend our way through the old city back to the hotel. The change in Allam's behavior is dramatic. At the beginning of the day, he was the gracious host, sharing his lovely city, taking us on a tour of the *souq*, showing us the sites. Despite the political talk that is always present, it felt like the times when friends come to Boston and I suggest, let's go on the swan boats! He had planned this relaxing day for us and when the fighting breaks out his radar changes abruptly and he becomes hyper-aware. Suddenly he is herding us like ducklings and immediately leading us home, all the while maintaining his sense of humor but with a sense of firmness in the face of real danger. Like others, he joins the ranks of men on their cell phones, assessing the situation, the level of risk. We are clearly right on the edge of where we should not be.

We traipse through the inside of the old marketplace, with the archways and thick white rock walls, into a protected hallway; the fighting is happening on the other side of these walls. We march up and down stairs that sometimes dead end, wander about a bit until the hotel suddenly appears around a corner. Ultimately, we gather in the hotel lobby and watch the scene from one of the second floor windows. While all of this noise, shooting, loud crashes, and booms are going on, Allam decides that it is best to go to his home which is further away from the activity. In the hotel, the mood is slightly cautious, a bit cavalier, but not fearful. I don't know how the Palestinian resistance functioned before cell phones, but news now spreads in seconds, where it is safe or dangerous, and what is the source of the conflict.

Factional Fighting

While we wait and organize our transportation, I ask how these fighters get their weapons. We hear repeated shooting and these are big, loud guns with large amounts of ammunition. Peering out the second floor window, I talk with one of the staff from the hotel who explains with an ironic smile that the fighters buy their guns from the black market that is sometimes supplied from Israel. According to him, there are black marketers selling powerful weaponry to the Palestinian militant resistance and then the Palestinian resistance uses these guns against the Palestinian Authority and Israeli civilians and soldiers. I suspect that this is a big business here and I have heard of the corruption on all sides and the opportunity for huge profits. The tragic irony of having Israelis selling guns to Palestinians who then use them on each other and other Israelis is just another one of those mind-boggling pieces of information.

Through the cell phone network we learn that a member of the Al-Aqsa Martyr's Brigade was in the police station, allegedly beaten and then released. In response, members of the Al-Aqsa Martyr's Brigade attacked the police station. This appears to be one of those situations where Palestinians are shooting at Palestinians and where the Palestinian Authority is trying to assert its authority over a more radical element in the city. The gun battle goes on for quite a while and is very close by. From the hotel window, we see men with machine guns running, a man right outside our window in the hotel entrance, holding his Kalashnikoff, on his cell phone, and making repeated calls. Ultimately, we hear the ambulances and later learn that seven people were wounded although no one died.

When the fighting erupted earlier, all the women disappeared and only young men were left out in the streets, running back and forth from the scene of fighting. It seems not only do these city folks deal with violence from the Israeli occupation; they deal with violence among themselves. I reflect that these are the young men born after 1967 who have known only checkpoints, closures, and curfews. They have seen their parents and grandparents repeatedly humiliated by Israeli soldiers and lost friends and family to a variety of catastrophes. Their parents were likely active in the First Intifada and they have grown up with little hope for a positive economic or social future. This moment is also a reflection of the ongoing breakdown of civil society, of the Palestinian Authority's weakness on the street, and the radicalization of young people who have little to lose and no experience with other kinds of choices.

When I have to leave the safety of the hotel and run down the steps to the car, my adrenaline peaks and my heart rate lurches upward. I have serious doubts about my sanity and that nagging question, what is a nice Jewish girl doing in a place like this, echoes in my ears. We get into the car and drive quickly away from the fighting, with this little edge of terror in our throats and a bit of gallows humor. Of course, we get lost and that is a touch unnerving, but the shooting is getting less intense and we are leaving it behind.

I feel such a sense of irony that we spent the morning in a discussion with this educated man who is devoted to democracy and to building a positive future for his people and then his people start shooting each other. The look on Allam's face, initially the gracious and witty host, turns to this mixture of maybe embarrassment, sadness, weariness, and disappointment. I suspect that these kinds of incidents on some level break his heart because he wants things to be so much better and there are so many obstacles between here and there.

A Lovely Dinner

After the wild ride towards his home, we head into the famous hills of the city. Allam, his wife, and teenage daughter live in a charming, well-appointed apartment with a stunning view of Nablus. Oddly, when the shooting stops, we are dropped into another world again. It is a "down-the-rabbit-hole" kind of experience. His wife, Khadeja, and a friend have prepared a fabulous meal that highlights local dishes and is outrageously tasty; chicken, fava beans, humus, okra, stunningly delicious and too much as usual. I think this must be how people cope, how people compartmentalize. Here we are, there are people on one side of the town trying to kill each other and we are having a beautiful meal in this lovely home. These kinds of contradictions are amazing and simultaneous. It is also interesting to me how quickly we put it all behind us. As soon as the shooting stops, we move on. Allam still has that weary look, but he is much happier and more relaxed in his own home with his family and friends.

We learn that his older daughter was married in November, 2004. Khadeja takes out the wedding pictures and we cluster around and admire her beautiful, well-coiffed daughter. With her classic features and elegant makeup, she looks like an Arab model stepping out of a fashion magazine, but the story of her wedding dress is a poignant example of the reality of life in this city. Last fall, Allam was on a speaking tour in the US that our medical delegation had sponsored. Given the limitations of shopping in the West Bank, while in New York he went to Macy's to buy his daughter her wedding dress. Consulting by cell phone, trying to figure out her size and desired style of dress, he buys her a gorgeous, white, beaded wedding dress and carries it back to Nablus for her to wear at her wedding.

The family story is even more complicated and in many ways, a classic example of the tortured paradoxes that face many Palestinians. The daughter met her husband at the university in Jordan and although he is Palestinian he doesn't have the required papers to enter the Occupied

Territories, he can only stay in Jordan. Consequently, the wedding had to come to him. Judging from the pictures and the home videos we watch, this was one of these lavish weddings with every relative invited, a band, hired traditional dancers, and enormous amounts of food. The camera sweeps across views of the well-dressed young and old, eating, dancing, including a particular dance that looked strangely like the *hora*. In fact, the whole affair reminded me of an over-the-top Jewish wedding. They did not lift the bride in a chair because she absolutely refused, but they did hoist the groom up on someone's shoulders and dance around him, so these customs go way back. It is wonderful to see this family really enjoying themselves and celebrating. Khadeja just sits at the edge of the couch glued to the TV screen, beaming at the pictures of her daughter, filled with mother pride, eyes twinkling at the video of all the guests who look so carefree and joyful.

We also see a film of the teenage daughter dancing. The family had a pre-wedding party in Nablus for the women who all dressed elegantly for each other and threw an all-women party, dancing and having a good time. Allam's entrancingly attractive younger daughter was filmed dancing in this very undulating style, almost like a belly dancer. Again, Khadeja is just beaming and the younger daughter perches on the couch with me, smiling and remembering that party where she danced and danced. I sense that in the midst of the stress and crises of living in the West Bank, the family took a break. They went to Jordan and they celebrated with abandon.

The very Palestinian side to this story is that the new husband cannot come to visit his wife's family in the West Bank because he does not have the required papers. Allam explains that the couple is planning to go to Australia where there are some relatives and the son-in-law plans to get an Australian passport. Then with his Australian passport, he can come and visit his mother-in-law in Nablus. I suspect that is one of the longest journeys that any son-in-law has had to take to meet his mother-in-law in her own home.

At the end of the evening, as if we hadn't had enough food, a huge plate of sweets arrives, again, fabulously tasty, with a subtle honeyed flavor, and very different from other desserts that we've encountered in the West Bank, accompanied by more Turkish coffee, and more tea with fresh mint. When we finally drive home, the streets are much quieter, and we hear announcements over the booming loudspeakers on the mosques. We are told that the voices are urging the people to be calm, that all Palestinians are brothers. They should lay down their arms. Allam spends much of the evening on his cell phone, assessing the level of safety on the streets and around our hotel, deciding if we are all sleeping on the floor of his living room or if we should leave the city entirely. He explains that this is the tone of his life; he is constantly changing his plans, his schedule, and his meetings, depending on "the situation."

The streets are quiet and we head to the hotel. In the car, Allam explains that the different factions are engaged in intense negotiations and so people have put down their guns and gone home. As we drive through the streets we are hit by the acrid smell of burning tires left from the tumult, the smell of street warfare and angry, frustrated men.

Smoking *Narjeelah* and Planning for Tomorrow

Back in the lovely Al Yasmeen Hotel, it is peaceful and quiet and a group of us sits around small round tables smoking *narjeelah*, a fruity smelling concoction mixed with a wonderful mellow tobacco. This is puffed through a water pipe and we pass the mouthpiece around in a common ritual of relaxation with friends. I of course start coughing wildly which breaks the spell and reminds me of the wild ups and downs of the day.

Tomorrow, I will go to Jenin to a maternity center, so I am hoping that the city stays quiet. I ask one of the hotel staff if he thinks the Israelis are going to seal up the city again, because Nablus is often placed under closure or curfew. The young man from the hotel says, "No, no. The Israelis are not going to come in. They like it when Palestinians are killing Palestinians." There is something so painful about his comment, the bitter feeling from this young man that on some level with the IDF, it is fine, the best Palestinian is a dead Palestinian.

Leaving the city, even if it is calm, is going to be a complicated affair. A PMRS ambulance is going to be bringing patients into the Nablus hospital, which provides a higher level of care than the surrounding region, because it is often very difficult for patients to get here due to the wall and the checkpoints. Tomorrow morning after discharging its patients at the hospital, this ambulance is going to pick up Khadeja, the obstetrician-gynecologist who is my guide, and then they are going to come and get me. I ask, what time will it come? Well, it depends on how many patients, it depends on how many checkpoints, it depends on how long the ambulance is held at the checkpoints, it depends on whether someone starts fighting with someone again. There are so many "it depends," and that is just another day in the life of a patient or a doctor or a person living in the Occupied Territories. Everything is always kind of up in the air.

As our "fun day" in Nablus drifts to an end, I marvel at the weight of the city's history, the many forms of violent and nonviolent resistance and just stubborn endurance that are seen in the course of one day. I wonder what happens to a society that is repeatedly restricted and under military siege. I wonder how a society will be repaired when its young men and women have suffered so many traumas and have so little hope. I am awed by the people who are able to maintain the normal bits and pieces of life and family and laughter in such a difficult setting. There is a victory to be had in the refusal to be humiliated, in the determination to dance with abandon at your daughter's wedding, in the belief that justice will ultimately be yours.

9

Restrictions on Access to Health Care: We Are Not Animals

THERE IS A STRONG BELIEF among many Israeli Jews and their Jewish and Christian supporters that in the name of security, in the absence of a "partner for peace," the time has come for a divorce from the Palestinian neighbors. After years of broken promises and dashed expectations, many favor building a separation wall, ostensibly to keep the Israelis on one side and the Palestinians on the other, thus unilaterally establishing concrete, electronic, and wire barriers and probably permanent borders. Without even beginning to discuss the many international legal controversies provoked by this project, this solution has many contradictions.[1] One irony is that it ignores the fact that because of the location of the wall, many Palestinians are actually being separated from *each other*. This occurs when Palestinians find themselves in the unfortunate position of living in the "seam area," the land between the Green Line and the wall, by living in East Jerusalem which is increasingly cut off from the West Bank, by living in a West Bank village caught between loops of the wall, or by being Israeli citizens.[2] Among many Jews, I find minimal questioning or even awareness of the Israeli governmental plans to solidify and make permanent the system of checkpoints, terminals, tunnels, permits, and other controls on the movement of Palestinian civilians. This is part of a publicly declared effort to protect the growing Jewish settlements in the West Bank as well as the residents living in Israel in vulnerable cities.

Talking with Palestinian students, physicians, administrators and patients, I am repeatedly moved by our commonality as human beings, rather than by our differences as Jew and Muslim, American and Palestinian. Traveling through the West Bank on the roads used by Palestinians, every time I am stopped at a checkpoint or roadblock, I can imagine the frustration of Bassem Al Natshehe, the passionate development director of Al Ahli Hospital in Hebron, who commented, "Every checkpoint you stop at, you feel humiliation. Everywhere you go, you feel humiliation." I often think of the 60-mile ambulance ride from Ramallah to Tulkaram with three obstetrician-gynecologists and a midwife after a women's health conference. Dr. Azzam Mahmoud, who trained in Romania and brought a Romanian doctor home as his wife, reflected on the endless bumpy ride and the multiple stops.

> If there is no occupation there is no problem. You see when you travel between two cities, five checkpoints. It is very big problem. I can't go where I want to go like every human. Why I must visit five checkpoints between two cities? They look at every Muslim or every Palestinian that he is a terrorist. We are not terrorist. Our people are very peaceful. We are very friendly. What you want from the man that you take his land, kill his boys, destroy his house, and you want to put him in between a wall? We are not animals. We are human. We are men and women.

I wonder if these plans for separation really make anyone safer and what are the implications for the people on the *other* side of these walls? How do these restrictions affect their ability to stay healthy, to provide and access care? What happens starting at the level of the individual psyche and extending into the overarching societal infrastructure when lines are arbitrarily drawn and barriers create an increasingly narrow noose around each professional school, clinic, or hospital? Can we imagine how this will affect future generations who grow up with shrinking visions of the possible and little knowledge of Israelis beyond the soldiers they confront at checkpoints, or bulldozing their olive groves or the roads to their universities and health care facilities?

I will start this exploration by examining several fragments in the life of a Palestinian medical student attending Al Quds University in East Jerusalem, then move on to the work of a family physician providing care in Qalqilya, a city in the northwestern part of the West Bank. Having gained some personal insights into the lives of these individual health care providers, I will then step back and look at the broader implications for the health care infrastructure, using an examination of my own experience providing health care in Gaza as a focus.

Moments in the Life of a Medical Student

East Jerusalem

ST lives in East Jerusalem, annexed by Israel from Jordan in 1967, at which time East Jerusalemites became Israeli residents, entitled to Israeli national health services, free public education, and access to work in West Jerusalem. She studies in Abu Dis, a neighborhood and closely related suburb of East Jerusalem. The Israelis annexed 10 percent of Abu Dis to East Jerusalem in 1967 and the community has been further divided and encircled by the ongoing construction of the separation wall. This built-up locality is contiguous with the city; its commerce and activities closely related and interwoven. Because of the inability of Palestinians to obtain housing permits in East Jerusalem proper, tens of thousands of residents moved into suburbs such as Abu Dis while holding their Israeli identity cards and receiving Israeli services. Thus, close relationships exist between East Jerusalem and Abu Dis through family ties, work, commerce, schools, and higher education.

These outer suburbs do not have a single hospital and rely on clinics and hospitals in East Jerusalem for their health care. The Palestinian hospitals in East Jerusalem provide the most advanced care in the Occupied Territories. They have functioned relatively independently from Israel, except for the recurrent and protracted episodes of closure and the loss of patients from the West Bank and Gaza who are unable to obtain the necessary permits or overcome the physical and financial obstacles to care.[3]

According to the Israeli human rights organization, B'Tselem, a chronic lack of investment by the Jerusalem municipality into Palestinian neighborhoods has left the area in a deteriorated state.[4] This has resulted in a marked disparity in social services ranging from the provision of sewage pipes and sidewalks to public parks and libraries when East Jerusalem is compared to West Jerusalem.[5] There has also been minimal interest by the Israeli government in the enforcement of laws or the maintenance of civil order in East Jerusalem. The government has actively placed severe restrictions on Palestinians building or developing land and has consistently sought to destroy Palestinian political and cultural institutions in East Jerusalem. In 2000,

57.5 percent of Palestinian East Jerusalemites were estimated to live below the poverty line.[6]

The 200,000 East Jerusalemites comprise 10 percent of the population of the West Bank. Between the legal restrictions and the expanding ring of Jewish settlements around East Jerusalem, they are increasingly isolated from their families and political, commercial, religious, and cultural connections to their compatriots in the West Bank. According to PHR-I, tighter restrictions on Palestinian civilian movement began in 1991 and worsened in 2000 with the Second Intifada, negatively impacting health care providers and their patients.[7] PHR-I notes that medical students often face barriers to completing their training due to difficulties in traveling to their universities and clinical rotations or in obtaining permits to study abroad. The issue is particularly egregious in Gaza where there is no medical school. If a Gazan student is discovered studying in the West Bank, he or she is "deported" back to Gaza as if the desire to obtain a university or postgraduate education is equivalent to criminal behavior.

Clinical Rotation in New York City

In 2004, ST, a medical student from Al Quds University in East Jerusalem, pursued a clinical rotation at Columbia Presbyterian Medical Center in New York City. While she was clear in her email negotiations that she was a Palestinian studying in East Jerusalem, her supervising resident at Columbia was quick to introduce her to another student, saying, "Guess what? He's also an Israeli." Despite the Israeli student's obvious discomfort working with an Arab student, ST felt that their relations were going well until a bombing in Be'ersheva, Israel, occurred. The Israeli student's mother called him while ST and he were walking to clinic to see patients together. ST recalls that the student kept repeating the story, "There was a bombing in Be'ersheva and all my family and friends live there." She remembers responding,

> "I'm really sorry; I don't know what to tell you. Is everyone OK? Did you hear about anyone who got hurt or something?" He said, "No, my Mom called and everyone is fine." "Oh that's good; I really don't know what to tell you." He went all around the hospital telling everyone we see, that this and this happened and there was a bombing. Then one of the residents he was talking to, he was telling her there was a bombing. She said, "But isn't

there a wall separating you people from each other?" Because no, the wall is not yet complete and that's why it should be complete. I couldn't take it. I was like, "Hey you, you're the last one to be talking about the wall! OK? The wall is not destroying your life as it's doing to my life, so you stop talking about the wall. OK, we know there's a bombing. It's not a big deal. Bombings happen every day, attacks, and the Israelis invade cities, they demolish houses every day. So this is the reality we are living, so stop!" I couldn't take it, I went to another room. So the resident, trying to separate us in order to resolve the conflict, sent him to see an inpatient.

That incident really struck me. In an attempt to get out of the conflict and try to live a pure medical and social experience, the first thing, I am confronted by someone from the other side. You can never escape.

The View from East Jerusalem

We are talking with ST in East Jerusalem, standing on the Mount of Olives, with a crazy mix of tourists, locals, and a photogenic camel, looking down at the walled Old City, the dazzling golden Dome of the Rock, the fountains and gardens of the Noble Sanctuary or Haram al-Sharif, and the famous Al-Aqsa Mosque. There is a vast cemetery, flat white stones cascading down the hill, divided into Armenian, Christian, Jewish, and Muslim sectors, the old white Church of Mary Magdalene with its golden onion domes piercing through the dark trees. ST is pointing out her home where she lives with her family, to the southeast, and the separation wall winding through Abu Dis, the neighborhood in East Jerusalem where Al Quds University is located. She describes how the concrete barrier was built 100 meters from her home so it is impossible for her not to see it and feel its impact everyday. It has also blocked a nearby street, so neighbors can no longer cross to see friends, shop, and conduct their normal lives.

Squinting in the sun, she points out the winding path of the concrete wall, how it snakes around the campus. "So when you are standing in campus, you can see the wall all around you. So it really looks like a cage. Here where it looks like it's not continuous, it goes between the houses." She explains that families that thought they were in Jerusalem suddenly found themselves "abandoned in the so-called West Bank because the wall denied them the right of staying in Jerusalem. They sued the Israeli government since they were paying all the Jerusalem taxes as stated by the law. It's very unfair to suddenly announce them as not part of the city."

ST recounts that when the wall was under construction it was planned to cut across the university sports grounds. "If the wall goes through it, this land will be literally confiscated, so it will no longer be the school's property." The university administration, professors, physicians, and students organized a protest and everyone started giving lectures on the proposed construction site. Students played football and danced the *dabkeh*, a traditional folk dance, bands performed. People slept on the site and even held graduation parties on the grass. They hired a lawyer and sued the Israeli authorities. At the end of almost a month, the wall was moved to the edge of the grounds. ST says with frustration, "It shouldn't be there in the first place. We moved it a few meters, how pathetic. This is how things end up with Israel. We have to accept the best way of humiliation and [it all] becomes a matter of negotiation. It was better than nothing."

She explains that the university campus is now totally isolated on the other side of the wall in the neighborhood of Abu Dis. It used to be a five-minute drive for her to get to school. Now, to avoid a prolonged commute on public transportation and an unpredictable checkpoint, ST has found a place to sneak through a break in the wall in a garden of a church, although she still often encounters Israeli soldiers on patrol.

> It's very hard for us when we want to take lectures or exams and we have to go to campus. Sometimes it is impossible for us to go there because of having to sneak through the wall. Then you have the soldiers checking people and making their lives harder. Your life, as unpredictable as it is, ends up being controlled by some Israeli teenager IDF's mood.

The wall has also affected the patients who need to come to the hospital. Because Arabs in East Jerusalem have Israeli health insurance, they tend to use Israeli facilities. Those patients who come to the high-level hospitals in East Jerusalem are thus often from refugee camps and the West Bank. ST explains, "They have to have permissions. It's very expensive to come with a taxi all the way around. When someone is sick they cannot come walking and jump over walls in order to access health care. Of course this had a long-term impact on the Palestinian health status." In 2004, ST found as the eight-meter high concrete slab barrier was under construction, the hospitals were left empty because the patients couldn't negotiate the multiple permitting policies and physical obstructions. The medical students spent long hours sitting in the nursing station with nothing to do. The hospital administrators now try to make arrangements for patients and their companions from the West Bank to come on specific days with permits for elective admissions and outpatient visits. The Israeli authorities are also creating new laws and a permit system that will make it difficult for Arab East Jerusalemites to travel to the West Bank, just as it is currently difficult for West Bank residents to travel to East Jerusalem. ST explains that this will require her to go to the District Coordination Offices (DCO), an Israeli security center that provides permits for a restricted period of time. Thus she might soon be required to have a permit to do a clinical rotation in Ramallah or Hebron as well as to visit family and friends in Jericho.

A Clerkship in Nablus

Medical students need hospital training, but access to clinical rotations outside of East Jerusalem was difficult even before these new constraints. ST describes wanting to take a clinical rotation with a physician in Nablus who is known to be an excellent surgeon and teacher. She tried to go to Nablus, but was turned away at the checkpoint.

> As usual people found a harder alternative and were simply taking risks crossing the border in that way. You would simply rent a donkey along with its owner, load it with your bags, and go up the mountains just in the middle of nowhere in order to make it to Nablus, a long and difficult route. Knowing that at any second soldiers might take notice of that and start shooting haphazardly, I decided to take the risk.
>
> As we went hiking in the mountains with the donkey in front it felt really strange to be doing this. I suddenly asked the guy leading us to stop and go back. I was living the "What if" phase of any life event; what if soldiers saw us, what if they shoot, what if I make it to Nablus but am not able to get out? What if another invasion takes place while I am in there, endless questions but no answers! On the way back to Jerusalem I was experiencing a complexity of feelings of hatred, denial, humiliation, disrespect, oppression, disappointment along with a strong desire to revolt, to disobey, and never surrender.

I look at ST with her fashionable blond streaked hair and trendy outfit, classy shoes, and urbane wire rim glasses. She looks like she could easily be from any cosmopolitan European city. She had said earlier, "Despite the fact that on many occasions I was mistaken for a European, I never hesitate to say and stress the fact that I am an Arab Palestinian who is trying hard to simply live the normal life of those my age, a basic right every Palestinian was denied since he was born." I try to imagine her with her modern look and historical legacy of stubbornness and endurance, sneaking through the rough mountains with her bags of medical books and sophisticated clothes slung across a plodding grey donkey.

Checkpoints in the City

Word has gotten around through the pervasive cell phone network and street chatter that the Israeli government has received a warning that two Palestinians from Gaza have come into Jerusalem planning a suicide bombing. Suddenly there are checkpoints throughout the city and all the entrances to Abu Dis are blocked. A number of medical students cannot get home, and a soft-spoken student says she is planning to "find a way, not in front of the soldiers, so that I can pass without seeing me." She explains that there are spaces in the wall between the concrete slabs where she sneaks through, but that she will not go through the church today because soldiers will be there. I ask her if she is afraid and she says, "No, I manage to do it a lot. It may be fearful for someone who's not going every day but I manage to do it." What if she is caught?

> I have a permission to Jerusalem so they will be more calm, maybe shout at me and then let me pass. If I don't have a permission, they would be more aggressive with me, like shouting too much. They may make me stay for hours just until they go, something like that. They don't hit girls, they hit boys mainly. Add to that, they force them to sign paperwork in order that they won't even dare to think to come to Jerusalem with no permit.

Another student on a cell phone learns that her mother who went shopping is now trapped in Abu Dis even though she has an Israeli ID. There is no negotiating and the closure can last unpredictably for hours.

Changing plans, we pile into ST's car heading downtown towards Salahadin Street when we are stopped by Israeli policemen at a temporary checkpoint. While they examine our documents, ST talks about other checkpoint experiences. She tends to be fearless and argumentative with the police or the soldiers, knows her legal rights, but ultimately capitulates for practical reasons. She recounts a dispute over being asked for her driving license by an Israeli soldier.

> "You're not a police officer, you have my ID and my license is of no business to you." Very confident he replied, "No I can do whatever I want. I can ask about anything I want." After getting into a long, pointless argument, he wouldn't let go of me till I give him what he asked for. This puts you under the spotlight; makes you aware of how weak you are. What a weird world that we live in that gives an Israeli teenager the right to boss me around. In order to pass I had to come up with my driving license. [I felt] no victory.

Our documents are returned and we are on our way, heading to a local internet café and student hangout.

ST has strong feelings about the young Israeli soldiers that she frequently encounters at checkpoints and roadblocks. She says that she actually feels sorry for these young recruits, that she can imagine how they feel, the distrust, the racism, the boredom, the finger on the trigger.

> It's unacceptable that these teenagers get the chance to control my life, but I also feel sorry for them, as someone their age should be doing something better for a life than standing at a checkpoint and humiliating people their age or older. Practically speaking they are being used by their government to inflict crimes in the name of security, putting their life on hold for two years or more to serve the occupation. There's a point of targeting this age group who are simply too energetic, enthusiastic, who have been taught that Arabs are enemies; Palestinians are terrorists whose dream is basically killing Israelis.
>
> Well, I would like to point it out clearly here that this is not the case. We are not trained to kill. We are not brought up to hate or take revenge. We respect human dignity. The last thing that would come to my mind is hurting an Israeli, not because I love them, because simply it's just not me. I wake up every morning knowing that there is someone out there trying to make my life miserable. This is their job. [I want to say to the soldiers] Go, get a school, go learn something, do something better for your life.

Political Issues on Campus

Talk turns to life on campus and ST, who started her involvement in dialogue and peace-oriented groups with Jewish Israelis when she was a teenager, explains that at a Palestinian university, students who have

Israeli friends are suspected of being collaborators. Her involvement with the peace group, Seeds of Peace, and her desire to communicate and "touch the human side" is often viewed with suspicion.

> Unfortunately it's hard to be on this front on your own when most of those in the university are busy with political groups that see such an ideology as weird and unaccepted. People tend to be pre-judgmental, hence you might be simply black-labeled the moment they learn that you have relationships with Israelis and you meet them on [a] regular basis.

She explains that the "black label" means that a student will not be trusted by his or her own friends, will be seen as someone who does not care about the rights of Palestinians. She admits that she knows many Israelis and is comfortable having social relationships, but has neither close friends nor enemies.

> It's impossible to get the conflict out of your mind especially with the current situation. Living in an Arab Palestinian conservative society and attending a Palestinian University automatically limits my relationship with Israelis. I am not in favor of being stranded from my community. I'm satisfied with the kind of relationship I have with the Israelis; at least I have a channel of communication with the other side.

ST reports she has multiple opportunities to meet with Israelis and she has had seminars and workshops on important issues such as talking about difficult topics, mediation, and negotiation. "There are skills that you need in order to interact with someone who for a long time was presented to you as an enemy and who practices this role very well. It's very hard to converse, people get emotional. You need to have self-control."

At the same time, she finds the students at the university are divided into two opposing camps; those who feel Israel should be returned to the Palestinians and those who support a two state solution with 1967 borders, East Jerusalem as the capital and the right of return for refugees.

> Of course, no one will think of it as one state, living together as friends and a peaceful environment because this is not realistic, because there's no way we can live with Israelis and be equal. They will always be dominating. They will always be trying to control us. We'll always be the side who's disadvantaged and this is so clear in East Jerusalem because Jerusalem is controlled by the Israeli government.

Nonetheless, ST states she would be happy to train with Israeli medical students but notes that her Palestinian school is not accredited by the Israeli health ministry. "I feel that it's really essential to bring the medical efforts together because when it comes to medicine, it's not about politics." She would like to be able to treat Palestinians in East Jerusalem, even if it's under the Israeli health ministry, "as long as I'm serving my people. Also there's nothing wrong with me serving the Israeli people if I have something to give, I don't think there should be a problem."

Conflict and Coexistence

This difficult emotional and political dance is illustrated in a story ST recounts while returning with us to Ramallah in a van from Hebron where several delegates had given medical lectures at Al Ahli Hospital. She describes her first year in clinical training, the first week on general surgery, the first day in the operating room. She anxiously went into the operating room just to observe, and found the patient was a young man who had been shot by Israeli soldiers in Nablus and now needed a bowel resection. The bullet had gone through his abdomen, his diaphragm, and out through his chest wall. The doctors attempted to operate on the young man in Nablus, were not successful, and transferred him to Mokassed Hospital in East Jerusalem where there are more advanced services and highly trained surgeons. ST describes the five-hour surgery in detail and almost fainting at the sight of the trauma.

After this experience she was scheduled to go to an Israeli/Palestinian peace organization in East Jerusalem to attend a discussion group. She debated skipping the meeting, "I was thinking, should I go see them or not? Why on earth am I doing this? Why am I coming here and I'm sitting with you and talking with you when I go through this internal conflict early in the morning and then come and just pretend that everything is OK?" She decided to attend and remembers telling the group that she was not there to be friends, but rather to describe her experiences from the morning, "to let you know what you're doing to me. Inside me I'm really very confused. It's very contradicting what I go through at different times of the day." She believes that it is important for the other side to know what is happening.

We need to confront. Then the facilitator, after that he came up to me and he was like, "I'm really sorry that you had to go through this. It's very interesting and it brings us to the issue of internal conflict and what conditions are you living in and then what you're thinking, what you believe in, and it's very brave of you just to decide and come."

This event did affect me a lot. It was so strong, empowering, made me feel eager to do something about what's happening. It's a responsibility for you to talk to Israelis; by avoiding, nothing will be solved. No, this is wrong. We need to communicate.

A Family Physician from Qalqilya

Fences and Walls

North of Jerusalem along Israel's narrow waist, the West Bank city of Qalqilya bulges westward, approximately eleven miles from Tel Aviv and nine miles from Netanya. In 2002, following a protracted siege and closure, the building of what has been called the "security fence," "separation wall," or "apartheid wall," was begun. In July 2003 it was completed, entirely enclosing the city like a giant concrete lasso.[8] This barrier divided Qalqilya not only from Israel, but also from the West Bank Jewish settlements of Zufin to the north and Alfe Menashe to the south, and from nearby Palestinian towns such as Jayyus, Habla, and the larger city of Tulkaram.[9] The 40,000 inhabitants of Qalqilya are connected to their neighbors through a long neck, like a bottle emptying out via a single checkpoint facing eastward.[10] This wall is more than a response to the Israeli fear of suicide bombers or the physical architecture of barbed wire and concrete slabs. Its impact on access to health care has been profound. It has disrupted not only the flow of patients, providers, ambulances, and medical supplies, but also the system of primary care centers and higher-level referrals, the cobbled-together network of UNRWA, Ministry of Health, and private NGO clinics and hospitals that serve the people of this area.[11]

The wall has added to the difficulties already created by the splintering of the West Bank into multiple cells, a patchwork of villages and cities separated by checkpoints and roadblocks, intermittent local curfews, and larger closures of entire towns or cities.[12] A Palestinian who wishes to travel from cell to cell must receive a special permit, which is often granted or denied arbitrarily. He or she then negotiates the physical hurdles as well as the distortion of distance created by the loops of the separation wall that weaves in and out, wrapping around Jewish settlements to include them on the "Israeli side" of the wall. PHR-I receives dozens of appeals each month from medical groups and patients unable to obtain care due to these multiple barriers, and the organization works through the civil administration, the Israeli Army, and Department of Defense in an advocacy role. PHR-I also generates appeals to the Israeli High Court when an individual's rights have been denied, not only to advocate for that particular patient, but also to open the debate regarding the policies of the security forces in a more public forum. The security policies have resulted in an unprecedented disruption of the internationally recognized right to provide and obtain health care in an occupied area. This has had an especially deleterious impact on preventive and emergency care, as well as on the referral infrastructure and specialty centers that were the foundation of the health care system.[13] This is exacerbated by what has been referred to as the "NGOization" of health care, where multiple organizations provide fragments of desperately needed care without an overall strategy, a sensible division of services, or a critical investment in the development of an autonomous, high quality, unified system.

Arriving in Qalqilya

The delegates have just unloaded our gear in a second-floor apartment in the city of Qalqilya after a lively wrestling game in a dusty dirt yard with an inquisitive collection of local children, when there is a knock on the door. Afraid the energetic children are back, we hesitate to respond. It has been an exhausting day. While one of our taxis made it from Tulkaram without any difficulty, the other was stopped at a temporary checkpoint, a vehicle and Israeli soldiers blocking the road, and held for an hour for no obvious reason before being allowed to proceed. We spent the afternoon exploring the West Bank side of the eight-meter high, concrete separation wall that completely encircles the city. The wall's grey, prison-like presence is interrupted by cylindrical guard towers and accompanied by a dirt military road, trenches, a muddy, garbage and rock-strewn no-man's-land, and rolls of barbed wire. It is utterly daunting and feels particularly ominous when an Israeli soldier in the guard tower fires warning shots over our heads to let us know that our presence and probably our cameras are not appreciated. From the second floor of a nearby abandoned home, we can see the Israeli bypass road and Jewish settlement beyond the wall, another layer of obstruction to Palestinians, and their rich agricultural lands. We are trying to absorb the magnitude of the emotional and economic impact of this imposing structure on the farmers and shopkeepers and children within this walled city. Our guide, Souad Hashim, when she is not describing the daily indignities and the level of destruction to property and lives, is worrying that we will not have enough blankets in the apartment and may be chilly during the night.

Dr. Hussein Shanti and Family

Reluctantly unlocking the door of our apartment, we are greeted by a family of children of various ages, each bearing a blanket, and their father, Dr. Hussein Shanti, dressed neatly in a dark suit and crisp white shirt with an opened top button and loosened tie. Bewildered, we welcome them in and are soon talking, showing the children the wonders of computer games and playful comic goofiness, sharing candy and baseball hats. The girls are shy, choosing the offered chocolate treats cautiously, the youngest boy takes his new baseball hat on and off and replaces it at hilarious tipsy angles. Dr. Shanti, his face weathered and weary with that look of premature aging often etched by chronic stress, his mustache neatly trimmed, eyes dark and expressive, starts to speak.

He explains that he is a family physician, trained in Italy 20 years ago. His private office is in Rasatya, a town about four kilometers or five minutes from his home in Qalqilya. Since the separation wall was built snaking into the West Bank to include the Jewish settlement of Alfe Menashe on the west or "Israeli side" of the wall, with Rasatya on the other side of this loop, his office is now one hour or 30 kilometers from his house. Because of the distance and his uncertainty about getting to work, crossing through checkpoints, he now sleeps in his office five nights per week, seeing emergencies as needed. "I work automatically." At 6 am he takes a taxi back to Qalqilya where he works in a government clinic run by the Palestinian Authority, seeing patients from 8 am to 2:30 pm, six days per week. Then he sees his family and returns to Rasatya.

He tells us that usually he sees patients with chronic diseases, pregnant women, and children and that he is able to perform basic screening tests. He adds that generally, babies born up to twelve weeks early are able to survive if their mothers can reach the UNRWA hospital in Qalqilya or the hospital in Nablus. The major problem he finds is that hospital-based childbirth is expensive and patients are having increasing trouble getting to the hospitals due to the checkpoints, roadblocks, and the wall. Some of his patients have health insurance through the Palestinian Authority, but many pay for care out-of-pocket. He is concerned about increasing cancer, anemia, diabetes, hypertension, congestive heart failure, renal disease, asthma, and depression "in all of us." He worries that two villages have been completely cut off from his private clinic and patients who come to see him often lose a whole day of work because they can't get through the gates in the wall which are unreliably open for brief periods during the day. He is also troubled by a chronic lack of supplies and medications. As an example, he talks about his difficulties providing asthma care, his lack of affordable medication, his inability to provide inhalers with spacers for appropriately taking the medication. He improvises by using a plastic cup as a spacer, placing this over a child's face. He completes his narrative by explaining that the working conditions are poor and the needs are great. "It is not easy." He explains that a small family in this region has six to seven children and that some women have up to 20 children. His mother had 22 pregnancies, eleven survived and there are 60 grandchildren. Like many Palestinians, the family connections are extensive and Dr. Shanti lives in the same building with three of his brothers and their families.

The residents of Qalqilya once relied on a brisk commercial relationship with Israelis who came to shop in the city, as well as on Palestinians obtaining work in agriculture and construction within Israel. Dr. Shanti estimates that 70 percent of Qalqilya is now out of work, one-third of the businesses have closed, and a large percentage of the population depends on food packages from the Red Cross and from Arab countries. Additionally, 65 percent of the arable land is located outside the wall and there are serious problems accessing the town's farmlands and harvesting adequate levels of food.

The Meaning of Separation

I think back to our tour of the wall earlier in the day, barbed wire often snaking across neat rows of vegetables, green houses adjacent to the no-man's-land, fields mutilated by the concrete wall. Much of the barrier route is not along the Green Line, but loops within the West Bank, annexing to Israel the most fertile agricultural lands and many of the sources of water.[14] In Qalqilya, besides the single major entry/exit checkpoint, Souad tells us that there are only two multilayered, heavy yellow metal sliding gates with barbed wire fencing. Only one of them is unreliably open twice a day for Palestinians who have obtained the hard-to-get permits to farm their own land on the other side of the wall. At one point, we are crowded around one of the gates with Souad and her spunky ten-year-old daughter who has entertained herself during the afternoon by running up to the imposing concrete barrier and scrawling graffiti with a magic marker. At the gate, she climbs up and is drawing Stars of David and then placing a firm "X" over them. Suddenly an Israeli army jeep pulls up and a woman in full battle gear jumps out, automatic weapon ready, and yells across the wire fence, "Can we help you?" Then, incredulous that we are on the *inside* and do not seek any help, she questions, "How did you get to that side?" The implication of her question clearly is that we are standing with this dangerous (educated, savvy, politically knowledgeable) Palestinian woman and her untrustworthy (vivacious, bright, articulate) daughter. We yell back, "Through the checkpoint on the other side!" The soldier, her face dwarfed by her oversized helmet, stares at us in amazement. Suddenly, Souad's daughter jumps up, waves, and shouts, "*Shalom hat!*" For a few minutes we just stand facing each other, a few meters but worlds apart, the word "separation" taking on a whole new meaning, marveling at the soldier's disturbing assumptions and this little girl's brief act of connection as well as resistance.

An Obstetrician-Gynecologist from Gaza

The Decimation of the Gaza Strip

The individual narratives of students unable to reach their classes, patients and providers trapped at checkpoints, supplies and equipment blocked by Israeli regulators, only reveal part of the story of the disruption of lives and institutions that has occurred under occupation. There is also a long-term impact to the policies of restricting the most ordinary, necessary activities of daily life and combining that with years of neglect and active de-development of critical institutions. This is well documented in Gaza, where the Israeli government's lack of investment into the medical infrastructure and education of personnel from the time of the 1967 occupation combined with the managerial and financial inadequacies of the Palestinian Authority governing since the Oslo Accords in 1993. These policies produced a perfect storm for the failure of the health care system. Added to these insults are the repeated assaults on the remaining institutions by Israeli closures and incursions that have left the medical system in shambles.[15]

Sara Roy, in "A Dubai on the Mediterranean," describes the 1,400,000 people living in the Gaza Strip, with the population growing by 3 to 5 percent annually, half the population under 15 years old, and access to health care and education diminishing at an alarming rate. She cites the World Bank, noting that Palestinians are in the midst of a massive economic depression with unemployment rising to nearly 40 percent overall, with some estimates up to 80 percent in parts of Gaza, resulting in approximately 75 percent of Gazans living in poverty. According to the World Food Program, approximately 42 percent of the Gaza population faces "food insecurity," defined as a lack of adequate and nutritious food for normal growth, and 30 percent are "food vulnerable," at risk of food insecurity. According to Roy, "Since 2000, the economy of the Gaza Strip and the West Bank has lost a potential income of approximately $6.5 billion and suffered $3.5 billion worth of physical damage at the hands of the Israeli army."[16] The destruction of homes, schools, hospitals, and agricultural lands, and the severe restrictions in movement by Israeli authorities since 2000 have had dramatic consequences on the population of Gaza. This distress comes on top of a seven-year history of repeated closures which have created massive increases in poverty and unemployment. Roy notes that the societal damage is so extreme because,

> the 30-year process of integrating Gaza's economy into Israel's had made the local economy deeply dependent. As a result, when the border was closed in 1993, self-sustainment was no longer possible – the means weren't there. Decades of expropriation and deinstitutionalization had long ago robbed

Palestine of its potential for development, ensuring that no viable economic (and hence political) structure could emerge.[17]

Post Gaza disengagement, the Israeli government maintains total control over the movement of people, produce, and commodities in and out of the Gaza Strip and continues to supply and thus have power over the availability and price of electricity, water, gas, and fuel. In 2006, Israeli forces reoccupied parts of Gaza and decimated more of the infrastructure.

Dr. Izzeldin Abuelaish

Statistics often do not convey the emotional gravity of human suffering and the personal consequences of the collapse of critical societal institutions. Meeting with Dr. Izzeldin Abuelaish, an obstetrician-gynecologist born in the Jabalya Refugee Camp in northern Gaza, provides us with an intimate glimpse into this conflict. A handsome man with an infectious smile, intense dark eyes, and expressive hands that are constantly in motion, Izzeldin explains that his family is from Huj, a former Palestinian village now in Israel, located between the Gaza Strip and Hebron. His father was an uneducated but wealthy farmer. His parents were deported in 1948 to the Jabalya Refugee Camp where he was born in 1955, followed by eight siblings. The family grew up in a two-room house with no plumbing or electricity. As a child, Izzeldin did odd jobs, selling sunflower seeds, washing cars, working in a factory. In 1970, his family home was demolished to widen the streets for Israeli tanks, and the family was temporarily homeless. Meanwhile, he attended an UNRWA school in the refugee camp, received a scholarship to study medicine in Cairo, graduated in 1983, and had further training in Saudi Arabia, England, and Israel. He is very proud of his work at the Israeli Soroka Medical Center in Be'ersheva, caring for Jewish and Arab Israelis, as well as occasional patients transferred from Gaza, and in Gaza where he has staffed clinics and hospitals. He has delivered babies for Palestinian women as well as Jewish women from the Gaza settlements. He is a believer in health care as a bridge in times of conflict and the doctor as a "messenger for peace." I first met Izzeldin while he was studying for his Masters at the Harvard School of Public Health and was impressed both by his sincerity and his unrelenting optimism.

The Israeli Incursion

Izzeldin lives with his wife and nine children in an elegantly built home at the edge of the Jabalya Refugee Camp. Three of his brothers and their families each have a floor of this recently constructed apartment. The first floor is an open space lined with pillows where men often congregate at the end of the day to talk, laugh, smoke *narjeelah* and cigarettes, and drink strong cups of Arabic coffee. Izzeldin's three oldest daughters have spent their recent summers at the Creativity Peace Camp in Santa Fe, New Mexico, where they have built relationships with Israeli girls living relatively nearby, but light-years apart by political standards. I feel like Izzeldin is trying to immunize his children against the poisonous reality around them.

In September 2004, the Israeli army moved into northern Gaza with tanks, bulldozers, and armored personnel carriers with the goal of stopping the firing of homemade Palestinian rockets into the Israeli town of Sderot, which resulted in the deaths of four Israeli citizens. According to the UN Gaza Field assessment of the IDF operation, Days of Penitence, air and ground attacks by the IDF continued for 17 days. They damaged homes, businesses, and schools in several densely populated refugee camps, restricted the movement of health and humanitarian workers, and leveled large areas of agricultural land, particularly olive and citrus trees, and public infrastructure including three factories and a mosque. The bulldozers gouged deep trenches in the roads and severed sewer, water, and electrical lines. An estimated 107 Palestinians were killed including 27 children, over 400 people were injured, and 675 made homeless.[18] Izzeldin describes the long anxious nights, the ominous hulking tanks parked outside his door. His children all slept in the middle of the house away from the windows and trigger-happy snipers, crying and comforting each other during the repeated shellings, F-16s shrieking overhead. He has just taken us on a tour of the devastated areas, pointing excitedly with a mixture of outrage and disbelief at the crumpled concrete walls, wire and plaster twisted and jutting through the wreckage, doors askew, fractured dinner plates flattened in the mud, the drifting, dank smell of sewage.

His long tapered fingers point, "Look here! Look here!" over and over again. "Yes, look here! These were farms, which have been demolished. Look here! The tanks were here and they went inside the camp and demolished all of those places, the houses and you will see now the houses. It's shocking to see."

El Morshed Educational Social Society

The Jabalya Refugee Camp houses approximately 100,000 refugees, living in crowded conditions almost three times the density of Manhattan. Their health care is provided primarily by the largely underfunded, understaffed UNRWA hospitals and clinics. Izzeldin takes the medical delegates to a homegrown voluntary social service organization called El Morshed. In 2003 a group of educated men and women in the community, psychologists, teachers, engineers, and social scientists, founded the clinic in an attempt to address the cultural, social, and medical needs of the desperate local population. Izzeldin volunteers his obstetrics and gynecology services every week and word has spread that a pediatrician and an obstetrician-gynecologist from America will also be seeing patients. We make our way through an overcrowded waiting room, mostly mothers and children, amid much chattering, screaming, little boys and girls running about. After the formal introductions from the chairperson of the board and other officials, the flood of patients begins, our pediatrician moves to the next room, and I sit beside Izzeldin, awaiting his translations, discussing cases, and trying to absorb the bizarre contradictions and intensity of the moment.

To my utter amazement, we are doing an infertility clinic in one of the most populous areas in the world. There is no exam room, minimal privacy, and frequent offerings of small cups of dense, sweet, black coffee. One woman is 41, her husband 60 years old, 14 years of infertility; another is 30 and her husband 37, eight years of infertility; another is 25 and her husband 33, nine years of infertility; another 40 and her husband 44, 18 years of infertility. One woman has had four pregnancies and three children died of a variety of congenital disorders; but maybe one died of dehydration? The patients gently lay before us precious scraps of paper with bits of often illegible medical testing information, fragments of grossly inadequate workups, pathology on numerous testicular biopsies. The couples save for years to undergo an IVF cycle, or to travel to Egypt for treatments of equally questionable quality. In Gaza there are no sperm banks and no facilities for freezing fertilized embryos. One woman has four daughters and has not conceived for four years; her husband is threatening to take a second wife if she does not provide him with that essential precious son.

Even Izzeldin loses his patience, condemning the doctors who do not keep adequate records, are ill-informed and often grossly incompetent; the substandard laboratories without quality controls, producing conflicting test results. He tries to weave the pieces together, to offer a glimpse of hope, to strategize what is possible to accomplish, who is insured, who can see him at another clinic where he can do a physical exam, an ultrasound. Where can he arrange an x-ray, hormonal studies? The patients are universally gracious and many reveal a worn look of guarded perseverance. Some of the women wear head scarves; some have faces that are covered, only their eyes expressing the pain and disappointment that has framed their lives. Gradually I am coming to understand that while I see a medically abysmal and hopeless catastrophe, each of these couples is trying to live a normal life. They are aspiring like families all over the world to fulfill their desire for children (hopefully with many sons), and this refusal to be defeated is actually an immense source of strength as well as a form of quiet resistance for which Palestinians are well known. I cannot tell how much of this feels slightly delusional and how much is the powerful secret to survival under impossible conditions.

I am feeling utterly disheartened at the level of need and our inability to provide even a fragment of meaningful assistance. I find our pediatrician examining a laughing child with Down's syndrome, surrounded by her enormous family and possibly half the neighborhood. He explains to me that she has major medical and developmental needs, none of which seem to be available in the Gaza Strip.

The Hard-to-Treat Cases

The next day Izzeldin takes us to see a group of difficult-to-diagnose and treat pediatric patients from the Jabalya Refugee Camp. Apparently we are being received as the big experts from America, a truly humbling experience. I spend most of my time with a family of two sweet, bright-eyed little girls and their concerned parents who arrive clutching a ream of medical reports and ultrasounds. Both of these children were born with a rare congenital hormonal disorder which causes the female genitalia to develop with some masculine characteristics, including an enlarged clitoris and absent vagina. In my 30 years of practice, I may have seen one case, today I see three. I quickly learn that the Jabalya Refugee Camp has one of the highest rates of intermarriage of first cousins in the world and thus there is an extremely high rate of genetic disorders and genetically related illnesses that are not even well understood. These girls' parents are first cousins.

We review the children's histories. The diagnosis and hormonal therapy appear correct but the parents have two questions for the American experts. Their first daughter had undergone the removal of her enlarged clitoris by an (unscrupulous) Gaza doctor because he explained that the clitoris "did not look right." The mother asks should they do this to their younger child. I launch into a series of diagrams and explanations and an emphatic, "No!" The second more profound issue is, will their daughters be able to marry? I translate that to: will their daughters be able to have intercourse and children? The creation and maintenance of a vagina in such a girl would be a major undertaking in the medical mecca of Boston, requiring special expertise and ongoing long-term follow-up. The possibility of this happening in Gaza is zero. Fertility is another complicated issue. As I continue explaining with more careful diagrams and details, I wonder what are the chances of these girls ever obtaining the repeated permits and funding and transportation to reach, for instance, Hadassah Hospital in Jerusalem, where such medical issues could be addressed. Again I suspect that the answer is extremely unlikely. Sorrowfully, I think about how women in this traditional society are defined by their ability to reproduce. I look at these cheerful girls with their dark curly hair and slightly shy demeanors and wonder what tragedy and disappointment awaits them. How do you explain this to their caring, ever-hopeful parents? But it was time to see the next child, a little boy who was admitted to a local hospital with a blood pressure of 220/190 (normal is less than 120/80), seizing, with a stroke and a number of other strange disorders. He obviously has some mysterious disease, perhaps a rare undiagnosed syndrome. His desperate parents have taken him to

Egypt where a major workup was unsuccessful at making a diagnosis. Perhaps the experts from America could help?

Living on Hope

The intensity of need in the Gaza Strip is clearly daunting, from the broadest level of institutional infrastructure and training to the details of patient care. Even after the much heralded Israeli disengagement from Gaza and the victory of Hamas in the Legislative Council, the Israeli government's strict closure of Gaza checkpoints and recent bombing campaign have created a new degree of economic chaos and a disastrous lack of food and medical supplies.[19] This is devastating to the civilian population and the incursions in 2006 have only brought the society closer to total collapse.[20]

The intersection between health care and politics is so clear in this tiny troubled area of the world. I wonder if Israelis and their supporters in the US understand the consequences and sheer brutality of repeatedly constricting and destroying a society. I wonder if any Israeli would accept this state of affairs for themselves or would he or she turn to increasingly militant resistance? The miracle is really that so many people choose hope and endurance over violence. I think back to Safwat Diab, a project manager at the Gaza Community Mental Health Program, who told me of a dream that he had.

> I wish one day it will happen, we go to the beach, with my kids. I will stay until 4 o'clock in the morning, just lying on the beach. Nobody will threaten me. No thoughts about conflict will happen. [No Israeli] helicopters or even any crazy, stupid Palestinians will do something. So all of these I see as similar because they are taking my pleasure. We want a civil society. We want security together. Both, and that will not happen until we Palestinians feel that we have [our] own independent state. [Until then], this will not happen.

10

A Visit to Gaza:
Working in a War Zone

IN 2005, THE GAZA STRIP, a tiny wedge of land approximately 26 miles long and a few miles wide,[1] hit the front-page news with emotionally laden stories about the Israeli disengagement, the uprooting of some 8000 Jewish settlers from their homes. While the grief of the settlers was big news, almost nothing was said about their neighbors, the 1.4 million Palestinians, two-thirds of whom were refugees from the wars of 1948 or 1967, now living in eight densely crowded camps.[2] The word "Gaza" also evokes images of militant Islamic factions, Hamas, Fatah's Al-Aqsa Martyrs Brigades, Islamic Jihad; angry young men waving their automatic weapons and launching Kassam missiles into vulnerable Israel border communities. It is easy to think of this area as an untamed region filled with danger, chaos, and people who are not like *us*. The US media embraced the message, highlighting the tremendous compromises and sacrifices made by the Israelis, the militant aggression of the Palestinians, and their lack of appreciation for the official end of Israeli occupation of the Gaza Strip. Reports still insist that the Palestinians are now responsible for their own economic and social recovery, that their ability to create a peaceful, flourishing society is the first test of their ability to govern themselves.[3] The disengagement was touted as the initial move towards the final peace agreement, the breaking of a political and military impasse. It was a time filled with possibility and hope, at least until the Hamas victory in the 2006 Legislative Council elections. To better understand this historical moment it is important to look behind the headlines and examine the realities on the ground. There is massive unemployment and poverty, and access to health care and education is rapidly decreasing. In the last five years, war and occupation devastated an estimated one-fifth of the economic base and thousands of homes were destroyed by Israeli incursions.[4] These facts alone should make us pause and reassess the possibilities for hope and the probabilities for a viable future.

Visiting the Gaza Community Mental Health Program

In March 2005, months before the disengagement began, the medical delegation received an invitation to visit the Gaza Community Mental Health Program (GCMHP) founded in 1990 by Dr. Eyad el Sarraj. From Erez checkpoint, we took a battered old taxicab south to Gaza City, driving past miles of abject poverty. Partial buildings stood awkwardly, either because the construction was never completed or the Israeli bulldozers and Apache helicopters had left their mark. Rusted automobiles lay junked along the road together with piles of garbage and bustling, chaotic automobile traffic intermingled with donkeys and horses all competing for rutted, muddy streets. Suddenly, there was the Mediterranean Sea, grey waves against a grey sky, children playing and actually swimming in the brisk water, a freedom recently granted by Israeli authorities. Our hotel was a remnant of British colonialism, built in 1946, with huge, over-stuffed, upholstered chairs and heavy dark furniture, oriental rugs, fans and cool breezes blowing through hibiscus flowers and the sweet smell of *narjeelah*.

We first meet with staff from the GCMHP in their four-year-old administrative center. The wide stairway with a path of patterned white stones leads up through flower gardens and graceful palm trees to a modern, multistory white stucco building with a red tile roof and an inspiring view of the sea. After the dark, sweet coffee and tea with fresh mint, we sit down with Dr. Samir Qouta, an articulate man who passionately discusses the importance of appreciating the cultural setting, family dynamics, and coping skills in order to understand Gaza. He states that the mental health program was established during the First Intifada when the youth were first described as the "children of stones." There are so many potent images of young boys hurling stones at oncoming towering Israeli tanks. What, he asks, are the boys' motivations and what are the consequences of their actions?

Staff at the GCMHP studied these children and their families and brought the children to the center for treatment of trauma. They found that the children are not only enraged and defiant but also deeply anxious, depressed, and vigilant. Throwing stones expresses their anger at Israeli soldiers who have had a major negative psychological and physical impact on their lives. The children internalize the meaning of occupation; the message carried by repeated humiliations, frequent injuries and death to friends and family, and the inability of parents to protect themselves or their families. The researchers found that the children sharply perceive the differences between their poverty-stricken lives in refugee camps and the privileged lives of Jewish settler children, whose lawns are watered, garbage is collected, streets and playgrounds are clean. The message of occupation devalues the lives of Palestinian children and their potential for a better life through these repeated traumatic incidents and horrendous living conditions. The researchers found that large percentages of children have witnessed their homes raided by Israeli soldiers, have seen the beating and humiliation of their fathers, have been exposed to tear gas, injury, and detention. This has led to a widespread rejection of the authority of the father and the search for other heroes who are perceived as more powerful. The throwing of stones is thus a form of therapy, of avenging the humiliation of the father, of rejecting the messages of the occupation and asserting the right to a better life. This transformation of injured pride and helpless frustration into active resistance comes at a huge price, for the Israelis react harshly with shoot-to-kill and breaking-bones policies that have taken a major toll on the children of Gaza. Thus, not only are they robbed of their mental and physical health, Samir explains, but they are also robbed of their childhoods. The children worry about their fathers, brothers, and themselves being beaten, arrested, and shot; they suffer tremendous fear and pain and exhibit epidemic levels of post-traumatic stress symptoms, especially bed-wetting.[5]

Psychological Consequences of Living under Occupation

The GCMHP first started studying and treating these children and then gradually drew in their families: mothers unable to control their children's aggressive behavior and bed-wetting, or their own losses and distress; fathers suffering their own post-traumatic symptoms after detention or imprisonment. The center started training programs to develop more professional staff and community outreach in schools and clinics to work on prevention. The research unit focuses on understanding trauma within the context of the political situation and culture of Gaza, with a particular focus on children, women who have been victims of violence, and men who have been imprisoned and tortured. As an example, in collaboration with Helsinki University, GCMHP is studying the effect of trauma on attachment by observing mothers and their babies. Initial fieldwork shows that trauma impairs attachment behaviors and causes emotional confusion within the mother/child dyad.

Samir notes that among Palestinian children studied during the First Intifada, children were exposed to at least one traumatic episode and 70 percent were exposed to four or five traumatic events, resulting in extensive psychological damage. This also impacts cognitive abilities, basic intelligence, and risk-taking behaviors. They also documented that the more trauma to the child, the greater the disorganization within the family, the more the children perceive their parents as rejecting and hostile, the less the parents are able to control their children.

The Second Intifada is distinctly different from the First because the Israeli military response is much more intense and the traumatized young children from the first uprising are now teenagers and young adults. Samir explains that the initial study during the Second Intifada looked at the south of Gaza in an area of confrontations and Jewish settlements. Fifty-four percent of the children developed acute levels of post-traumatic stress syndrome and needed psychological intervention. He continues by discussing one study where researchers showed children a picture of Fatma, a child who is thinking about some troublesome issue, and asked, how can this child solve her problem? Thirty percent of the children responded that the child could become a martyr. He observes that this is a measure of the prevalence of trauma and the lack of security, where even children feel involved in the struggle and consider martyrdom as an option.

This is really the atmosphere of the political violence, and the children are really so strange. Sometimes even in their playing you can learn a lot from children, during their drawings, you can find a lot more than the research itself.

For example, once I was in my home and I observed what are the children playing, usually they are playing in the street, so they are playing for three hours, the game is called Martyr. They divide themselves into two parts, Israeli and Palestinian, and there is confrontation and then one of the children is killed and becomes a martyr. Then they started to call for the martyr, praying, go to the mosque, do funerals, and then repeat the play again between them. I observe them from my balcony; it's about three hours because they are each one to be a martyr. This is really how the nature gives the child the ability to cope. Sometimes he believe himself hero, and sometime he believe himself as a victim.

Samir comments that this dynamic fluctuation of moods, aggression, anxiety, and fear, can create psychological problems. At the same time, the throwing of a stone at a tank in the fantasy of the child is an act of power, a challenge that is "very important in the coping self and also ventilation, the process inside the child."

Samir continues earnestly describing an experience he had with his own nine-year-old daughter. He lives in eastern Gaza and owns a small plot of land that had 23 large, old olive trees. One evening Israeli soldiers cut down the trees and he was feeling both sad and shocked. His daughter looked at him and asked if he was sad and he replied of course. "And you? Look what she told me. 'My father, don't be sad, we shall cultivate this olive again.' So you can hear, get some hints about what the children think, despite their loss. Sometimes their ability to cope and to see the situation is better than adults'." This same daughter several years earlier tried with her mother to visit her dying grandmother, but the Israelis had closed the road between Gaza City and Rafah. They waited twelve hours and finally returned unsuccessfully in the evening. The child said to her father,

"You have to come to remove the blocked stones from the road. I have to go to see my grandmother before she dies." So, now she looks to father as power. But she doesn't know that my power cannot face her fantasy that I have ultimate power, that I can move the big stones from the road in order to go. It was difficult to answer. I told her tomorrow you will visit. I'll go with you to visit. Tomorrow she goes with her mother, because it is difficult for me to leave here, and they waited for two or three hours and they [Israeli soldiers] let them pass.

Another study evaluating the recent levels of post-traumatic stress syndrome in the population examined 700 children and found that 43 percent of the community suffers from acute levels of this disorder. "This means that all the professionals in Gaza, in Palestine, have to work with those children in the families, in the schools, in order to help the children to ventilate and to achieve more adaptive behavior, otherwise if this trauma will be inside of them they will affect their life, their career, their future." Samir, his dark eyes framed by wire-rimmed glasses, his mustache neatly trimmed, continues sipping his tea. He explains that while most research focuses on children, the research group has also examined adults who were arrested and jailed. They found that the majority have experienced some form of physical or psychological torture and that 30 percent of the survivors suffer from post-traumatic stress disorder, with insomnia, headaches, intrusive thoughts, and depression. They also wanted to understand why the other 70 percent are able to cope. Researchers found that if the "ex-political prisoner" is able to see himself as a hero and the meaning of his experience centers around resistance, then he is more likely to avoid stress symptoms and behaviors. Those who do suffer are most likely to benefit from individual counseling, but the treatment is still hampered by the social stigma of mental illness. Individuals who do come for counseling feel defeated, they have lost their pride and sense of heroism. Thus counseling must address many levels of pain.

Research and Intervention

The GCMHP is not only involved in research, but also intervention. Samir discusses a program in the Jabalya Refugee Camp in the north of Gaza where teachers and children are trained to solve problems through negotiation. They act as peer counselors and use mediation to solve issues among the schoolchildren. Psychologists will evaluate the program as a potential for community intervention. Samar introduces us to Rula Abu Sofia, a dynamic research assistant, with a Bachelors of Science in civil engineering and a degree in business administration. She is eager to discuss a project using a quality of life assessment tool developed by the WHO, customized "for the conditions in Palestine, because of the ongoing conflict and the specialty of living in war-like conditions." She explains that they plan to examine the impact on young people of limited educational choices and opportunities to travel focusing on, "their desires, their dreams, more on the conditions of women, the differences between them in the camps and the villages." Their hope is to develop programs designed to improve the quality of life. She feels this will highlight the need to open the borders between the Gaza Strip and the West Bank so that students can travel freely and men and women can have equal educational opportunities.

Rula continues animatedly, explaining that one month ago four students from Gaza who were studying at Birzeit University in the West Bank were "expelled" and sent back to Gaza during their final year of study. Campaigns by the university and Friends of Birzeit have been unsuccessful. She admits that she was once one of those "illegal" students.

> We were confined to stay in Ramallah; we are like illegally living in Ramallah for the sake of education. I have personally spent four years during the Intifada since November 2000 'til August 2004 in Ramallah without being able to come back to Gaza. If I dare to do that, I will never get the opportunity to go back and complete my study. Lots of people are facing that.

Research and Reality

The delegates are interested in how this research translates into programs and Samir explains that the GCMHP works with other NGOs and human rights groups in Gaza. They study the phenomenon of trauma and develop optimal therapeutic approaches that influence policy and programs in other NGOs. He admits that their role on the frontline is much more modest.

> You can't change policy, you can't prevent war but you can help in the schools, the human rights organizations, advocacy lobbying. We can work with the council at the school, at UNRWA. We have several activities, like a small hole in the dark that can give some highlight and some findings about the crisis of the children, the traumatized families.

He adds that they have done work with TV programs, speaking frankly about the crisis for the traumatized children and their families, the responsibility of the Health Ministry, and the possible interventions.

We want to know how the issue of domestic violence is addressed in a war zone such as this. We are surprised to learn that the level of violence fluctuates with the political atmosphere. Samir notes the more active the conflict, the less domestic violence because there is a sense of communal cohesion and struggle when the enemy is perceived on the outside. He explains when there is a lull in the fighting, he sees more violence, especially between families.

> Here the community is so crowded, and usually fights between families and inside families are really a problem. If you go to the camps, there's a lot of fights. There are families of about ten or twelve members. This kind of crowdedness gives the chance for domestic violence. Usually, if there is a problem between families and there are some people that have been injured and killed, this problem becomes exaggerated because we have not one extended family; we have *hamula*, a group of extended families. So the parties interfere with this process and the fights are bigger. What makes this problem is that security does not put an end to such issues. There is an example that one member of the family had been killed and the Palestinian Authority put the criminal in jail for a long time, without going to court. So what does the family who lost do? They go to jail, enter the jail, take the person who had killed, and they kill him in the same place that their member was killed. So you can imagine what kind of Authority we have.

Rula adds, "This is because of the state of lawlessness that we are experiencing. The Authority is there but the authority of families is much bigger and stronger and the Authority is not able to put control on all these actions."

Disengagement and the Control of Borders

Our conversation shifts to the upcoming Gaza disengagement and the staff reminds the delegates of the vast uncertainties that lie ahead and the potential for chaos. They see a need to reclaim water resources, improve access to the Mediterranean for fishing, and relieve the crowding in the refugee camps, and they perceive a desire to regain access to the West Bank. They are also concerned with the management of the borders. Samir describes current experiences with the Rafah Gate at the border of the Gaza Strip and Egypt, the only way Palestinians can leave Gaza. He says that Israelis currently control movement across that border.

> Usually in this situation, many times there are crowded people who are traveling and the people when they go back [to re-enter Gaza] they are stuck at the border sometimes one, two days, sometimes a week, sometimes a month. Some of the people are stuck in the border six weeks. Some of the people die on the border. Some of the people give birth, have children, and

there is a very well-known story that a woman has a child and they called the child in Arabic 'Crossing.'

Rula adds that there is a commonly expressed sentiment, "Hell is a part of Rafah Gate." She explains that Gazans returning from Egypt may be trapped at the border controlled by Israelis.

> They are stuck, locked between. They are stuck over there with no services, no infrastructure, nothing, like 3000–4000 people each time in one hall with no services, no bathrooms, nothing. They are just living on some humanitarian aids that some organizations can get in to them and that's it. They would be stuck for three weeks, a month recently in December when they closed it. A lot of them will be in Egypt because that's the only way to get through to the rest of the world, through Cairo airport.

Meeting Dr. Eyad el Sarraj

It is time to go upstairs and meet with Dr. Eyad el Sarraj, a renowned psychiatrist and human rights activist, born in Be'ersheva, formerly Palestine, in 1944 and forced to live in Gaza after the war. He subsequently obtained an MD from Alexandria, Egypt, and psychiatric training in London. Winner of numerous human rights awards and author of extensive publications on mental health, civil society, peace, and politics, he was also arrested and tortured in 1996 by the Palestinian Authority for condemning their violations of human rights of dissidents. Despite his impressive credentials and challenging life, his persuasive manner is modest and warm. He welcomes us graciously into his nicely appointed office, floor to ceiling curtains draping the windows, an oriental rug under a long coffee table piled with literature, a few strategic ashtrays, and of course another round of coffee and tea. He lights the first of many cigarettes and we begin. He talks about the difficulties of mobility for the population, and the extreme poverty which adds another barrier to obtaining counseling; even if the session is free, the family may not be able to afford the taxi. To stress the level of need, Eyad reviews more devastating research findings; in his latest study, 30 percent of people in Gaza had more than eight symptoms of post-traumatic stress disorder, anxiety, or depression and were in need of intervention. As we explore the work of the program, he states,

> We always treat children within the family context and we even treat victims of torture, for instance, or women who are victims of domestic violence. We

try also to do it within the context of the family. We try to be facilitators. Sometimes it's a question of communication within the family, sometimes you have to change a little bit of the dynamics of the relationship within the family, but family is central. We don't have a social welfare system. We are tribal still and the family is the most important frame of security for people. We have to use it.

We started here in the first of March 1990, and it was in the wake of the First Intifada. It was basically to try and help the children who at the time were victims of the Intifada. We very quickly realized many of these children have fathers who were humiliated or even tortured in Israeli prisons and part of the problem of the children was the problem of their fathers. So we started to care for the fathers and then we realized that the mother was also abused by the same father who was tortured in Israeli prisons. So we started to have special projects for the women. Today we have these three main projects: women, children, and victims of torture.

Eyad explains that as the group started to document and research the impact of trauma and violence on children and adults, he also started a training program. Initially he was the only psychiatrist in the Gaza Strip and now the GCMHP has a staff of over 200 people and they created a postgraduate diploma program in community mental health and human rights. Together with other universities ranging from Tel Aviv to Flanders (Australia), they have developed an academic council, designed curricula, and shared teaching staff. GCMHP is funded by Scandinavian countries, Switzerland, Holland, NGOs in Europe, sometimes by the EU itself, and by individual contributions. Eyad reiterates,

> We link mental health to human rights because it is only logical to expect problems when people live in an oppressive environment, either at home or in the street. We believe strongly that human rights are the basic structure of our concepts as much as peace, democracy, and respect for the rule of law. We cannot improve mental health without having these. This is why we are very active in the community, in the political community and non-governmental community. We try to lobby on behalf of women for instance, on behalf of children, in terms of legislation and so on. We are active in defending victims of human rights violations.

Working within the Family Structure

Eyad is very clear that his data does not apply only to Palestinian families and children, that violence and trauma have the same impact on children anywhere in the world. He states Israeli children who are injured or exposed to violence will have similar responses. Post-traumatic stress disorder, anxiety, difficulties in relationships between parents and children are universal. "So there is no real difference when it comes to human tragedy." He also finds that everywhere women are more communicative and in touch with their feelings and that men, "are more narcissistic and full of themselves and they want to show themselves as macho and heroes and strong and so on." As a result of this resistance and the dynamics within families, mothers are the single most important factor when it comes to communicating with the children. "The father gives orders, comes home very late or leaves home early. He's there but not there, but the mother is there and she's warm. We found that children who have mothers who are communicative and warm, and the children are traumatized, fare better than children who are also traumatized but they don't have communicative mothers." He finds that supporting the mother is not difficult because women like to express themselves and "once the psychologist is skilled enough to handle the situation like a mirror to the client, so she can see herself in a different light and then start to reflect and come back again with new ideas and new insight into her own self, then she changes also. Her own relationship with the rest of the family will change."

The *muezzin*'s call to prayer drifts across the room as Eyad reaches for another cigarette. The delegates want to understand more about the relationship between husbands and wives and the stressors in this environment. He reports,

> Women are just belongings to men and men do not like others to interfere with their belongings. Some very conservative men do not like any interference even if it is under medical service or mental health service. We [are] not welcome sometimes to go and see a woman we know needs help. The husband or the father-in-law or whatever is there, sometimes will tell you, "you are not welcome. Go away. We don't need you." This is why the best way to approach a man is through the children. We bring the child and we say I want to help the child because usually they have problems. Then you ask the mother to come in and she easily comes and then you ask the help of the father to come into one session. When he comes into the session, he starts to feel that this child is not his, it's a different child. Because for the first time ever the child is sitting there equal to him and he can say whatever he wants to say without being beaten or hushed. This is

usually an eye-opener for the father. For one whole hour, he is sitting there with a little child who is equal to him.

Collaborators, Drug Addiction, and Self-esteem

The process of emotional healing first starts with individual sessions with the child that may include drawing, talking about dreams, and then they move into the family setting. "But the best thing is when you have the family, mother, father, children, sitting together for the first time as equals and I believe this is the real teaching of democracy." We ask about his relationship with conservative religious leaders in Gaza and Eyad explains that some have been supportive. During the First Intifada, he dealt with two extremely sensitive issues: collaborators with Israel and those involved with drug addiction and trafficking, primarily morphine, cocaine, and tranquilizers. While Hamas was killing collaborators and drug traffickers, Eyad saw them as patients in need of help and he intervened on their behalf. He points out that many of the leaders of Hamas were physicians who were his colleagues during their years of training. "So we struck from the beginning a kind of relationship based on mutual respect and openness. I was involved in the community life. I feel always responsible for whatever is happening, even if it is beyond my profession. Whenever there was something, I would go there and give my advice or share opinions." He developed an agreement with Hamas leaders that they would not kill anyone for these offenses without sending the accused for treatment and Eyad would then argue that the patient was now under his supervision and needed time for therapy. "Of course the stigma of being a drug addict in this place is so strong that you know it is worse than the stigma of being gay. To be a gay here also is very stigmatizing, but to be a drug addict is like a collaborator, the worst of the worst, working for the enemy."

He clearly remembers his first case which involved a collaborator. The man was referred from Shifa Hospital because his doctor felt that he was depressed and needed psychiatric help.

> Now in the process of therapy, he told me that he received a threat on his life. So immediately, I went to Dr. Rantissi [a Hamas leader] and I told him, "This man is mine; you don't touch him, because I am treating him. Right? That's number one."

"Second, I am against all these things you are doing, killing people without being really careful about the evidence, court, so on and so forth, and of course, on top of that, I am against the death penalty anyway." So I was arguing all the time. He said, "OK, this man is yours, we are not going to touch him."

I know the story of that young boy. When he was twelve, he saw his father being killed by a knife. Some people came, masked people at night and killed his father by cutting his throat in front of the little boy. He felt at that time, his father was his hero. He couldn't believe it. When he grew up a little, he knew that some people said it was Hamas that killed your father because he was a collaborator [with Israel] and he couldn't believe it. When he was 16 or 17, he wanted to take revenge. So what did he do? He went to the Israelis and said I want to work with you so I will know from you. I will help you, if you help me to know who were the killers of my father.

The Israelis used him, they didn't tell him of course who killed his father, but used him as some informer. They used to send him into demonstrations and he would tell them the names of people who were in the demonstration, or spy on somebody and then go and give a report, and the Israelis would give him some money. After some time, he felt guilty, he is doing something wrong. This is a very harsh society too. At that time, Hamas declared a kind of amnesty for collaborators if they confess publicly. So he went to the major mosque in Gaza, after the prayer on Friday, he stood up and confessed, that I am a collaborator. I stopped. I want now redemption. He was shunned by his family because the family felt stigmatized, how could their son be a collaborator? So they chucked him out, and when he wanted to go back to his cousin, they had a quarrel and the cousin broke his jaw. This is why he went into the hospital and it is how he came to me. But I saved his life.

I am intrigued with his comments about Hamas, and Eyad adds another complicated observation.

Here, this is something very important to know, Palestinians do not feel that they did not defend their country. They feel that they have struggled and that gives them a kind of self-esteem which is protective against the ill effects of trauma. So, this is important to remember. You know sometimes people go around here and say, how can these people be nice and hospitable and warm and ask you to come and drink coffee when all around is this disastrous life and terrible situation? Sometimes people cannot even afford to buy a piece of bread.

First, it's a culture that by duty you have to be hospitable to strangers. Second, we have a strong self-esteem because of the resistance. You know, I am one of the people who feels that our armed resistance was not successful and in many ways was wrong, particularly suicide bombing in Israel was morally wrong and politically wrong, but as far as self-esteem is concerned, I am proud as a Palestinian that we Palestinians did not surrender.

Psychiatry and Human Rights

The delegates are intrigued by the relationship between physicians and some of the most notorious Hamas leaders. Eyad explains that all of these physicians may have a shared sense of responsibility beyond their profession, to feel for the needs of their people. He notes that he first learned about human rights when he was studying medicine, when he worked at his first psychiatric hospital in Alexandria, Egypt. "It was not an introduction to psychiatry as much as it was an introduction to human rights because I saw *One Flew Over the Cuckoo's Nest*. I saw it there and I said this is impossible. This kind of treatment for mental patients is shameful. It's an affront to humanity. I will not tolerate it. Since then I became a human rights activist." He sees his basic mission is to instill hope and to direct people's energies into something constructive, despite the enormous challenges.

> The situation sometimes becomes overwhelming because of the fact that people generally are not hopeful about peace. You see peace for the Palestinians means one word: dignity. Peace in Israel means security. I said today on Israeli TV, that Israeli security forces will always be doing exactly the opposite, destroying the security of Israel by not creating peace. Peace means dignity for people. By treating the Palestinians in such an undignified manner, the Israelis destroy the security of Israel because these people become suicide bombers, violent, malicious, and so on.

He fears that when the Israelis leave Gaza, they will focus their attention on consolidating their settlements in the West Bank.

> What is happening now on the ground is that Israel is settling the West Bank at such a pace that it will be impossible to have a Palestinian place there. This will create a new cycle of violence. I am very optimistic in the sense that I believe in the nature of humanity, that the positive energy and life will win over destruction and evil and death. The situation today is so serious, because not too long from now, if the situation in Palestine is not settled with dignity, Palestinians, Arabs, and Muslims will acquire weapons of mass destruction. They will use them and they will use them everywhere.

Eyad reminds us that he predicted suicide bombing long before it started to happen because he sensed the anger, despair, and hopelessness from his own patients. Now he is more fearful of people acquiring weapons of mass destruction unless,

> They feel dignified and happy and secure and in peace. Because at the end of the day, Arabs, not Muslims, believe that death in dignity is better than living in humiliation. They believe strongly that you have to die in dignity rather than to live as a slave. If you cannot walk with your head high, if you are living in a shameful situation, you better die.
>
> This is the essence of suicide bombing. People are ready to sacrifice themselves for this. Today it is a small bomb; tomorrow it is an atomic bomb, or germs or whatever. The wall and the settlements are not protecting Israel. Never. Not the F-16s and not the tanks. What will protect Israel is me, a dignified Palestinian. This is why I say the Israeli security forces are doing exactly what could destroy the security of Israel.

Despite all of this tough talk, Eyad is also deeply sympathetic to the history of Jews and Israel. He explains that he feels so much for Jews as victims because he himself understands what it means to be a victim. He believes that Jews are victimizing Palestinians because of their own experience of victimhood; Jews suffer from a "victim psychology."

> I hope I'm not patronizing by saying this but without Israelis and Jews standing up before it is too late and confronting this issue of victimization in Israel and among the Jews, it will be too late. You know, Israel can survive with bombs for ten years or 20 years, for 100 years, but then it will be destroyed, because it is living as an alien place among the Arabs and the Muslims. Only when Israel becomes part of this land, and the Israelis become part of it, when they treat me as an equal human being, then Israel can survive, that is the only condition.
>
> The problem with Israel is victimization and power. Together they make dynamite. Some Palestinians were tortured in Israel severely, but came out as community leaders. Others became traumatized victims.

He sees the same patterns in the Palestinian Authority. Some of the people previously imprisoned and tortured in Israeli jails become officers and interrogators, victimized and powerful at the same time. The officers then create their own victims among their own people.

> Why? In order to combat the victimization within themselves and the feeling of shame and humiliation, they have to project it onto somebody else. This is exactly what Israelis have been doing to the Palestinians. Instead of facing it inside themselves, they're projecting their victimization onto the Palestinians so they feel proud of themselves. You don't want to deny the history; you want to relate to the history, the helpless Jew going into his death. They

feel ashamed of that history. They felt they have to be powerful. Victim with power without sanity is very dangerous. This is what the Palestinians have been doing. It's a cycle, goes from one generation to the other, from one nation to the other.

The conversation moves to the upcoming disengagement plan, which Eyad welcomes, but sees as only the beginning of the story. He states passionately that he wants hope, he wants a future, and that must include a sovereign Palestinian state on 22 percent of Mandatory Palestine. He worries about Palestinian violence, which only justifies Israeli actions confiscating land, destroying homes, and building the wall, which will ultimately destroy the West Bank. Once the world discovers that the possibility of a viable state in the West Bank has been destroyed, that Gaza has turned into a giant prison, he fears "the whole Arab and Muslim world will erupt."

> Now they [the US and Britain] are talking about democracy, fine, good, democracy is good. But dignity is not just democracy. Dignity is when I feel as an equal human being and I have my rights, my land. I personally don't give a damn about land or nationalism or religion, but I tell you about the feelings of people who consider these are very important. Land, religion, nationhood. Exactly like the Israelis now. Of course, reaction, action, reaction. Create security, a peaceful state that does not infringe on other people's rights, and the Palestinians and the Muslims are now ready to accept Israel in its borders.
>
> The disengagement plan again. If it is only turning Gaza into a big prison, it will be a non-starter. What is the point of adding a few hundred *dunams* to Gaza when there is no economy, when there is no freedom of movement, when there is no hope, when there is no dignity? It will be only the beginning of a new cycle of violence.

Grappling with Violent Resistance

The delegates want to know more about Eyad's understanding of Hamas, which at this point had not taken part in the upcoming elections. He clarifies that Hamas, an acronym for the Islamic Resistance Movement, is purely a Palestinian offshoot of the international Islamic militant group, the Muslim Brotherhood, dating back to the 1980s. It was originally a religious movement with a political agenda, focused on developing "good Islam," but it formed a military wing during the First Intifada. They became an underground movement dedicated to an all-out war against Israel. Now, Eyad feels that Hamas leaders have much more confidence, have wide popular support as an incorruptible organization, and are ready to become a political party, to enter into elections and form a new government. Most importantly, "Hamas was fighting for the dignity of people." Hamas has a wide social support network which helps poor families, families who have lost their homes, families where men have been killed. The new generation of Hamas leadership "are highly respectable people in their own communities; doctors, engineers, professors in the universities." He sees a process of political maturation occurring that could transform Hamas into a political party.

Eyad notes that Israeli forces killed many of the more moderate Hamas leaders, such as Sheikh Ahmed Ismail Yassin and Abdel Aziz al-Rantissi.

> Hamas is a political movement, and now, after all the armed struggle and so on, now they have to confront the reality. The reality is there's a vacuum created by the collapse of Fatah and the Palestinian Authority. Who's going to fill that? Hamas will not take chances. Hamas will go into this. There is a problem, of course, with Hamas. Hamas has a leadership outside in Syria and Hamas has a leadership inside. There's a conflict between the two. Who's in control, particularly after the death of al-Rantissi and Sheikh Yassin? They settled that quickly by saying we have two kinds of leadership, one outside and one inside. It's not a healthy situation especially that these people outside work in Syria, which is a military dictatorship, corrupt regime. So Syria now is playing this kind of game. You hurt us in Lebanon; we will hurt you in Israel. So this is another element when you come to Hamas.

At the same time, Eyad is strongly opposed to the militant attacks and suicide bombing promoted by Hamas. "For me this is terror and it should be condemned. Full stop. No question about it. It plays into the hands of Sharon. It is wrong, morally wrong from a human rights point of view. From the Islamic point of view it is wrong. From the political point of view it is wrong."

Trauma and Resilience

Looking forward, given the grim political and socio-economic picture and the extremely traumatized population, what does Eyad feel he can offer his patients? He explains that he is always amazed by the resilience of his patients, by their ability to cope with such an extreme level of suffering. He hopes he can extend help to the people in need, to work with the Ministry of Health, WHO, UNRWA, and others. He is working on having access to the schools in Gaza in order to reach the children and he hopes to build and improve his professional staff. He predicts that the influx of financial support that will be coming into Gaza post-disengagement will create a new dynamism unless there are restrictions of movement between Gaza, Israel, and the West Bank. Then the "bubble will burst and very quickly." He warns,

> We should use this opportunity to build the infrastructure in Gaza, to build the democratic peace movement, and also struggle with the rest of the Israelis who want peace, the Jewish communities who want peace and who want to make sure that Israel is going to survive in security. Security that will not be provided by guns. Never. This is our mission and this is what I believe we should do.
>
> We will continue to create and instill hope and create alternatives. I'm working now on a project for the children to have sea sports, I want to create an atmosphere for children to go and play in the sea, swim. I have just been told, unfortunately, that wind surfing is not allowed in Gaza by the Israelis. It's illegal and jet skiing is not allowed and boats are not allowed more than nine horsepower or something. All these are restrictions, but still, we can teach our children to swim, to play on the sand, to play diving, to play whatever sport is available.
>
> You have to create alternatives; you have to create sports clubs, as much as you create jobs for the old people. I'm creating five new centers in Gaza for the children to learn English and computers, not only to learn English and computers, but also to convey a message and to allow them a platform to express themselves. The most fundamental issue when you deal with people who are traumatized is to allow them to speak about themselves freely. This will be reflected in their self-confidence and if they have a problem with trauma it will come out. If we don't care for this generation of victims, they will create a new generation of victims. So we have to do a lot of work now.

Eyad reflects on the difficulties of working in the schools, the endless bureaucracy and stupidity, the fact that the Ministry of Education follows Jordanian law in the West Bank and Egyptian law in Gaza. During occupation, the Israelis refused him access to the schools as did UNRWA which was following Israeli recommendations. "Because the Israelis, military people, said that we were going to manipulate the children to be militants. They thought we were going to use the children for political propaganda." Then the Palestinian Authority took over and again refused them access. "They thought we were going to use the children to put forward the message of human rights, have respect for the rule of law, and this will be against the Palestinian Authority, so they denied us access to the schools." I finally ask him why he is not crazy and he replies, "Who has told you I am not crazy?" With a smile and another cigarette he retorts, "You know, I love this place because I grew up here. I love the sea, I love the people and I love justice and I have something to do. I have to do it. It is so exciting and rewarding and fulfilling. Every time you meet a child and make him smile, that for me is the biggest reward on earth." Then he tells us a story where we learn that his name, "Sarraj," means "the person who puts light into the lamp." What could be a more fitting name for this extraordinary doctor?

11
Visiting Rafah: Just the Bad Face

URING OUR DELEGATION'S VISIT TO Gaza, we face our most painful confrontation between official explanations, intellectual understanding, and the power of brutal emotional insight. Thus, this becomes partly a story about wildly conflicting narratives and our ability to appreciate "truth" in a complicated and troubled area of the world. The following chapter is an illustration of this clash of "facts" and the cascade of assumptions, judgments, and sympathies that follow. It is useful to examine this moment in history closely, as it provides a microcosm for the kind of double-speak that is dominant in the military, media, and international opinion. I will review the IDF report on a military operation in Rafah in 2004 and compare this with the findings of an international human rights organization. I will then describe my own experiences in 2005 visiting a clinic in nearby Khan Younis, interviewing a family from Rafah, and surveying the devastated area with members of the medical project.

Operation Rainbow

On May 18, 2004, the IDF launched a military operation called "Operation Rainbow." It was officially designed to destroy the terrorist infrastructure operating in southern Gaza and the tunnels between Egypt and Gaza, as well as to avenge the deaths of 11 or 13 (depending on the source) Israeli soldiers killed in the Gaza City neighborhood of Zeitoun and in the Rafah buffer zone.[1] On May 2, a Palestinian attack also killed a mother and her four children in the nearby region of the Kissufim Jewish settler road.[2] According to the official IDF website, since the Oslo Accords, the IDF has retained control over a narrow strip of land between the area in Gaza under Palestinian control, and the border of Egypt. This area is 12.5 kilometers long with four kilometers running parallel with the border of a densely populated town and refugee camp called Rafah, and is referred to as the Philadelphi Route.[3] The IDF website reports that this tiny stretch of land has been a center for the smuggling of weaponry and explosives, drugs, and goods from Egypt into Gaza, mainly through a tunnel system, "the gateway to terror," dating back to the 1980s.[4] The IDF website has detailed descriptions of how the tunnels are constructed and how the local population contributes to this underground operation and economy. The IDF and the Palestinian Authority agree that the primary motivation for families allowing tunnel traders to build exit shafts in private homes is their desperate need for money. According to IDF sources, the weapons are then used by Hamas and the Popular Front for the Liberation of Palestine, often aided and supported by the Palestinian Authority.[5] From September 2000 to October 2003, the IDF forces claim to have uncovered over 90 smuggling tunnels.[6]

On May 11 and 12, 2004, two Israeli armored personnel carriers were attacked in the Zeitoun neighborhood of Gaza City and the Philadelphi Route near Rafah. The IDF, using soldiers from a number of battalions, heavy armored personnel carriers, tanks, helicopters, and armored Caterpillar D9 bulldozers, began a massive operation. It started adjacent to the border in congested areas of mainly concrete homes with asbestos roofs. Military activity then extended into the Tel al-Sultan neighborhood in northwestern Rafah more than a kilometer from the Egyptian border and abutting the Jewish Gush Katif settlement bloc and the Brazil and Salam neighborhoods in the east.[7] It should be noted that the Israeli armored Caterpillar D9 bulldozer is produced in the US and sold by the US Foreign Military Sales Program. The vehicle weighs approximately 64 tons, stands just over 13 feet tall and is more than 26 feet long. It is specially modified with armored protection by the Israeli state-owned Israel Military Industries and sometimes has features such as machine guns or grenade launchers. These modifications allow the bulldozers to work in dangerous battle zones and to resist mine blasts, and indeed no operators were killed between 2000 and 2004. The front blade is more than six feet high and fifteen feet wide.[8] The bulldozers used in Rafah were also equipped with a "ripper," a blade on the back used to destroy roads by dragging the blade down the middle of the street, creating an over five feet deep disruption of asphalt and dirt and severing water and sewage pipes.[9]

Israeli authorities claim to have killed more than 40 militants and 12 civilians (but state that some may have been killed by Palestinian cross-fire), and injured an unknown number of people. The IDF apparently does not keep statistics on civilian injuries and deaths caused by their activities. A well-publicized incident occurred when several hundred (some report thousands of) Palestinian protestors approached the Israeli positions and seven protesters were killed according to the IDF, which states that the Palestinian group included armed militants.[10] Most IDF forces left on May 25 and by June 1 the military operation officially was concluded. As of May 23, one smuggling tunnel filled with explosives had been located, and two more tunnels were subsequently found.[11] Later the IDF admitted that one tunnel was actually an incomplete shaft and another was located outside of Rafah, unconnected to any of the home demolitions. The IDF reported that 56 homes were demolished and stressed their focus on military- rather than civilian-related targets despite the challenge of facing insurgents who blend into and are often supported by the local population. They highlighted their efforts to promote humanitarian aid, facilitate movement of ambulances, and support the distribution of food and medicine by international NGOs and welfare organizations.[12]

What Really Happened in Rafah?

In contradiction to the reports by the IDF, the extensive brutality, massive damage, and lack of the legal requirement of absolute military necessity, created a worldwide outcry. "Absolute military necessity" is an internationally recognized obligation that demands that civilian costs be proportionate to concrete combat needs. The residents of Rafah claim that the substantial destruction was an attempt to collectively punish the camp as a whole and to undermine support for insurgents opposing the Israeli occupation.[13] In early May, when the plan for demolitions was first discussed in the Israeli press and sporadic demolitions had started, international condemnations were heard from UN Secretary-General Kofi Annan, Irish Foreign Minister Brian Cowen speaking for the European Union presidency, and US Secretary of State

Colin Powell. As the operation continued, the *New York Times* cited a report by the Israeli Justice Minister, Tommy Lapid, in which Lapid compared the destruction of homes in Rafah to Nazi atrocities and warned of the possibility of war crimes charges against Israel in the International Court of Justice.[14] While numerous organizations ranging from the Israeli human rights group, B'Tselem,[15] to the Palestinian Center for Human Rights,[16] have made similar comments on the events in Rafah, I would like to highlight the detailed report by Human Rights Watch (HRW), a well-respected international organization.[17]

Human Rights Watch Report

Based on careful research from over 80 sources and on-site examinations, HRW reports that between 2000 and 2004 the IDF demolished an estimated 1600 homes in Rafah, leaving 16,000 people homeless. Caterpillar D9 bulldozers were used during repeated night-time raids to demolish blocks of homes and expand a "buffer zone," often without warning and irrespective of the actual threat of a particular home or its inhabitants. In May 2004, the Israeli military recommended expanding the "buffer zone," using the justification that smuggling tunnels and threats from militant organizations required a greater military response. According to many analysts, the widespread and indiscriminate destruction of homes and neighborhoods was both illegal and consistent with a desire to create a wide-open border area to facilitate Israeli military control. HRW said the home destructions are

> based on the assumption that every Palestinian is a potential suicide bomber and every home a potential base for attack. Such a mindset is incompatible with two of the most fundamental principles of international humanitarian law: the duty to distinguish combatants from civilians and the responsibility of an Occupying Power to protect the civilian population under its control.[18]

Using photographs, satellite images, and witness testimony, HRW was able to document that the deep incursions into Rafah in May 2004 resulted in the destruction of 298 homes and appeared to be consistent with retaliation for the earlier deaths of Israeli soldiers. It also appeared to be a dramatic flexing of military muscle, perhaps related to the upcoming Gaza disengagement. While the IDF has a right under military law to close smuggling tunnels and prevent hostile attacks, HRW notes that the considerable destruction was inconsistent with the stated rationale for the attack and that multiple violations of international humanitarian law occurred before and during the assault. In Tel al-Sultan, northwestern Rafah, 76 percent of the roads were destroyed by bulldozers and tanks and there was extensive damage to water and sewage pipes, disrupting water supplies for six days.

The Smuggling Tunnels

There is much controversy surrounding the size, significance, and extent of the smuggling tunnels. HRW interviewed people from the IDF, Rafah residents, Palestinian Authority members, participants in a variety of armed Palestinian groups, foreign diplomats in Israel, Israeli and foreign journalists, and authorities on contraband tunnels and subsurface soil. While there is no disagreement that tunnels do exist to smuggle contraband, initially mostly cigarettes, doves (a favored pet), alcohol, and drugs, and more recently small arms and explosives, it appears that the IDF grossly exaggerated the threat in order to rationalize extensive home demolitions. If closing the tunnels was the only goal, the IDF could have used non-destructive methods for detecting and destroying tunnels similar to those used along the US–Mexico border and the Korean demilitarized zone, and well documented by the US Army Corps of Engineers. The IDF clearly chose not to use this approach.

> They were unwilling to provide details of what they had tried and why such measures were unsatisfactory, but they maintained that incursions into Rafah and the destruction of tunnels and/or shafts under homes was the most effective means to close the tunnels down. According to IDF spokeswoman Maj. Sharon Feingold, the IDF takes "the utmost care to pinpoint the tunnels and do as little damage as possible."[19]

Israeli authorities have also repeatedly claimed that since 2000, 90 tunnels have been discovered in Rafah; however, when pressed for details, it seems that these claims refer to tunnel egress shafts rather than actual individual tunnels. These shafts may connect to pre-existing tunnels or are sometimes dead ends, contradicting the impression of a vast honeycombed, active tunnel network. Oddly enough, until 2003, the IDF did not actually close the tunnels, but demolished the Rafah homes containing the entrance shafts (whether the tunnel was functional or inoperative), sometimes after the Palestinian Authority had already sealed the tunnel with cement. This caused destruction in the general area and immediate homelessness to the residents and often their neighbors, but largely left the tunnel system intact, a tactic that was obviously collectively punitive to the population but not necessarily militarily effective. This raises the question of how great a danger these tunnels posed in the first place.

The Egyptian authorities have also monitored the tunnel system from their side of the border in collaboration with Israel. The Egyptians informed HRW that there are a limited number of tunnels and they are mostly inactive. The degree of smuggling into Rafah was considered insignificant when compared to the bilateral overland smuggling of people, drugs, and goods along the lengthy Israeli–Egyptian border, which is largely in a desert area and has not been in the headlines.

Armed Conflict in Civilian Areas

There is no controversy that Rafah is an area of dangerous and intense conflict between Israelis and Palestinians. It is clear that the IDF uses heavy machine guns, rockets, and tanks in civilian areas, that the shooting is often indiscriminate, disproportionate, and sometimes unprovoked, and that bullet holes are frequently sprayed across entire buildings rather than clustered around windows or other possible sniper positions. Palestinian armed groups, which include Islamic Jihad, Hamas, Fatah, and the Popular Resistance Committees, regularly attack IDF positions and patrols along the border and the former Jewish settlements using mostly Kalashnikov rifles, rocket-propelled grenades, and improvised explosive devices. Both groups use strategies that put civilians in the middle of hostilities, and local civilian opinion ranges from supportive to critical of such operations, although there is public consensus on the need to resist occupation in some manner.[20] HRW noted multiple instances where the IDF converted civilian buildings into sniper locations, forcing the residents to stay in the building with the soldiers, or the snipers wrecked and defiled the contents of the home after seizing it, or used local civilians as human shields during home searches. Palestinian militants clearly place civilians at risk by operating in densely populated areas, but HRW could not find evidence of firing from occupied homes or forcing residents to give up their homes to the armed groups.

There are no reliable comprehensive statistics on military and civilian deaths from this conflict. However, the Palestinian Central Bureau of Statistics reported 393 deaths in Rafah between 2000 and 2004, including 98 children of less than 18 years of age. Twenty-nine percent of the civilian victims were women and children so the estimates of civilians killed are probably much higher as one cannot assume that all the male fatalities were armed men. During the same period, ten or eleven Israeli soldiers were killed in Rafah.[21]

The Philadelphi Route

The Philadelphi Route along the border, "is better understood as two distinct areas: a shielded *patrol corridor* (between the border [with Egypt] and IDF fortifications) and a *buffer zone* (the space between IDF fortifications and the houses of Rafah),"[22] according to HRW. Since 2000, there has been a gradual expansion of the area controlled by the IDF through repeated demolitions of homes on the periphery of Rafah, which was once a tightly knit community of families, originally refugees from 1948. The IDF built a metal wall, 26 feet high, with guard towers, all located inside the demolished area, approximately 275 feet from the actual border. This created an ever-widening buffer zone between the patrol corridor and the refugee camp, free of Palestinians and filled with the rubble of their demolished homes. There was also a doubling of the width of the patrol corridor. Approximately 15 percent of Rafah's previously built-up area was destroyed for this expansion and, ironically, this brought the Israeli soldiers closer to the camp and to potential hostile fire. This is what happened on May 12, 2004, within the buffer zone when Israeli soldiers conducting anti-tunneling maneuvers in a vehicle containing explosives for destroying tunnels met their death at the hands of an Islamic Jihad rocket-propelled grenade, and "Operation Rainbow" subsequently commenced.[23]

May 18–24, 2004

HRW reports that in May 2004, 298 homes in Rafah were destroyed, 166 between May 18 and 24. The details are chilling and quite consistent with multiple other sources and satellite photographs. Homes in areas such as Brazil, which is distant from the border, were extensively destroyed by armored Caterpillar D9 bulldozers. Residents were allowed to flee but not given time to remove their belongings. The IDF also devastated roads, agricultural fields, olive groves, greenhouses, and the Rafah zoo, which was meticulously secured prior to demolishing.[24]

> The IDF claims its forces came under attack from Palestinians using anti-tank weapons, explosives, and small arms. Based on interviews with 35 Rafah residents and two members of Palestinian armed groups, information provided by the IDF, public statements by Palestinian armed groups and the Israeli government, and after surveying the affected areas, Human Rights Watch believes that armed Palestinian resistance to the May 18–24 operation was light, limited, and quickly overwhelmed within the initial hours of each incursion. Both sides made tactical choices to maximize their respective advantages: the IDF limited their operations mostly to [the Rafah neighborhoods of] Brazil and Tel al-Sultan, where they were not expected, and Palestinian armed groups laid ambushes in the densely populated heart of the original camp, where they would be more likely to engage the IDF at close quarters. As a result, throughout the operation, there was minimal direct engagement between the IDF and Palestinian armed groups.[25]

The massive Caterpillar D9 bulldozers plowed through neighborhoods to clear tank paths and reduce the risk of roadside bombs, regardless of the lack of specific threats, and destroyed countless homes for no obvious reasons. In the neighborhoods of Tel al-Sultan and Brazil, the bulldozers tore up 51 percent of Rafah's roads and destroyed the electrical grid, water, and sewer systems, creating water shortages and massive medical and public health emergencies. Attacks were also undertaken by Apache helicopter gunships and Merkava tanks. HRW also noted multiple other abuses that included illegal killing of civilians including children, the use of civilians as human shields, and opening fire on a demonstration protesting the siege of Tel al-Sultan, killing nine people, including three children under the age of 18 and wounding 50. While the IDF claimed that armed militants were in the crowd, eyewitness reports and videos of the incident contradicted this statement. Eyewitness reports found that numerous Palestinians were shot while attempting to obtain water for their families during the days of curfew.

Between May 12 and 24, HRW documented approximately 3800 people made homeless by IDF activities and UNRWA reported temporarily housing approximately 2500 people after the May operations. Available housing and funding for rebuilding quickly reached crisis proportions, with the added difficulty of a lack of available land in the area of Rafah and the vulnerability of newly rebuilt homes to subsequent demolishing. Some people stayed in the homes of already crowded relatives or returned to their partially damaged homes in an effort to prevent total demolition by maintaining their dwellings as officially "inhabitated." Ambulance drivers and staff from the local Abu Yousef al-Najjar Hospital reported IDF restrictions on the movement of medical personnel and with the siege of Rafah, due to the minimal capacity of the local hospital, dead bodies were stored for five days in shops and a vegetable refrigerator. Dr. Ibrahim Al Hbash, director general of the Shifa Hospital, the main hospital in the Gaza Strip, placed the hospital under highest emergency in preparation for receiving patients from Rafah after the report of the shooting at the large demonstration. The injured never arrived and did not even reach the newly built European Union hospital in Khan Younis, because the IDF did not allow free passage of ambulances. Reporter Tamar Gozansky visited Shifa Hospital and did note dead and wounded from the incursion into Zeitoun. The wounded were injured by missile and gunfire during home demolitions and three were crushed by tanks.

There is little evidence to suggest substantial or persistent armed resistance to these incursions or respect for the human rights and basic humanitarian needs of the Palestinian victims, most of whom were civilians. Although the international community's condemnation was significant, there was a distinct lack of action from governmental leaders or organizations. On May 19, 2004, the UN passed Security Council Resolution 1544, 14 to zero, urging respect for international humanitarian law and decrying the consequences of the massive home demolitions. The US abstained, although it did not block the resolution. Even more importantly, there was no change in the 2004 US/Israel funding agreements for foreign military financing of $2.15 billion, economic assistance of $480 million, or any punitive modifications in a three-year $9 million loan guarantee to defray debts from previous guarantees. European Union–Israel trade agreements also were not significantly threatened.[26]

I wonder, what is the impact of this kind of empty rhetoric? In the face of this military catastrophe and humanitarian disaster and the absence of substantial international consequences, where are the persistent voices of outrage from the US and Israeli media? Where are the protests from political organizations, the cries of horror from US ministers as well as rabbis and mainstream Jewish community groups who cry "Never again!" Does that kind of moral outrage only apply when Jewish blood is shed? Where is the condemnation from the US Congress and elected officials regarding the obscene use of our F-16s, Apache helicopters, and Caterpillar bulldozers? Where are the heartbreaking human-interest stories of dead children and families searching through the rubble of their lives on the front pages of US newspapers? Where are they? I wonder, is there no one who values Palestinian life? Are there no accepted limits to Israeli military aggression? How do you explain this to a child from Gaza?

Khan Younis, Just North of Rafah

The day after the delegation's visit to the GCMHP, we travel to a satellite community clinic in Khan Younis, just north of Rafah, to talk with several articulate and dedicated clinicians. Dyaa Saymah received his masters in psychology from the Islamic University in Gaza and Dr. Nemer Abu Zarqa trained in psychotherapy at Tel Aviv University, forensic psychiatry at London University, and general psychiatry at Cairo University. Both men speak with an earnest intelligence about the workings of the center. They discuss the committees on children, drug abuse, human rights, and women. They review their negotiations with traditional healers who offer Koranic readings to cure emotional wounds, their difficulties in obtaining expensive new psychiatric medications, their lectures at schools, parents' meetings, sports clubs, public meetings, and on Palestinian TV. They talk about treating all patients as human beings who are suffering and in need of psychiatric care, whether they are victims of trauma, collaborators and their families, ex-political prisoners, or Hamas fighters. The delegates follow the process for a new patient, starting with the referral and a multidisciplinary evaluation, diagnostic assessments and the development of treatment plans and community follow-up. Dyaa and Nemer discuss many cultural issues: husbands who will not allow their wives to seek therapy, the general society's lack of education about mental illness, people's tendency to seek help for physical complaints when the underlying issues are depression, anxiety, marital discord, and trauma.

They review the debriefing and screening process for post-traumatic stress disorder, particularly after the incursions and home demolitions in Rafah the previous year.

I study Nemer's square face, his thin mustache, dark sweater, warm professional manner; and Dyaa, clean-shaven, handsome, with laughing eyes. We are in that comfortable emotional place, professionals reviewing cases, distant from the gut-wrenching feelings of dealing directly with human suffering. That veil is slightly torn when Nemer recounts the story of two brothers.

> I remember once two brothers were together and there was a conflict and one of them was shot by the Israeli soldiers. He sees his brother full of blood and he carried him with his hands to the hospital. He came here to this clinic complaining of insomnia, severe avoidance to the situation, to everything related to the trauma. Later when he became better he tried to talk more about the story, how he carried his brother. Emotionally he was a little bit depressed, anxious, afraid of the soldiers, afraid of gunshot. We treat him, first by relaxation technique because he was anxious and give him anxiolytics [drugs to decrease anxiety], antidepressant medication, and tried to get him to talk more about the trauma and so he became much more better.

We move on to the question of how many Palestinians deal with bereavement, how "martyrs" of all ages are paraded through the streets, making every violent death an act of political resistance and a show of Islamic force. Both men feel that creating the feeling of martyrdom is useful to the family in the grieving process, that the community outpouring supports the family. Developing a sense of pride, "a hero boy," is part of the mourning and coping mechanisms of this culture. At the same time, Nemer freely admits, "If you lost somebody in the family, even if the people around give support, but you lost somebody, you lost a man from the family, and it is difficult for the whole life. Because also we are people, people the same all over the world. We have the same feelings." Dyaa adds, "I think that as a proudness, it helps in the beginning, because it brings so many social supports to this family. I think in the long term it doesn't help." He stresses that at first the family benefits from the increase in respect and public acknowledgement. This healthy defense mechanism helps overcome the initial suffering. Ultimately, "a death is a universal phenomenon around all the world. We are all affected by death, loss of family members, and we are all going into grieving process."

As often happens when we talk with professionals in this area of the world, a more personal story emerges in the course of conversation. Nemer explains that his sister lost her child, Hussein Abu Akar. Israeli tanks invaded the Khan Younis Refugee Camp and this seven-year-old boy and Nemer's ten-year-old son, Ali, went to investigate the tanks as young curious boys will do. "Because they are children, they don't know what it means, what the tanks do and they stand behind the tanks and they start to just look at the tanks, and they [Israelis] shoot them and my sister's son was killed." Nemer's son tried to put his hands on the wound, saw the blood and felt his cousin's bowels protruding through the wound. He started crying and ran to get his aunt. Together they went to the hospital to find that Hussein was dead.

> But my son was psychologically disturbed. He had nightmares, he had terrors and he told me that he has, in the dream, he ask about ambulance, ambulance, ambulance! He called the ambulance to save Hussein, his friend, because they were standing together. Maybe 40 days after the killing of Hussein, my son went to the Israeli checkpoint because people go there on the holiday when the school is finished. He sits with some children and those children buy some biscuits and chips for the people who enter the checkpoint. The Israelis saw them and they told the people to bring all the children to the soldiers. They took my child. He is ten years old, and they left the others. When he was afraid and he tried to run away, they caught him and they took him to the checkpoint. After two hours, they put him in the tank and they opened the computer and there was the film where Hussein was killed and my son was standing near Hussein and the soldier asked him, "What you do here with Hussein?" He said, "I look at the tank." "What do you like to see?" He said, "I don't know. I just would like to see the tanks, I look at the tanks." After about four hours my wife went there with a lot of people to ask about our son, saying "This is a child. What are you doing? Why did you take him?" They released my son. The soldier closed the computer. This happened in this area. There are a lot of cases like this. You know this is a war, and during the war you can see everything.

I ask Nemer how as a father and as a psychiatrist, is he able to help his son with these compounded traumas, a young boy living in a challenging and violent society. He explains that being a father and a psychiatrist are two very different things, but together they make an important combination.

First of all I say that we lost Hussein but we have to save Ali. When he started to complain and to tell me that he has nightmares about the event, he saw Hussein, and he saw the trauma, I am afraid he will develop post-traumatic stress disorder. He is traumatized. I try to help him, take him with me to different areas, try to tell him to talk about the experience, about his role in the Intifada, what you can do during the Intifada, why you go there, what happened. To talk about his feelings and his expectations, all these things. I observe his behavior; observe his sleep, his eating, his relationships. I try to give him some advice to avoid those situations where the soldiers are, where the clashes are in this area, and thanks be to God he became much better. He is about eleven now.

Everybody in the world, every human being, needs peace. This is part of our life. The important part of our life. No intelligent man in the world would like to be killed or injured or to kill others or to harm others, but I give you the reality. We have no trust with each other because of the last many years of violence. We kill them and they kill us, we harm them and they harm us, there is little confidence with each other. Our children have no trust with the Israeli side and they look at them as an enemy because they see many Palestinian children killed in the school. You heard about cases here, schoolchildren, six years old, in the school of my daughter. She is my neighbor. She was in this school and the bullets entered the classroom and she was killed on the seat at her school. So children look at Israelis as the enemy because they don't see the good face of the Israelis, they see just the bad face, the violent face, the soldier, the bullets, the gunshot. So they look, they don't see the other good hand, the health services, the good relationship with the Jewish in Palestine since they were neighbors in Yaffa, in Tel Aviv, everywhere they were together, Jewish and Palestinian, and they were as one nation. We are all of us, we live in this country and we were together but now the conflict has disturbed everything I know.

Home Visit in Rafah

Dyaa introduces us to Khitum Abu Shawarib, a social worker trained at Gaza Islamic University and at Birzeit in the West Bank, who is going to accompany our delegation on a home visit to a family they are both treating. Her oval face is framed in a cream colored *hijab*, her makeup expertly applied, and she is dressed modestly in a loose sweater and long, dark skirt. Khitum explains that this family consists of seven children, ages two to twelve, and their mother, who is an elementary school teacher. The eldest son suffers from stuttering, trichotillomania (compulsively pulling out his hair), and enuresis (bed-wetting). Although all the children and the mother were affected, the eldest son's

dramatic symptoms began after the father was killed and the family's
home was severely damaged during Israeli incursions.

> Their mother firstly didn't know how to deal with the children. She
> became nervous, she beat them, shouting. Sometimes she took them to
> their grandfather's home because she also works as a teacher and she didn't
> know how to deal with them. As the children suffered from trauma, she
> also suffered from trauma. At the first visit, I talk with her and tell her, you
> are suffering with trauma, not your children.

Khitum started her home visits doing therapy with the mother. Not
only was the mother dealing with the loss of her husband, but also
she had to move from house to house, going from the border between
Israel and Egypt to near the border of Rafah City, and assume full
responsibility for the seven children. Her own family could not give
her much support because they too were suffering and it was difficult
for them to visit as they all lived in "hot areas." Dyaa adds,

> When the parents themselves are traumatized, they are [in] massive need
> for help and psychological support and they cannot show any love and
> intimacy emotions towards their children. One of the consequences of the
> trauma is the family structure and the family role here is totally changed.
> We sometimes ignore the suffering of the parents.

He stresses the importance of attending to the needs of the parents
as well as the children and finds that re-establishing a healthy family
structure is often reflected in improved mental health for the traumatized
children.

Passing concrete-strewn construction sites, horses, farms, greenhouses,
and a newly built mosque, our van pulls up in front of a recently built
home. The garden is brown earth with newly planted saplings, the first
floor white stucco, the second bare concrete, a decorative grate covers
the only visible window and the front door is off a low porch edged
with squat white columns. We are greeted graciously by the mother,
an attractive, delicately featured woman who immediately begins the
ritual of feeding us cookies and drinks. I look around the room with its
arched doorways, dark curtains tied back, and a tall long-leafed plant in
the corner. There is a small adjoining kitchen with mosaic tiles running
along the borders of the room and around the refrigerator which is
decorated with plastic stickers of colored fruits. The room soon fills
with brightly dressed, animated children, and several older teens and

adults, standing, squirming, sitting on white plastic chairs, the couch adorned with a patch of lace, the walls all white and everything in the process of becoming a home.   .

After initial introductions in which we explain that we are a Jewish delegation, the tape recorders and cameras emerge, and the mother starts to speak. The mother explains that her family is from the Rafah area; they are not refugees, and were living beside the Egyptian/Israeli border. At that point, the oldest child was eight years old. Dyaa translates for the mother who explains that starting in 2000, living near the Egyptian border became intolerable due to the frequent shooting and night-time bombing.

> The children always were crying, shouting because they are afraid of the sound of shooting and bombing. He [the oldest son, Abdullah El Shaer] starts to develop symptoms like enuresis, loss of appetite, sleep disturbances, and nightmares. Many nights they had to evacuate the home because of the invasion and escape to another safer area. After just one year of the beginning of the Intifada, the IDF start to demolish the houses in the area and every night there was a home demolishing inside the area, their neighbors' houses. She mentions that the big problem for her was the questions of her kids. Why they are shooting? Why demolishing our houses? Why hitting us? Why we are living in these conditions? We need to move from this house, we need to become safer in another area.
>
> Two years they are living in the same conditions. It is getting worse and worse, every night the same scenario again, and shooting, demolishing, and the kids start not to sleep and always the same questions and she has got no answers for these questions. After three years her husband was killed by the Israeli forces and just one month after her husband's killing, Israeli forces demolished three houses very close to their house by bombing and they cannot live in it [their home] because it's cracking, so they left the house.
>
> Her husband was a farmer, his land is in this area and he built this [new] house because he expected that the original house would be demolished. He just was killed, was close to the borders and was shot. He was not in political activities and was just a farmer. Suddenly she heard about his death unexpectedly and she was surprised of this.
>
> She mentioned that the peace message is presented in all religions in this world and all religions want peace, to live in peace and quiet. We don't like this war and she hopes that all the Jewish people are like you and understand that we need to live in peace and we will get rid of all this struggle and all this blood.

The mother explains that during the "miserable period that in one month I lost my husband and I lost my house," she had to move temporarily for six months to her family's home while construction on this new home was completed. She describes a system of social support where neighbors and friends worked and gave financial support to complete the building. Her neighbors are all relatives and they all had homes demolished, but they rebuilt their homes here, away from the border and next to their farms. She describes initially feeling nervous and angry. Her children were aggressive towards each other and increasingly "violent to everything." She met Khitum at a public meeting dealing with women's issues and started counseling, becoming aware that her nervousness and anger were a consequence of her traumatizing experiences and personal losses. She found that she was able to regain the role of the mother and to build a more constructive and healthy family dynamic. Everyone started feeling better except Abdullah who is soon to start treatment at the clinic in Khan Younis with Dyaa. Besides his emotional problems, she also notes a marked deterioration in his work at school. Dyaa continues the translation.

> She says that it is a very hard job because there are seven children and without a father, and she is supposed to be the father and the mother of the family and a teacher also to get the income of the family. So in the beginning it was very difficult, but time by time the children understand they must be cooperative. They can help in some minor things and she can arrange everything before going to school and after coming home from school. She says that she has a very strong belief in God that he will help her to overcome these hard circumstances.

She makes an interesting comment that when she taught in the school in Rafah, the students were generally more aggressive, easily provoked, both nervous and violent. In the new village school which is in a less dangerous area, the students are quieter and when they hear the sounds of bombing, helicopters, or F-16s, the girls in particular become startled, hypervigilant, and anxious.

The house fills with more neighbors and the children are starting to wiggle with curiosity and the challenges of sitting still. Shyly, Abdullah agrees to answer our questions. He has a sweet, thin, childlike face and is wearing a black knit hat with a big "A" and a shirt that ironically has "HAPPY BOY" emblazoned across the front. He talks quietly and rarely makes eye contact. He speaks about school and his favorite pastime, playing soccer with his cousins. When he grows up, he wants to be a doctor. He has no questions for us, but his mother interjects that he is embarrassed because of his stutter. His eyes fill with tears and he retreats to the couch at the back of the room, curling into himself and his depression, only to emerge from his overwhelming gloom when one of the delegates starts showing him photos on his digital camera. He is, after all, only a child. One by one, other siblings step forward, much more engaged, talkative, giggling, lovely innocent faces with large brown eyes and stories to tell about school, homework, playing with cousins, missing dead friends. It seems they all plan to be doctors as well.

The Demolished Area

After more comments from the growing cluster of relatives and neighbors, we set off in the van to see Abdullah's old neighborhood in Rafah. Despite all of my preparation, I am totally unprepared emotionally for my sense of horror and grief each time we get out of the van and explore the piles of rubble, framed against the dark metal separation wall with Egypt in the distance. In every direction, there is a swath of flattened destruction; concrete tumbled at odd angles, wires jutting into the blue sky, multistory solitary fragments of apartments, each floor a different color, pictures still standing vigil on the walls, fragments of doorways and streets. I try to imagine a residential area; homes tightly clustered together, schools, stores, children playing in the street. In this wretched havoc hundreds of lost shoes, bits of underwear, a child's doll, bright yellow lego pieces, a computer game, fractured plates lay in the jumble, a testament to the chaos and the rapid flight of the families as the bulldozers came crashing through. For the first time during this trip, I completely lose my composure and start sobbing, filled with a deep sense of shame, ashamed to be Jewish, ashamed of the behavior of the Israeli government, and ashamed to be the citizen of the country that made this possible. I can't imagine a better method to humiliate and enrage an entire generation of Palestinians. This seems such an obvious recipe for disaster, for despair, for growing militancy. I cannot fathom how such a military operation makes life safer for Israelis.

Fortunately for me, we soon attract a small crowd of children, mostly barefoot, curious, and not used to visitors. With Khitum translating, I learn that this one family with ten children is related to Abdullah and they have now returned to inspect the remains of their home. One little girl defiantly says she was not afraid when she heard Israelis shouting and nearby tanks, but her sister cried. Khitum comments that denial often works well for children. We are invited into their damaged house, the walls inside and out spattered with bullet holes, the water tank destroyed and leaning sideways in the dirt. We clamber up the metal stairway, followed by a growing parade of children. The mother is wearing a traditional, long, delicately embroidered dress, surrounded by a cluster of her children. The little ones are coy and friendly; the young men look at us with angry, sullen faces and refuse to engage. We stand with her as she looks around, holding her head and keening quietly, "Why did they do this? Why did they do this?" The vividness of the suffering, the magnitude of the poverty, and the utter hopelessness and devastation are overwhelming.

Khitum's Story

We return to the van and Khitum explains that she was here during the invasion.

> I was [staying with] my husband's family. I visited them and when I was with them the invasion happened. During the middle of the night, we escaped from the house. Apache helicopters were above us and Israeli tanks were behind us. We were running in the road. I was very afraid, especially because it was the first time I saw this thing and I am carrying my small daughter, running and running in the night. The next morning, I run to another safer area, but it was a very long night. I was very afraid because the tanks were behind us. The next night we escaped from the home and in the morning we returned. The next night was easier than the first night. After that invasion, I refused to come back to Rafah.
>
> [My husband's family] still live here, in their home, because they haven't another choice. It's very bad and very dangerous. They are six kids, the youngest one, she's twelve years old. She's very afraid. When she hears bombing, she starts crying, she cannot walk, and she cannot sleep. I work with her [psychologically]. The father, he works in the Jewish settlement. He works in the clothes factory, paid by the hour, no benefits and no health insurance. His relation with his boss is very good; he gets paid five shekels [approximately $1.10] an hour. Sometimes the settlement is closed and they refuse to let them enter. During the month, he works about one week. Maybe he goes to the settlement and returns without working. At 5 o'clock

he must go to the settlement, stop at the settlement gate. Maybe they allow them to enter the settlement at 8 o'clock.

She explains that each day the bosses pick the workers they want and turn the remainder of the men away. Despite Khitum's calm exterior, the daily grinding trauma and poverty weigh heavily on her story.

As we head north back to the hotel, conversation becomes more relaxed and personal. Khitum explains that she is married to a lawyer, "a very kind man," who fell in love with her, but did not approach her for seven years. Finally he called her and proposed on the phone! She exclaimed that she didn't even know him, but after dating for four months, she too fell in love and they were married. She explains that he is different from most men. "Maybe, but my husband does not act as a boss. Never. It's unusual in our society. His personality is very different from other men." Their daughter is in daycare while she works and she is now pregnant with her third child. Her older daughter was born four weeks early and died of prematurity after a two-month hospitalization. Her doctor has told her that there is a 70 percent chance this next baby will be a boy, but she is hoping for another girl. She wants a sister for her daughter and she also admits, laughing shyly to herself, that she actually prefers girls. "I think the life for a woman is better or more beautiful than the life of a man, because of babies and emotions and the nature of life. Especially in our society." Besides, she adds, "I like girls because I see them like flowers."

Part Three
The Implications of Knowing:
Complicity and Dissent

12
Finding the Voice for a Just Peace: Seeing the Human Face

WHILE WRITING THIS BOOK, SO many extraordinary events have erupted and evolved in the Middle East. Not long after Arafat took his final breaths in a hospital in France, his arch rival, Sharon, briefly sputtered and then sank into unconsciousness. Angry Jewish settlers were dragged from their homes in Gaza while the total Jewish settler population in the West Bank continues to explode. Hamas won a democratic election to the Legislative Council that was largely interpreted as a vote against the corruption and ineptitude of Fatah. Israeli Prime Minister Ehud Olmert rode to narrow victory with a plan to unilaterally make large Jewish settlement blocks in the West Bank permanently part of Israel. Fatah and Hamas are on the brink of civil war and the Palestinian economy is dying under a worldwide economic boycott. After years of skirmishes, forces in Gaza and Lebanon captured Israeli soldiers, Hezbollah launched rockets into Israel after Israel struck back, and then the IDF unleashed a massive retaliation targeting much of the infrastructure and civilian population. Lebanon lies in ruins and many fear a destabilization of the entire Middle East as well as a long-lasting humanitarian catastrophe. Civilian casualties in Israel, Gaza, Lebanon, and the West Bank continue to climb.

I listen to the news differently now, under every headline I see real people, mothers, fathers, and children caught in this drama. A horrific suicide attack in Tel Aviv; Israeli snipers kill somebody in Nablus. Were the victims or perpetrators somebody I know, their child, their mother, a son wrapped in explosives, lost in self-destructive rage, or a different son fingering the latest in military hardware and cold-blooded hatred? Everything feels much more personal as I struggle with this complicated affair; bearing witness to multiple narratives, feeling complicit, confused, guilty, and outraged all at once. I am awash in emails and internet sites that only heighten my anxiety and despair. May 10, 2006, I receive an urgent press release from Physicians for Human Rights-Israel: "Report: Collapse of the Palestinian Health Care System,"[1] followed by more emails from Palestinian health care providers I know describing appallingly desperate conditions. Who is dying from lack of medication, chemotherapy, dialysis, maternity care, essential services? How many people are hurting because the Palestinian Ministry of Health that provides general health care for 65 percent of the population cannot even pay for basic salaries?[2]

Shortly thereafter, reports of the dire consequences of the Israeli bombing of the electrical power plant in Gaza, the public health catastrophe, and the food and water shortages start pouring in.[3] Manar, a student from the Deheisha Refugee Camp in Bethlehem, now studying in the US, writes me vividly troubling emails while visiting her family. She describes heavily armed Israeli soldiers invading the camp, streets mostly empty of young men who are all in jail or have been killed while throwing stones, the scarcity of food, the intermittent electricity, and the growing poverty and desperation. No one has received a salary in months and increasing outrage and defiance prevail. After a description of a harrowing and humiliating journey and hours of harassment at multiple West Bank checkpoints, she concludes one missive with, "If you don't hear from me, I'm in jail or killed by Israeli bullet."

So how do we comprehend and analyze what is happening in this region? It is important to look at the environment in which we as Jews and US citizens attempt to have this troubled conversation. Despite all the emotional anguish, it is imperative to explore the marketing of "pro-Israel" messages, the challenges of having a critical dialogue in this environment, and the social and political consequences and possibilities as we look towards the future.

A Question of Marketing

Using a focus on my personal experience, I will examine how the dimensions of political and cultural attitudes are shaped by exploring a few remarkable, iconic items that have crossed my path. As I pick through the stacks of mail, email, newspaper clippings, and announcements, my gaze is caught by a strange blue plastic food bag clip that reads: KEEP YOUR PASSION FOR ISRAEL FRESH IsraelActionCenter@jcrcboston.org. Too often, the difficult problems facing Israel and its relationship to the Palestinian people are presented as more a question of misunderstanding and bad public relations than as substantive, critical analysis. Marketing and image making have replaced an honest discussion involving the serious issues facing a vibrant but complicated Israeli society and its own security concerns. This is all painfully intertwined with documented Israeli human rights violations, the horror of Palestinian suicide bombings, Palestinian difficulties and aspirations, and the contribution of the US to this tangled morass. I would like to share with you two extraordinary but illuminating reports that I acquired in the course of my exploration.

"Israel in the Age of Eminem: A Creative Brief for Israel Messaging" is a research project by Dr. Frank Luntz, a well-known communications expert and pollster.[4] The work was commissioned in 2003 and funded by a coalition of foundations and philanthropists who are avid supporters of Israel. They expressed concern for Jewish identity and attitudes towards Israel in young people aged 18 to 29, and, "the outbreak of anti-Israel activities on a number of campuses across North America."[5] Using focus groups and reactions to ads, flyers, promotional information, and websites, "The report is designed to help you appeal to the roughly 80 percent of the young, secular Jewish population whom we are currently not engaging."[6] The report stresses the importance in "Israel advertising" of showing faces that look "American" rather than Middle Eastern, of maintaining an edgy sophistication, exhibiting a "kind of attitude and irony," most successfully generated by people in the entertainment industry rather than traditional un-hip Jewish organizations. Luntz notes, "The net effect is that we must now sell the Israel many of us loved during the Six Day War to an audience who grew up after Rabin and during the second Intifada."[7] Additionally he adds, "For most readers of this document, a visit to Israel would be filled with spirituality, wonder and inner-peace. For these Jews today, an Israeli trip would be full of 'stress and anxiety.'"[8] While emphasizing the importance of Birthright trips where young Jews are given a free but narrowly focused trip to Israel, he also urges the use of cultural events to engage youth. The report cites the successes of events as diverse as Tibetan Freedom Concerts, Christian rock music, and *The Vagina Monologues*, but also favors comedy performances, monologues/theater, and tours by Israel's top DJs, techno musicians, and dancers to deliver an upbeat "pro-Israel" message. The report concludes with an evaluation of ads aimed at young Jewish audiences and ends with the "Ten Commandments" for successful Israel advertising to younger audiences, including presenting "facts" in a simple, straightforward, and I would argue, hopelessly one-sided fashion.[9] At no time is there any acknowledgement that there are serious issues to be addressed in understanding this tormented conflict and that conflicting narratives coexist which desperately need to be examined, understood, and grappled with if there is any possibility of real understanding.

A more insidious document was also produced by Luntz in 2005, *America 2020: How the Next Generation Views Israel*, for The Israel Project.[10] This is a well-funded, right-wing, international educational organization "that works to strengthen Israel's image in order to help protect Israel, reduce anti-Semitism and increase pride in Israel." [11] This report focuses on interviews with graduate students at elite US campuses who were often found not to be "pro-Israel," sometimes overtly hostile, and often sympathetic to Palestinian suffering and aspirations. Luntz again discusses the crisis on campuses, alleging suppression of "pro-Israel" views and an anti-Israel bias in the media. He warns that this misperception breeds "latent anti-Semitism" and hostility towards the "Israel lobby." He notes, "Many on the political left put the Palestinians on a pedestal and consider their cause one of basic human rights denied by an oppressive Israeli regime."[12] He worries about the danger if future leaders of America are not adequately "pro-Israel" and assumes that those with center to right politics in fact have a more "balanced" view. Luntz explains that pro-Israel organizations are fighting back on campuses, however,

> The fact is, we are losing the communication war in the elite media, and it will cost us the support of a generation of elites. The enemies of Israel may always exist; the names may change but the threat will not. Unless we stand up, speak out and reverse this trend, the next generation of American leaders will not see Israel as an ally. They will see Israel as a burden – and one that may not be worth carrying.[13]

As an example of these dangerous misconceptions, he states, "[The students] refer to Israel's security fence as a 'wall' so what is entirely a defensive measure is now seen as offensive and aggressive. They actually believe that Israel's security measures create more problems than solutions – and that the fence is a particularly ugly symbol of 'division,' 'oppression,' and 'occupation.'"[14] Luntz deplores the "Palestinian public relations advantage,"[15] and warns, "This belief is fueling the perception that the Palestinians are the underdog."[16] He cites the graduate students' lack of interest in viewing FOX or MSNBC, "the two cable news networks most sympathetic to Israel,"[17] and deplores the popular BBC as an important news source for the elite students. "The problem is [the students] make little distinction between the violence inflicted by Arab terrorists and the preventive efforts and/or retaliation of the Israeli army."[18] Luntz then develops a careful marketing strategy to win the hearts and minds of this cohort of Jewish Americans. He states that to reach this audience it is important to stress the message of peace and to show sympathy for the suffering and aspirations of Palestinians and that, "all Israel asks in return is an end to terrorism."[19] Another important message is that, "Israel accepts the Palestinians right to exist. We ask the same from the Palestinians,"[20] and that students need something to blame that is not Israel. Luntz suggests blaming the corrupt Palestinian government for their woes and reminds us that, "It's not just a conflict, it's culture."[21] He reiterates the oft-quoted but ill-founded statements that Palestinians teach their children to hate, that Arafat walked away from an excellent offer at Camp David, and stresses the Israeli suffering from suicide bombing. He suggests that it is important to venture into the Christian community to push the "pro-Israel" message, grounded in the convergence of values and the Biblical claims for a Jewish state. He recommends using attractive women to deliver the message, no accents except British, and an emphasis on appearing reasonable. Messaging is critical: "They're disputed territories, not occupied territories ... Arabs not Palestinians."[22] Luntz concludes his report by analyzing TV and media advertising and issuing guidelines for effective marketing.

> There's a reason the Palestinian message creators have the advantage right now. They are reaching out with *emotion* to win our hearts, while those who support Israel are trying to win the argument. Jewish organizations and those who seek to influence the public debate in favor of Israel must accept

the fact that outside-the-box, unconventional advertising is imperative for reaching the future elite.[23]

Luntz and the Israel Project are representative of many powerful organizations that seek to shape the discussion in an extremely dangerous fashion, setting up a false dichotomy between the good but victimized and poorly understood Israelis and the bad but pitiful Palestinians who are in reality oppressive terrorist ideologues. This broad historical and political sweep does little to acknowledge the complexities, mutual suffering, and grave imbalance of power that exists and dehumanizes Palestinians beyond recognition. It ignores the serious questions that Palestinians have as they watch more and more of their land being appropriated while questioning whether the Israeli government actually recognizes the Palestinians' right to a viable existence. It ignores the economic and psychological cost of the occupation on Israelis. In this kind of analysis, the mutual catastrophes that led to the founding of Israel on land already occupied by Palestinians, the Arab resistance to bearing the tragedy of the Holocaust, decades of massive Israeli military dominance, multiple failed "peace processes," the consequences of a long-standing, brutal occupation, and the crippling of the Palestinian economy, do not even enter the equation. Palestinians are equated with Arabs everywhere, ignoring the individual histories, mistakes, and grievances of different Arab-speaking peoples and feeding into the general anti-Arab, Islamophobic feelings that are prevalent in the US. Treating the Israel/Palestine conflict and the increasing awareness and sympathy for the experiences of Palestinians as a marketing problem in a society that is dominated by an unquestioning support for Israeli policy borders on the ludicrous. We do Israelis as well as Palestinians and ourselves a grave disservice if we buy into this simplistic, nationalistic explanation. This approach also raises serious questions about our own Jewish values and our long-standing humanist traditions.

A Tempest in Academia

Another example of mainstream Jewish hostility to open discourse can be seen in the response to the March 23, 2006, article published by John Mearshiemer and Stephen Walt in the *London Review of Books* and as a working paper on Harvard University's Kennedy School of Government website.²⁴ "The Israel Lobby" examines what drives US policy and diplomatic support in the Middle East. It explores the impact of special interest groups, organizations, and individuals that are united in a demand for strict, uncritical support for the most right-wing of Israeli policies and unfettered direct economic and military aid to Israel. The authors refer to the Israel Lobby as a group that includes the American Israel Public Affairs Committee (AIPAC), the Conference of Presidents of Major Jewish Organizations, Committee for Accuracy in Middle East Reporting in America (CAMERA), Jewish Institute for National Security Affairs (JINSA), Washington Institute for Near East Policy (WINEP), and the David Project. They include more campus-focused organizations such as Caravan for Democracy, Israel on Campus Coalition, and Campus Watch. While the authors have no argument with effective lobbies working to influence US governmental policy and public opinion, they state that their goal is to start an honest public debate on this explosive topic.

> There is a moral dimension here as well. Thanks to the Lobby, the United States has become the de facto enabler of Israeli expansion in the Occupied Territories, making it complicit in the crimes perpetrated against the Palestinians. This situation undercuts Washington's efforts to promote democracy abroad and makes it look hypocritical when it presses other states to respect human rights. US efforts to limit nuclear proliferation appear equally hypocritical given its willingness to accept Israel's nuclear arsenal, which only encourages Iran and others to seek a similar capability.
>
> Besides, the Lobby's campaign to quash debate about Israel is unhealthy for democracy. Silencing sceptics by organising blacklists and boycotts – or by suggesting that critics are anti-semites – violates the principle of open debate on which democracy depends. The inability of Congress to conduct a genuine debate on these important issues paralyses the entire process of democratic deliberation. Israel's backers should be free to make their case and to challenge those who disagree with them, but efforts to stifle debate by intimidation must be roundly condemned.
>
> Finally, the Lobby's influence has been bad for Israel. Its ability to persuade Washington to support an expansionist agenda has discouraged Israel from seizing opportunities – including a peace treaty with Syria and a prompt and full implementation of the Oslo Accords – that would have saved Israeli lives and shrunk the ranks of Palestinian extremists. Denying the Palestinians their legitimate political rights certainly has not made Israel more secure, and the long campaign to kill or marginalise a generation of Palestinian leaders has empowered extremist groups like Hamas, and reduced the number of Palestinian leaders who would be willing to accept a fair settlement and

able to make it work. Israel itself would probably be better off if the Lobby were less powerful and US policy more even-handed.[25]

There is much to be applauded in this article and much that warrants serious debate. Does US foreign policy toe the line of the Israel lobby to the detriment of US self-interest or does the US use Israel as both proxy and scapegoat for its own foreign policy agenda? What is the impact of major oil and military/industrial interests in the region? What about the growing power of evangelical Christians who promote very right-wing policies drenched in apocalyptic fundamentalism? How did the ideologies of these two highly respected academics affect their analysis? There are many important issues that deserve in-depth and critical deliberation. I also become understandably nervous whenever someone talks about the power of Jewish money or describes a loosely organized lobby that neo-Nazis, not to mention neoconservatives, could interpret as a sinister Jewish cabal running the banks and secretly manipulating the world stage. Similarly, it is important not to overstate the influence of this lobby and thus relieve the largely non-Jewish neoconservative groups that actually run this country of the responsibility and consequences of their efforts.

So what was the response? Progressives hailed this article, posted it on a stream of active websites and blogs, and praised the authors for exposing the influence of these various organizations on public discourse, the US congress, and their intimidation of media and peace activists. The work was vigorously debated, the political analysis and historical accuracy scrutinized, and the blunt tone critiqued.

While a respectful debate about "The Israel Lobby" percolated mostly through academia and the blogosphere, there were also shrill charges of anti-Semitism and a vicious, bullying, personal smear campaign. Academics such as Alan Dershowitz and organizations such as the Anti-Defamation League charged the authors with "lying," "bigotry," and "anti-Zionist drivel." The ferocity of these diatribes and distortions is a clear example of the consequences of straying beyond the narrowly defined acceptable public debate, which is indeed exactly one of the premises of the original article. Some of the criticism was more muted, charging that "The Israel Lobby" contained statements that may not be anti-Semitic in intent but may be anti-Semitic in effect. These kinds of comments have a chilling impact on debate; they may initially sound reasonable, but are actually deeply inhibiting to public discourse. After all, no one wants to be called an anti-Semite, but we need to be able to bring to light difficult issues without public or self-censorship.

It is also important to examine the ugliness this controversy provoked, the use of the accusation of anti-Semitism and intellectual intimidation, the predictable hysteria that erupts in response to serious critiques of Israeli policy. The danger is not only in the stifling of healthy debate about topics that are dear to us, but more importantly in the fact that the Israel lobby is actually politically far to the right of the majority of US Jews as well as Israelis. Thus, an extremely effective, well-funded lobby in Washington and beyond exists that wields a huge amount of influence, but does not reflect the constituency it purports to serve or speak for and is in fact supporting a foreign policy that many US Jews find increasingly dangerous. While this article may have lacked nuance and by most accounts was unblinkingly harsh, US Jews need to ask, do we as a subgroup within US society want to be in an alliance with mostly WASP neoconservatives, Christian fundamentalists, and right-wing Jewish ideologues? Silencing debate using moral blackmail is also inconsistent with Jewish values and the traditions of debate that form the basis of our own rich heritage. As the Israeli government claims all the rights and responsibilities of nationhood, it is time to realize that Israel is not entitled to special treatment and that clinging to our singular place in history as "righteous victims" only exacerbates Arab and Muslim hostility.

The Brandeis Art Exhibit Controversy

So how does this dynamic look on a more local level? Brandeis University in Waltham, Massachusetts, is a vibrant, world-class, nonsectarian university founded in 1948 under the sponsorship of the US Jewish community and named for the late US Supreme Court Justice Louis Brandeis. The university, where half the students are Jewish, has taken brave and enlightened steps to increase dialogue on Middle East issues. It recently established a partnership with Al Quds University in East Jerusalem and a number of West Bank Palestinian NGOs, and appointed a number of Israelis as well as Palestinian Khalil Shikaki to the Crown Center for Middle East Studies. Brandeis granted an honorary doctorate to Tony Kushner, coeditor of *Wrestling with Zion: Progressive Jewish-*

American Responses to the Palestinian/Israeli Conflict and author of the screenplay *Munich*. In April 2006, Lior Halperin, an Israeli army veteran and Brandeis student taking a class called "The Arts of Building Peace," organized an exhibit of pictures and comments by young Palestinians from the Aida Refugee Camp near Bethlehem and, with the assistance of a Brandeis professor, mounted the exhibit entitled "Voices of Palestine" in the Goldfarb Library. The drawings and brief commentaries reveal the trauma as well as the incredible yearnings, and political and personal aspirations of these young people living under a violent and ugly occupation. On viewing this installation, I was struck by the number of drawings that showed the destruction by Israeli tanks and bombs and the ravages of the separation wall mixed with expressions of fervent Palestinian nationalism. This sharply contrasted with the children's poignant dreams of becoming doctors, dentists, engineers, pharmacists, and journalists. Viewers were invited to write their thoughts to these teenagers in the spirit of developing conversation and understanding.

Within days of the opening, Lior reports that she was called by Daniel Terris, director of the International Center for Ethics, Justice and Public Life. While explaining that he was active in bringing the voices of Palestinians to the Brandeis community, Lior states he reported that the exhibition was causing a "mushroom of criticism." A dozen or so students had complained that the pictures were jarring and lacked context, and this controversy could be used by right-wing forces to threaten the university's other efforts to improve dialogue. Daniel asked Lior to take down the exhibit and she replied, "I refuse to be silenced." The next day, reportedly at the behest of senior administrators, the drawings were gone. The subsequent protests and controversy made the front page of the *Boston Globe*,[26] a story on WBUR, Boston's local NPR station,[27] an interview with Amy Goodman on "Democracy Now,"[28] and produced a barrage of supportive and angry emails and letters to the university. So how did an exhibit of children's art hanging in a university library provoke such a passionate and hostile response?

On May 3, 2006, the *Boston Globe* reported, "University officials said the paintings depicted only one side of the Israeli–Palestinian conflict," that "they wanted to make sure the Israeli–Palestinian conflict is presented in a balanced manner."[29] Lior countered that, "the university censored an alternative view." Dr. John Hose, Associate Vice

President for University Affairs, explained in a May 4 email that the installation occurred immediately before final exams, some students were confused and upset, the drawings were in a prominent physical location that deserved a "larger educational context," and the issue was "context" and not "balance."[30] On May 5, Daniel Terris composed a lengthy letter to the Brandeis community in which he stressed the incredible work being done on campus to encourage the discussion of a range of perspectives on the Middle East. Nonetheless, despite what he described as the best of intentions, he raised concern for the controversial images and personal statements, "That some members of our campus community would likely find troubling." He worried that in the absence of "context or explanation"[31] the exhibit might have an unexpected negative impact on understanding and dialogue and inflame long-standing tensions.

Lior's instructor, Cindy Cohen, also wrote to the students, reflecting on the questions raised by the exhibition and the use of art for peacebuilding. She stressed the positive impact on both the children and the audience and the possibilities for building relationships through art.

> Voices from Palestine provided an opportunity for members of the Brandeis community to encounter a perspective on the Israeli–Palestinian conflict that is rarely given full expression here. Even for those who completely disagree with the political messages implicit within it, it offers the opportunity to learn about a point of view. If we disagree with the assumptions behind the children's expression, how might we communicate those disagreements in a way that the children might hear? Even for those who profoundly disagree, can we hold those disagreements without demonizing the children or the adults who work with them?[32]

She reflected that it is critical to craft events that are most likely to reach beyond "people's defenses. We must take into account the sensitivities of the people we are trying to reach."[33] She questioned whether the exhibit could have been better contextualized, whether the project could have had a greater effect if it had creatively acknowledged the range of views of the audience.

This entire episode speaks to the difficulties of presenting a sympathetic picture of Palestinian life and the sparks that are ignited when lines are crossed, even in a liberal academic institution. I seriously doubt even during the high stress time of final exams, that an emotionally upsetting exhibit of children's art from Sudan or East Timor would have elicited such a response. For all the hand-wringing and thoughtful reflections, the response to this topic clearly concerns the topic itself. Many of us note that when Michael Oren and Daniel Pipes, two right-wing defenders of Israeli governmental policy, recently spoke on campus, there was no outcry from the Brandeis administration for "balance" or concern for the feelings of less right-wing Jewish or dare I say Arab students. When students are upset or challenged by a book or a course, they are urged to wrestle with the ideas rather than close their eyes. Likewise, an art exhibit is not designed to make people feel comfortable; art is often meant to provoke and to stimulate critical thinking and to touch emotions. That was apparently too much of a threat for the Brandeis administration. In my more sinister moments, I wonder what political and financial pressure was placed on Brandeis by donors and alumnae who sought to stifle this painful and difficult conversation and felt a little student project was easily expendable. Interestingly the exhibit was transferred to the Massachusetts Institute of Technology (MIT), where it was installed without controversy. MIT does not have a deeply rooted Jewish identity and apparently could tolerate the conversation with more equanimity. What does this say about tolerance and open-mindedness in our own Jewish community and our ability to empathize with the suffering of others?

Trying to Have a Conversation

My ability to understand the role of Jews in the Diaspora and our relationship to Jewish Israelis and Palestinians living on both sides of the Green Line is complicated not only by silencing within our own communities, but also by our own internal pain and self-censorship. Though most Jews have risen up the economic ladder beyond our immigrant forefathers in the garment industries, and the days of changing our names from "Kleiner" to "Kenmore" in order to find work are long gone, we often behave as a deeply wounded and emotionally defensive people. This existential trauma embraces centuries of anti-Semitism, the horrors of the Shoah, and extends to the boatloads of European refugees and the frightening, tenuous early days of the founding of the State of Israel. It is born of the machinations and betrayals of the dying Ottoman Empire, the British colonial enterprise, UN partition efforts, two world wars, newly formed Arab states, multiple smaller military conflicts, and growing national and religious movements. Jews are neither the sole victims nor the sole victimizers in this complicated history. By listening to the many narratives, I have come to feel that reducing this story to a battle between good and evil is disastrous and does not help us understand or work towards resolving the current dilemmas. I also believe that for Jews, religious and secular, in this era of ethnic politics, with the US dominating and funding much of the discord, this conversation is no longer optional.

A few years ago, I stood with a group of Jews at a "Solidarity with Israel" rally in Boston, holding a sign that read, "I STAND WITH ISRAEL, AGAINST SHARON, AGAINST OCCUPATION." A white-haired *bubbe* marched up to me shaking her fist and yelled with a thick Yiddish accent, "You should have died in the camps!" I can only weep at her level of raw, wounded rage. I suspect that in order to heal as individuals and as a people, we need to face our agonizing historical wounds and at the same time to acknowledge the pain, contradictions, aspirations, and equal humanity of Palestinians caught up in our catastrophe. Perhaps, "Never again!" needs to be embraced in its most universal sense to mean we must never again forget the ability of ordinary men and women as well as governments to commit unspeakable acts of cruelty. Each terrible ordeal stands on its own. I ask you, nonetheless, is it possible for us to acknowledge that our Jewish day of coming home was the Palestinian day of mass displacement? Our day of independence was their day of misfortune. Our new towns and cities are built on the rubble of their destroyed homes and villages. Is it possible to comprehend that the occupation begun in 1967, like all occupations, is a corrupting and atrocity producing situation starting at the level of the individual and extending to the policies of the state? Is it within our capacity to understand that Palestinian hostility is often a response to Israeli land acquisition and aggression and that as Ben Gurion and Moshe Dayan admitted in the early days of statehood, they too would have fought back if they had been Arabs? Surely if Jews as a people hungered for Zion for 2000 years, we can imagine the yearning of a family dispossessed 57 years ago. Increasing military might, humiliating and suffocating an entire people, and building concrete walls will not resolve this human dilemma.

The State of Israel has made tremendous accomplishments as a unique ingathering of Jewish refugees, as a leader in the world of science, health care, literature, music, art, and religious renewal. At the same time, something is seriously wrong. Arthur Neslen, in *Occupied Minds: A Journey through the Israeli Psyche*, reports that almost 10 percent of Israelis suffer from post-traumatic stress syndrome, tourism has decreased by 80 percent, 20 percent of Israelis are living below the poverty line, the economy is in recession, and antisocial behavior is on the rise.[34] The Israeli Bureau of Statistics now states that more Israelis are leaving the country to live in the Diaspora than are arriving. "[Israeli] Feminist organizations such as New Profile argue that Israeli civil life has been disfigured by military dominion; weaponry, militant self-righteousness, paranoia and patriarchal hyper-vigilance have all spilt back into a society with few resources to cope with them. They say that the occupation has come home."[35] I fear that Jews in the Diaspora support that which is most extraordinary about Israeli accomplishments and at the same time act as complicit enablers for that which is most pathologic. Many of us are aware of the betrayal, incompetence, aggression, and mendacity of a variety of Arab leaders in the twentieth and twenty-first centuries yet we rarely apply the same standards to British, French, US, or Israeli leaders. For Jews, calling attention to these discordant standards is so difficult because it threatens our existential core, our cherished narratives, and challenges who we want to be: good people with moral vision and compassion who only wish for a safe haven and an end to bloodshed.

We deeply cherish these humanist "Jewish values," but what exactly does that mean? Are these beliefs rooted solely in our religious traditions? How can it be that religious leaders such as Rabbi Arik Ascherman from the Israeli organization, Rabbis for Human Rights, who oppose home demolitions and the separation wall and fight for the rights of the poorest in Israeli society, are quoting from the same Biblical texts as the right-wing religious settlers grabbing hilltops and threatening Palestinian children on their way to school? I suspect that while our principles may have foundations in religious texts where one can find abundant calls for justice and the primacy of human values, our ethical traditions also stem from our historical place in society; Jews as victims, outsiders, the disadvantaged, and displaced. In the US, we know that many Jewish immigrants arrived at Ellis Island oppressed economically, marginalized socially, and already politically radicalized. They were disproportionately represented in progressive political and labor movements, and their children and grandchildren filled the ranks of the white Freedom Riders in the south and the movements in the 1960s and onward for civil rights, ending the Vietnam War, and a variety of student and liberation groups. Jews in the US have long prided themselves on their commitment to issues of social justice and fighting inequality, to *tikkun olam*, healing the world. For some reason, however, that commitment does not extend to the Palestinian people. Too often, I find that some combination of fear, hubris, and blindness, a kind of intellectual and emotional ghettoization, characterizes the conversation of many Jews when it comes to the thorny issues of Israelis and Palestinians. I fear now, although Jews have mostly "made it" in America and some of us have even entered the gated communities of the elite and powerful, and we even have a state we call our own, something more important has been lost. Have we sacrificed Jewish values in the name of Israeli nationalism and aggressive expansionism? Is Israeli nationalism our new fundamentalism?

Public Discourse in Israel

Vigorous debate about these issues takes place in Israeli public discourse in a much more lively and open fashion than in the US. Israeli historians such as Ilan Pappe and Tom Segev have written well-documented books reopening the one-sided narratives created by the victors and their allies, and exploring the multi-layered history that can bring us closer to understanding and empathy. Gideon Levy and Amira Hass, two Israeli journalists, have long reported on the brutal consequences and contradictions of the Israeli occupation. In 2005, a renowned, politically centrist newscaster, Chaim Yavin, the "Walter Cronkite of Israel," produced a brutal, eye-opening five-part documentary, *The Land of the Settlers*, that caused an uproar on Israeli TV. Israeli movies such as *Another Road Home* by Danae Elon and Palestinian movies such as *Paradise Now* by Hany Abu-Assad, and *Arna's Children* by Juliano Mer Khamis, the son of an Israeli Jewish mother and a Palestinian father, can engage us in a personal, nuanced exploration of these most difficult issues. In a May 15, 2006 article in *Haaretz*, a major Israeli newspaper, former Knesset speaker Avraham Burg stated:

> The Jewish people did not survive for two millennia in order to pioneer new weaponry, computer security programs or anti-missile missiles. We were

supposed to be a light unto the nations. In this we have failed. It turns out that the 2000-year struggle for Jewish survival comes down to a state of settlements, run by an amoral clique of corrupt lawbreakers who are deaf both to their citizens and to their enemies. A state lacking justice cannot survive. More and more Israelis are coming to understand this as they ask their children where they expect to live in 25 years. Children who are honest admit, to their parents' shock, that they do not know.[36]

Facing the Contradictions

So how do we in the Diaspora absorb this painful reality? What is our responsibility for a state that claims to speak for all of the Jewish people and for the policies of our US government that broadly endorses actions many of us find deplorable? Perhaps we need to examine honestly the national mythology that we have embraced. Looking at history, it is apparent that the plucky little nation of pioneers and survivors, a tiny democracy in a neighborhood of repressive, hostile regimes, was at its beginnings often attacked but not universally hated. Indeed Israel was much admired for its idealism and modern progress. Little was known of the Palestinian experience and grappling with the Holocaust was just becoming part of the international agenda. There were no Israeli debacles in Lebanon and no settler movement in the Occupied Territories. It may be time to admit that Israel is now 57 years old and the times have changed. In an article in *Haaretz*, on May 2, 2006, Tony Judt observed:

> We can see, in retrospect, that the victory of Israel in June 1967 and its continuing occupation of the territories it conquered then have been the Jewish state's very own nakba: a moral and political catastrophe. Israel's actions in the West Bank and Gaza have magnified and publicized the country's shortcomings and displayed them to a watching world. Curfews, checkpoints, bulldozers, public humiliations, home destructions, land seizures, shootings, "targeted assassinations," the separation fence: Today they can be watched, in real time, by anyone with a computer or a satellite dish – which means that Israel's behavior is under daily scrutiny by hundreds of millions of people worldwide. The result has been a complete transformation in the international view of Israel. What is the universal shorthand symbol for Israel, reproduced worldwide in thousands of newspaper editorials and political cartoons? The Star of David emblazoned upon a tank.
>
> Such comparisons are lethal to Israel's moral credibility. They strike at what was once its strongest suit: the claim of being a vulnerable island

of democracy and decency in a sea of authoritarianism and cruelty; an oasis of rights and freedoms surrounded by a desert of repression. But democrats don't fence into Bantustans helpless people whose land they have conquered, and free men don't ignore international law and steal other men's homes.[37]

What will happen if we boldly face these kinds of harsh critiques without flinching? There are indeed many countries with repressive leaders and human rights violations much more severe than Israel. Israel's violations of human rights, however, are a violation of both international law and a series of UN resolutions designed to protect a refugee population living under occupation and specifically protected by the UN and the Geneva Conventions. While Diaspora Jews did not flock to Israel as the early Zionists had hoped, we have our own strength and purpose as members of a large non-Israeli segment of the Jewish population. Possibly with the less tangled vision born of distance and personal safety, Diaspora Jews can offer support to Israelis and Palestinians who refuse to be enemies and who continue to warn of an urgent and predictable catastrophe. As an example, let us examine the outlines of a proposal that has been at the center of all of the many peace plans that have come and gone.

Examining the Two State Solution

We know that for years no matter who is in power, in repeated polls the majority of Israelis and Palestinians support some version of a two state solution; a safe, secure Israel living in peace beside a nonviolent, viable Palestine, with borders based on the pre-1967 borders, and some sharing of Jerusalem. Even former Prime Minister Sharon spoke of ending the occupation and lately Prime Minister Olmert has offered a unilateral version he calls the "realignment" or "convergence plan." Let us also acknowledge that Palestinians and Israelis are equally human, sincerely weary of the years of war, and that most are ready to live in peace and share the land. Let us remember that in the past, Israel has framed this conflict as primarily an issue of security, in which democratic, peaceful Israelis are seen as victims of inexplicable Palestinian terrorism. Unfortunately, that particular framing has eliminated from the discourse the original dispossession of Palestinians, the creation of hundreds of thousands of refugees that now number in the millions, and the brutal consequences of the occupation. Many analysts believe that the recent Hamas victory partially reflected a desire by Palestinians for peace talks to be negotiated from their own perspective as well, and they argue that negotiations will only be successful if both parties' claims are treated as equally legitimate. Thus it can be argued that this negotiation is not only about Israelis seeking security from Palestinian terrorism, but also about Palestinians attempting to survive and, not surprisingly, to resist the vastly superior power of Israeli occupying forces.

It is important to summarize the realities on the ground in order to grapple with what is happening. Jeff Halper of the Israel Committee Against House Demolitions, in February 2006, questioned the viability of a Palestinian state as currently envisioned by the Israeli government.[38] He described the West Bank as a collection of "cantons" (a word used by Sharon),[39] isolated by Jewish settlements and bypass roads; he cited four million Palestinians living in territory without contiguity, lacking control over water, borders, and their own freedom of movement, and isolated from Jerusalem as well as Gaza. He noted that Israel has established a military presence in the Jordan valley by creating a security zone along the eastern border of the West Bank. How can Israeli Prime Minister Olmert and his predecessors call for a modern, democratic Palestinian state when they have helped maneuver the Palestinian territories into isolated, nonviable cantons? It seems to me that disengagement and unilateral separation are not just responses to suicide bombings; they are also part of an active Israeli occupation and expansion into more Palestinian lands. Convergence is not a retreat, but entails moving some 70,000 of the West Bank Jewish settlers into other areas of the West Bank and resettling them behind a separation wall and barbed wire, and consolidating and incorporating more than 400,000 settlers living in the settlement blocs in the territories as officially, permanently part of Israel.

Israeli author Amos Elon, in his article "What Does Olmert Want?" describes how the separation wall divides some 200,000 Palestinians in Greater Jerusalem from their families, universities, businesses, and property in the West Bank.[40] He notes that tens of thousands of Palestinians on the other side of the wall will be separated from their orange and olive groves, their sole source of livelihood. How will Palestinians be able to engage in economic development and political stabilization if they are in actuality living in a giant open-air prison? They may live in most of the rooms, but the Israeli military controls all the corridors and the outside walls, entrances and exits, the sky and the sea. How will Palestinians survive when they are separated from Jerusalem, which accounts for approximately 40 percent of the Palestinian economy, and they lose access to their water, their richest agricultural lands, tourist sites, and many essential resources? If what remains is a truncated mini-state, how will this Palestine sustain its battered population, let alone address the needs of millions of refugees living in horrendous camps in nearby Lebanon and Syria? Why would any Palestinian settle for this?

When this latest plan fails, as I suspect it will, when poverty, desperation, and violent acts of aggression increase, when the refugees displaced in 1948 and 1967 produce another generation living in appalling, hopeless conditions, who will be responsible? I worry about all the contradictions. Most Israelis working to preserve their Jewish majority want the Palestinians to be as separate from them as possible, but 20 percent of Israeli citizens are already Palestinian and their birthrate is higher than the Jewish population. How does the desire for a Jewish majority with favored social and economic status conflict with the desire for democracy? At the same time, the policies of the Israeli government involve acquiring as much land as possible in the West Bank for Jewish settlers who live among the Palestinian population. Many would argue that the policies of the Israeli government have deliberately created a "Greater Israel" with clusters of Palestinian population centers in pockets of nonviable enclaves, surrounded on all sides by Israeli Defense Forces. Where in this is the possibility of an economically viable Palestinian state? I worry that this is an inherently destabilizing situation and in fact, no solution at all. I sometimes wonder whether Israeli policy will destroy the possibility of two viable states living side-by-side and instead produce de facto a single state. From my vantage point, current policies are moving Israel farther away from democracy and into a dominant, theocratic, militarized state with total control of a disempowered, hostile subgroup, some already second-class citizens, others living in enclaves that cannot survive or flourish. Is this state consistent with "Jewish values?" These predictions may seem harsh, but like Israelis active in the peace movement, these are the kinds of questions that Jews in the Diaspora need to have the courage to ask.

Getting Less Than We Deserve

The Lemon Tree is a beautifully told documentary written by Sandy Tolan, which describes the interwoven lives of Dalia Eshkanazi, whose Bulgarian refugee parents emigrated after the Holocaust to Israel and came to live in Ramla in a former Arab house that was the childhood home of Bashir Khairi.[41] At one point, Dalia remarks, "In a peace plan, *everybody will have to do with less than they deserve.*"[42] The more I learn of the history of this conflict, the more I believe that Jews and their friends in the Diaspora need to support the voices of moderation, to honor everyone's humanity, to recognize the traumas that all of the players bring to the table, and to understand the imbalance of power. Many Israelis believe in Israel's Biblical and historical right to all of the land west of the Jordan River: Israel, "Judea and Samaria." Likewise, many Palestinians dream of returning to their homes overlooking the Mediterranean Sea. Through the course of the last half century, most Palestinians have come to accept a state on 22 percent of their ancestral lands. Can we understand that "negotiating" about how much of that remaining fragment they are still entitled to feels untenable? For most Palestinians, the historic compromises were already made in 1948 with massive dispossession and the loss of 78 percent of the land to the Jews who constituted 30 percent of the population and owned 6 percent of the land. Because Israeli security is predicated on Palestinian hope and the possibility of justice, I argue that it is long overdue to say, enough! It is time to speak loudly and clearly and work forcefully towards ending the occupation. This means truly dismantling Jewish settlements and ending economic restrictions on Palestinians, and recognizing the importance of Jerusalem for Jews, Christians, and Muslims. It is time to begin unconditional negotiations with Palestinians, starting by calling Hamas's bluff and offering something substantial in return for recognition of Israel and a cease-fire.

We need to face the unresolved problem of Palestinian refugees. As I struggle with these emotional minefields, the Jewish response to the right of return for Palestinians is usually an absolute loud "no," with talk of a "demographic threat" to the Jewish majority, an end to Israel as a Jewish state, and so forth. Since I am trying to examine the wounds that will not heal until they are addressed, how can I not think about this one, particularly since Jews have repeatedly been a community of refugees themselves. Many Palestinian friends have said to me that the most important step for them is official Israeli recognition of the country's role in Palestinian displacement and suffering and an apology. I think of the model of South African truth and reconciliation commissions as a mechanism for communal healing. To overcome such an immense hurdle would require tremendous international support. It is important to note that there have already been numerous creative proposals involving some combination of return and compensation.[43] These ideas do not involve creating more injustice, forcing Jewish families to leave their formerly Arab homes. If we see everyone as equal human beings and if we can engage in a resolution that is not a zero sum game, but one in which everyone gains something, then there is so much that is possible. But time is running out. The wounds are growing deeper.

Looking to the Future

At home, after the invasions and occupations of Afghanistan and Iraq, the US government is facing growing criticism both from its citizenry and beyond its borders. In order to repair its broken relationships with the rest of the world, the US will undoubtedly have to reassess its unwavering support for Israeli policies that are seen by the world as destabilizing and instigating Arab hostility. I worry that if we as Jews do not tolerate criticism of Israeli policy, then all Jews will be seen as culpable for whatever catastrophes lie ahead. Surely history will teach us that Israel cannot claim a special moral dispensation because of past suffering, and then behave immorally, that the US government will not always be there offering large amounts of economic and military aid, that misusing the term anti-Semitism to characterize criticism of Israeli behavior ultimately renders the concept meaningless.

What is our responsibility as Jews in the Diaspora? We need to work within our communities and our political worlds to create an environment in which both Jewish and Palestinian narratives in all their complexity, contradictions, and pain can be heard and addressed. We need to be responsible for a government that speaks in our name whether or not we are willing participants. We need to support debate in synagogues, churches, mosques, and political forums that is as lively and diverse as that in Israel, to see the consequences of our behavior in the wholeness of US foreign policy. We need to write letters and emails, make phone calls, join dialogue and activist organizations, and support peace organizations in the US, Europe, Israel, and Palestine. We need to encourage and lobby our own Congress people to be emboldened, to broaden the dialogue without making that courageous stand an electoral suicide. We need to remember that we are new members in the country club of the powerful elites in the US, the new "white folks," and we can easily become unacceptable outsiders again if supporting Israel no longer enhances US interests. Making strong alliances with supporters of moderation in Jewish, Arab, Christian, Muslim, secular, and religious communities is critical to recapturing the conversation and building bridges. We cannot afford to let the right wing set the parameters of this debate.

Perhaps when the horrors of the pogroms in Europe, the repressive regimes in North Africa and many Arab states, and the grim realities of the Holocaust recede into history, a new generation will arise. Perhaps this generation, aware of the appalling excesses of the Israeli occupation of Palestine, can reopen the books of history and re-examine treasured Jewish beliefs. It may then be possible to see the face of the Palestinian "enemy" as equally human and equally entitled to what we would want for ourselves and our Israeli brothers and sisters. This is no longer a question of Israel's right to exist, but rather a question of how it exists and the cost of that behavior for its own citizens, for the region, and on the international stage. A Jewish physician colleague once told me I was "a danger to the Jewish people." I argue that doing this kind of work, calling attention to uncomfortable realities, trauma, resilience, and the desperate need for healing, is fully within Jewish tradition and critical to the survival of Israel. I treasure my legacy of endless questioning, soul-searching, and respect for human rights and dignity combined with a responsibility for healing the world. Perhaps we can repair our internal wounds by opening our hearts and minds, and mend our external hurt and fear through acts of reconciliation and advocacy, refusing to be enemies, always seeing and remembering the human faces that are so much like our own.

Glossary

Al Nakba: Arab term for the Arab-Israeli War of 1948, literally translated, The Catastrophe

Aliyah: Jewish immigration to Palestine and later Israel

Ashkenazi: Jews from Central or Eastern Europe

Balfour Declaration: British document in 1917 promising the establishment of a Jewish national homeland in Palestine without impacting the rights of the indigenous population

British Mandate: League of Nations established British authority over Palestine and other territories formerly belonging to the Ottoman Empire in 1922

Bypass road: road built by Israel in the Occupied Territories that is open only to vehicles with Israeli license plates

B'Tselem: the Israeli Information Center for Human Rights in the Occupied Territories established in 1989 to independently research and document human rights issues in the Occupied Territories in order to affect Israeli public opinion and official policy

Checkpoint: manned or unmanned obstruction ranging from a vehicle to an extensive military terminal where Israeli military examine permits and decide passage; affects all Palestinians and others in the Occupied Territories, does not affect Israelis traveling on bypass roads to Jewish settlements

Closure: practice of restricting movement in or out of a city, town, or village, often applied by Israeli soldiers to Palestinian cities for hours to months and enforced militarily

Coalition of Women for Peace: coalition of nine Israeli women's peace organizations, composed of both Jews and Palestinians, founded in 2000 to promote human rights and social and economic equality for all the citizens of Israel and a just and lasting peace between Israel and Palestine. The group focuses on an end to occupation and promotes an active role for women peace-makers.

Curfew: practice of restricting movement in or out of homes, often applied by Israeli soldiers to Palestinian civilians for hours to months and enforced militarily

Deir Yassin massacre: 1948 massacre of 254 Palestinian civilians by the Irgun; episode used as psychological warfare to instill fear in remaining populations

Democratic Alliance: also referred to as the Palestinian National Initiative, *Al Mubadara*, founded in 2002 by Dr. Mustafa Barghouthi as a "third force" in Palestinian politics, supporting a durable peace and nonviolent resistance, opposing Fatah as corrupt and undemocratic and Hamas as extremist and fundamentalist

Diaspora Jews: Jews living outside of Israel

Druze: a distinct Arab community, an offshoot of Islam. In Israel they live mostly in the north including the Golan, serve in the army, but are not socio-economically equal to most Israeli Jews.

Fatah: most prominent faction of the Palestine Liberation Organization, dedicated to establishment of Palestinian state

First Intifada: 1987–93 Palestinian uprising against Israeli occupation

Geneva Conventions: set of international agreements that govern international behavior and ethical conduct during war and the treatment of soldiers, civilians, and occupied territories, first signed in 1864

Green Line: originally the armistice line drawn after the 1948 war and later the border between Israel and the territories occupied in the 1967 War (West Bank, Gaza Strip, Golan Heights)

Gush Emunim (Bloc of the Faithful): religious national movement supported by right-wing secular forces in Israel, founded in 1974 to promote Jewish settlement in the West Bank and Gaza and ultimate annexation to Israel

Hadassah: large Zionist women's organization in US founded in 1912 to raise money for Israel

Haganah: main Jewish underground resistance movement founded in 1920s

Hamas: Movement for Islamic Resistance, radical Islamic movement founded in 1988, military wing, Izz al-Din al-Qassam, responsible for guerilla war and terrorism in Israel, provides extensive social welfare, won election to Palestinian Legislative Council 2006

Haram al-Sharif: area in the old city of Jerusalem that encompasses the Al-Aqsa Mosque and the Dome of the Rock on the Temple Mount

Irgun: Jewish underground resistance 1937–49, founded with goal of establishing a Jewish state, heavily involved in terrorist attacks against Palestinian population

Islamic Jihad: militant Islamic movement in the Occupied Territories, source of many suicide bombings in Israel

Israeli Defense Force: Israeli military founded in 1948 from the Haganah, the Irgun, and Stern Gang, post-high school service is mandatory, followed by reserve duty for men

Jabotinsky group: followers of Ze'ev Jabotinsky, right-wing, militaristic leader of Revisionist Zionism who also established a paramilitary youth movement called Betar during the British Mandate in Palestine, advocated the "Iron Wall" policy towards dealing with indigenous Arabs, precursor to the Likud party

Kadima: Israeli political party formed by Prime Minister Ariel Sharon·when he left the Likud party in November 2005, platform includes unilateral disengagement with the removal of some Jewish settlements from parts of the Occupied Territories, the maintenance of Jerusalem and large Jewish settlement blocs in the West Bank under Israeli control, and the establishment of permanent borders between Israel and Palestine

Kibbutz: village based on collective production and consumption, prominent in early Jewish socialist settlers in Palestine

Knesset: 120-member Israeli parliament or legislature with a wide array of political parties, power created through formation of coalition governments

Labor Party: Israeli parliamentary bloc derived from Mapai, the Zionist-socialist party founded by Ben Gurion in 1930, after various merges, renamed in the 1970s

Law of Return: Israeli law that any Jew has the right to Israeli citizenship

Likud: Israeli parliamentary bloc, coalition of right-wing parties founded in 1973

Mandate Palestine: *see* British Mandate

Mizrachi: Jews coming from Arab countries

Muslim Brotherhood: political group in Islamic world founded 1928 in Egypt, fought on behalf of Palestinians in 1936 and 1948; after 1967, re-established as counterforce to Fatah, later split into Islamic Jihad and Hamas

Occupied Territories: Gaza Strip, West Bank and East Jerusalem, Israel took control of these territories in the 1967 War

Oslo Accords: 1993 agreement between Israel and the PLO: PLO recognized as representative of Palestinian people, redeployment of Israeli troops out of Palestinian cities and population centers, recognition by Palestinians of Israel's right to exist and renunciation of armed struggle, beginning of normalization of Israel's relations with Arab neighbors and Palestinian responsibility for economic and social needs of its population and for Israeli security, "final status issues" (borders, settlements, Jerusalem, refugees) delayed during interim period

Ottoman Empire: also known as Turkish Empire, encompassed much of Middle East, parts of North Africa and southeastern Europe, 1299 to 1923

Palestinian: currently an ethnic and political description of Arabic-speaking people, Islamic, Christian, or *Druze*, with origins in Mandate Palestine

Palestinian Authority: governmental body running legislative and executive affairs in the Occupied Territories as established in 1993 by the Oslo Accords

Palestinian Center for Human Rights: organization based in Gaza City, established in 1995 by Palestinian lawyers and human rights activists to document and investigate human rights violations and provide legal counsel and research; promotes development of democratic institutions, civil society, and the right of self-determination according to UN resolutions and international law

Palestine Liberation Organization: founded 1964 to represent Palestinian independence struggle, traditional leadership replaced by Fatah headed by Yasser Arafat, identified with struggle for statehood, right of return of Palestinian refugees, anti-occupation

Palmach: elite commando units of the Haganah founded in 1941

Popular Front for the Liberation of Palestine: secular, leftist, national liberation movement, founded by Dr. George Habash in 1967 as a guerrilla organization dedicated to armed struggle against Israel, inspired by Marxism and Latin American revolutionaries, the first group to hijack airplanes for political purposes

Popular Resistance Committees: secular and fundamentalist Palestinian militant organizations in the Gaza Strip organized in 2000, to defend Palestinian refugee camps during Israeli incursions and attack Israeli military and civilian targets in and adjacent to the Gaza Strip

Refugee Camps: defined living areas in the West Bank, Gaza, Lebanon, Syria, and Jordan for Palestinian refugees from the wars of 1948 and 1967 and their descendants, under the care of UNRWA

Right of Return: internationally recognized law that is specifically protected by the UN for Palestinian refugees that states that refugees should be able to return to their homes or receive compensation for property if they choose not to return

Sabra: Hebrew slang for a Jew born in Palestine or later Israel, refers to the prickly pear which is thorny and tough on the outside and sweet and succulent on the inside. *Sabra* or prickly pear is also a Palestinian symbol; however, in Arabic it also means "patience"

Second Intifada: 2000, second Palestinian uprising against the Israeli occupation

Separation Wall (Fence, Barrier): militarized, electronic, and barbed-wire fence and concrete barrier under construction by Israel to improve security; in 2004 the International Court of Justice found construction of wall in Occupied Territories, along with inclusion of Israeli settlements, "contrary to international law" and called upon Israel "to make reparation for all damage"

Sephardi: Jews originating from areas surrounding the Mediterranean and the Arab world, also called Orientals or Jewish-Arabs, includes Jews from Spain and Portugal

Settlements: Jewish communities established within the Occupied Territories primarily since 1974, usually with full government and military support, approximately 20 percent are religious or ideological, the remainder are attracted by economic incentives, all create "facts on the ground" that impact future negotiations

Temple Mount: also called Noble Sanctuary, Jewish holy site in Jerusalem where First and Second Temples were located, also site of Muslim holy shrines, Dome of the Rock and Al-Aqsa Mosque

Two state solution: principle of many peace proposals that has as its foundation the creation of two separate, viable states, Israel and Palestine

UN Resolution 181: 1947, partition of British Mandate in Palestine into Jewish and Arab states

UN Resolution 194: 1948, repatriation and compensation of Palestinian refugees from 1948 war, internationalization of Jerusalem; Israel's acceptance into UN was contingent on accepting 194

UN Resolution 242: 1967, inadmissibility of acquisition of territory by war, just resolution of refugee problem

UN Resolution 338: 1973, called for cease-fire, affirmed 242

UN Resolution 446: 1979, affirmed Israeli settlements in the Occupied Territories are "illegal" and should be dismantled

UN Resolution 476, 1980, called the annexation by Israel of East Jerusalem and its declaration as Israel's "undivided" capital a violation of international law

United Nations Relief and Works Agency: established in 1949 as a temporary body to deal with refugees, but soon became major employer and provider of social services (food, medicine, housing, education) in refugee camps

Brief Time Line

1882–1903	First wave of Jewish immigration to Palestine
1903–1914	Second wave of Jewish immigration
1917	Balfour Declaration promises Jewish homeland in Palestine
1922	British Mandate in Palestine, Egypt gains independence, British and French diplomats divide up Arab portion of defeated Ottoman Empire
1930s–1940s	major Jewish immigration to Palestine/Israel from Germany and Central Europe
1933	Hitler comes to power
1936–39	Palestinian uprising with brutal suppression by British
1937	Peel Commission promotes partition plan
1939	White Paper restricts Jewish immigration and land purchase
1941–45	Jewish genocide in Europe, commonly known as the Holocaust
1947	UN Resolution 181 proposes partition into Jewish state on 56 percent of land and Palestinian state on 44 percent of land
1948	Israel proclaims independence, Arab armies enter Palestine, Israeli uprooting of 750,000 Palestinian refugees begins (*Al Nakba*), Israel victorious over Arab forces, David Ben Gurion elected first Prime Minister
1949	Armistice signed between Israel and Arab states, border of Israel established along the "Green Line," Israel claims 78 percent of historic Palestine
1950	West Bank annexed to Jordan
1956	Suez War, Israeli-Franco-British War against Egypt, Israeli occupation of the Sinai
1957	Israeli retreat from the Šinai
1964	Palestine Liberation Organization (PLO) founded
1965	Fatah founded, first military action
1967	Israeli-Arab War, also know as the Six Day War, Israel occupies the West Bank, Gaza Strip, Syrian Golan Heights, Egypt's Sinai Peninsula, creating 200,000–250,000 new Palestinian refugees
1968	Fatah takes over PLO
1969	Golda Meir elected Prime Minister of Israel
1970	Civil war between Jordanian army and PLO, Black September, PLO crushed by Jordanian army and expelled to Lebanon
1970–73	Mass immigration to Israel from the Soviet Union
1973	Yom Kippur War between Egypt, Syria, and Israel
1974	PLO recognized as legitimate representative of Palestinian people by UN, settlement movement of Jews into Occupied Territories (*Gush Emunim*) founded, Israel gives up small part of the Occupied Territories to Syria and Egypt

1977	Camp David Accords between Israel and Egypt, Peace Now founded in Israel
1979	Sinai Peninsula returned to Egypt
1979	Palestinian Medical Relief Society founded
1982	Remainder of Sinai returned to Egypt, Israel invades Lebanon, PLO leads Lebanese-Palestinian resistance, PLO expelled to Tunis, massacre of Palestinians in Sabra and Shatila Refugee Camps in southern Lebanon by Lebanese Christian militia
1985	Israel withdraws from most of Lebanon
1987–91	First Intifada
1988	Jordan secedes from West Bank, Hamas founded, Palestinian Declaration of Independence with official recognition of two state approach, Physicians for Human Rights-Israel founded
1989–90	Mass migration of Jews and non-Jews from former USSR
1990	Gaza Community Mental Health Program founded
1991	Gulf War, Iraqi scud missiles land in Haifa and Tel Aviv, Madrid Conference between Israelis, Arab states, and Palestinians
1993	Oslo Declaration of Principles (also called Oslo Accords) signed in Washington
1994	Peace treaty between Israel and Jordan
Mid 1990s	Emergence of Arabic language satellite TV stations
1995	Israel and PLO sign interim agreement, Palestinian control over parts of Occupied Territories, Israeli Prime Minister Yitzhak Rabin assassinated, Benjamin Netanyahu elected
1996	Yasser Arafat elected President of the Palestinian Authority
1999	Ehud Barak elected Prime Minister of Israel
2000	Israel withdraws from southern Lebanon, Israeli/Palestinian summit at Camp David, Second Intifada begins
2001	Ariel Sharon elected Prime Minister of Israel, Mitchell Plan calls for freeze on Jewish settlement construction in Occupied Territories, Israeli-Arab negotiations at Taba lead to substantial agreements but no final treaty
2002	Major Israeli incursions into the Occupied Territories and reoccupation of Palestinian cities, Saudi Peace Proposal adopted unanimously by Arab League, Israel begins construction of separation wall
2003	Road Map adopted by the Quartet, representing the US, European Union, Russian Federation and the United Nations, Geneva Accords proposed by Yossi Beilin and Yasser Abd-Rabbo
2004	Yasser Arafat, President of the Palestinian Authority, dies
2005	Israel removes Jewish settlements from Gaza but maintains control over borders and much of economy
2006	Prime Minister Ariel Sharon suffers major stroke, Ehud Olmert elected Prime Minister of Israel, Hamas wins majority of seats in Legislative Council in the Occupied Territories; with provocation by Hamas and Hezbollah activity, Israel invades Gaza and Lebanon

Notes

Chapter 1

1. http://www.vopj.org/personalnarr.htm (accessed 4/2/06).
2. http://www.seruv.org.il/MoreArticles/English/GuyGrossmanEng_1.htm (accessed 4/2/06).
3. http://www.peacenow.org.il/site/en/peace.asp?pi=69&docid=548&pos=6 (accessed 4/2/06).
4. Adam Keller, 'Bil'in's Struggle on the Ground, Among the Public, at Court,' *The Other Israel* (ed. Adam Keller), No. 123/124 (January 2006).
5. http://www.vopj.org/personalnarr.htm#The%20Conflict%20Today (accessed 4/2/06).
6. Jeff Halper, "Israeli Violations of Human Rights and International Humanitarian Law in the Occupied Palestinian Territories," paper presented to the European Parliament, Brussels, June 2001.
7. Marc Ellis, *Israel and Palestine – Out of the Ashes: the Search for Jewish Identity in the Twenty-first Century*, London, Pluto Press, 2002.

Chapter 2

1. Ruchama Marton, "The Right to Madness: From the Personal to the Political – Psychiatry and Human Rights," in Neve Gordon (ed.), *From the Margins of Globalization: Critical Perspectives on Human Rights*, Lanham MD, Lexington Books, 2004, pp. 195–221.
2. Marton, "The Right to Madness," p. 196.
3. Marton, "The Right to Madness," p. 197.
4. Marton, "The Right to Madness," p. 207.
5. Marton, "The Right to Madness," p. 199.
6. Marton, "The Right to Madness," p. 210.
7. Marton, "The Right to Madness," p. 209.
8. Marton, "The Right to Madness," p. 209.
9. Marton, "The Right to Madness," p. 216.
10. Ruchama Marton, "The Psychological Impact of the Second Intifada on Israeli Society," *Palestine-Israel Journal*, February 2004, p. 73.
11. Ruchama Marton and Dalit Baum, "Transparent Wall, Opaque Gates," in Michael Sorkin (ed.), *Against the Wall: Israel's Barrier to Peace*, New York, New Press, 2005, p. 213.
12. Marton and Baum, "Transparent Wall, Opaque Gates," p. 213.
13. Marton and Baum, "Transparent Wall, Opaque Gates," p. 214.
14. Marton and Baum, "Transparent Wall, Opaque Gates," p. 214.

15. Marton and Baum, "Transparent Wall, Opaque Gates," p. 215.
16. Marton and Baum, "Transparent Wall, Opaque Gates," p. 216.
17. Marton and Baum, "Transparent Wall, Opaque Gates," p. 216.
18. Marton and Baum, "Transparent Wall, Opaque Gates," p. 219.
19. Marton and Baum, "Transparent Wall, Opaque Gates," p. 219.
20. Marton and Baum, "Transparent Wall, Opaque Gates," p. 220.
21. Marton, "The Psychological Impact of the Second Intifada," pp. 75–6.
22. Ruchama Marton, "Doctors and the Duty of Intervention," *Palestine-Israel Journal*, Vol. VI, No. 1, 1999, pp. 57–62.

Chapter 3

1. http://www.peacenow.org.il/site/en/peace.asp?pi=43&docid=62&pos=1 (accessed 4/3/06).

Chapter 4

1. http://www.seruv.org.il/english/combatants_letter.asp (accessed 8/14/06).

Chapter 6

1. http://www.btselem.org/english/Freedom_of_Movement/Checkpoints_and_Forbidden_Roads.asp (accessed 8/15/06).
2. http://www.machsomwatch.org/docs/Counterview.pdf (accessed 8/15/06).
3. http://www.btselem.org/english/Freedom_of_Movement/Statistics.asp (accessed 8/15/06).
4. http://www.btselem.org/english/Publications/Summaries/200503_Gaza_Prison.asp (accessed 8/15/06).
5. http://www.machsomwatch.org/ (accessed 8/15/06).
6. http://www.machsomwatch.org/eng/summariesEng.asp?link=summariesEng&lang=eng (accessed 8/15/06).
7. http://www.machsomwatch.org/docs/Counterview.pdf (accessed 8/15/06).
8. http://www.pngo.net/pngo.htm (accessed 8/15/06).

Chapter 7

1. http://www.maram.org/pdf/brings-maternityhomes.pdf (accessed 4/11/05).
2. http://www.maram.org/pdf/brings-maternityhomes.pdf (accessed 4/11/05).
3. http://www.phr.org.il/phr/article.asp?articleid=73&catid=45&pcat=45&lang=ENG (accessed 4/11/06).
4. http://www.upmrc.org/ (accessed 8/22/06).
5. http://www.palestinemonitor.org/factsheet/effect_of_closure_on_health_care.htm (accessed 7/9/06).
6. Personal communication, Mustafa Barghouthi, MD, 2004.
7. http://www.mideastweb.org/palestinianwomen.htm (accessed 9/22/05).

8. http://www.womenforpalestine.com/020403v2/pp_vfp_pwanv.htm (accessed 4/4/06).

9. http://www.mideastweb.org/palestinianwomen.htm (accessed 9/22/05).

10. Yakin Erturk, *Integration of the Human Rights of Women and the Gender Perspective: Violence Against Women*, Report of the Special Rapporteur on violence against women, its causes and consequences, Addendum, Mission to Occupied Palestinian Territory, United Nations Economic and Social Council, 2 February 2005, p. 18.

11. http://www.mideastweb.org/palestinianwomen.htm (accessed 9/22/05).

12. Yakin Erturk, *Integration of the Human Rights of Women and the Gender Perspective*, p. 19.

13. http://www.ccmep.org/2003_articles/Palestine/111003_occupation_patriarchy.htm (accessed 9/22/05); http://www.whrnet.org/docs/interview-loubani-0311.html (accessed 9/22/05).

14. Ilan Pappe, *A History of Modern Palestine, One Land, Two Peoples*, Cambridge, Cambridge University Press, 2004, pp. 237–9.

15. http://www.mideastweb.org/palestinianwomen.htm (accessed 9/22/05).

16. http://www.ccmep.org/2003_articles/Palestine/111003_occupation_patriarchy.htm (accessed 9/22/05); http://www.whrnet.org/docs/interview-loubani-0311.html (accessed 9/22/05); http://www.miftah.org/Display.cfm?DocId=7966&CategoryId=21 (accessed 8/22/06).

17. Yakin Erturk, *Integration of the Human Rights of Women and the Gender Perspective*, pp. 13–14.

18. Yakin Erturk, *Integration of the Human Rights of Women and the Gender Perspective*, p. 19; http://www.miftah.org/Display.cfm?DocId=7966&CategoryId=21 (accessed 8/22/06).

19. http://www.miftah.org/Display.cfm?DocId=7966&CategoryId=21 (accessed 8/22/06).

20. http://www.ccmep.org/2003_articles/Palestine/111003_occupation_patriarchy.htm (accessed 9/22/05); Yakin Erturk, *Integration of the Human Rights of Women and the Gender Perspective*, pp. 2, 15, 20.

21. http://www.sonomacountyfreepress.com/palestine/women2.html (accessed 9/22/05); http://www.miftah.org/Display.cfm?DocId=7966&CategoryId=21 (accessed 8/22/06).

22. Yakin Erturk, *Integration of the Human Rights of Women and the Gender Perspective*, p. 17; http://www.miftah.org/Display.cfm?DocId=7966&CategoryId=21 (accessed 8/22/06).

23. http://web.amnesty.org/library/print/ENGMDE150162005 (accessed 7/9/06); http://www.ccmep.org/2003_articles/Palestine/111003_occupation_patriarchy.htm (accessed 9/22/05); http://www.miftah.org/Display.cfm?DocId=7966&CategoryId=21 (accessed 8/22/06).

24. Yakin Erturk, *Integration of the Human Rights of Women and the Gender Perspective*, p. 20.

25. http://web.amnesty.org/library/print/ENGMDE150162005 (accessed 7/9/06); Yakin Erturk, *Integration of the Human Rights of Women and the Gender Perspective*, p. 6; http://www.miftah.org/Display.cfm?DocId=7966&CategoryId=21 (accessed 8/22/06).

26. http://web.amnesty.org/library/print/ENGMDE150162005 (accessed 7/9/06);
    http://www.miftah.org/Display.cfm?DocId=7966&CategoryId=21 (accessed
    8/22/06).

27. http://www.miftah.org/Display.cfm?DocId=7966&CategoryId=21 (accessed
    8/22/06).

28. http://web.amnesty.org/library/print/ENGMDE150162005 (accessed
    7/9/06).

29. Yakin Erturk, *Integration of the Human Rights of Women and the Gender
    Perspective*, p. 15.

30. http://web.amnesty.org/library/print/ENGMDE150162005 (accessed 7/9/06);
    Yakin Erturk, *Integration of the Human Rights of Women and the Gender
    Perspective*, p. 16.

31. http://www.ccmep.org/2003_articles/Palestine/111003_occupation_
    patriarchy.htm (accessed 9/22/05).

32. http://web.amnesty.org/library/print/ENGMDE150162005 (accessed
    7/9/06).

33. Yakin Erturk, *Integration of the Human Rights of Women and the Gender
    Perspective*, p. 10.

34. http://web.amnesty.org/library/print/ENGMDE150162005 (accessed 7/9/06);
    Yakin Erturk, *Integration of the Human Rights of Women and the Gender
    Perspective*, p. 12.

35. http://web.amnesty.org/library/print/ENGMDE150162005 (accessed 7/9/06);
    Yakin Erturk, *Integration of the Human Rights of Women and the Gender
    Perspective*, pp. 10, 14–16; http://www.miftah.org/Display.cfm?DocId=796
    6&CategoryId=21 (accessed 8/22/06).

36. http://www.miftah.org/PrinterF.cfm?DocId=7845 (accessed 4/4/06).

37. http://web.amnesty.org/library/print/ENGMDE150162005 (accessed 7/9/06);
    Yakin Erturk, *Integration of the Human Rights of Women and the Gender
    Perspective*, p. 9; http://www.miftah.org/Display.cfm?DocId=7966&Categor
    yId=21 (accessed 8/22/06); http://www.miftah.org/PrinterF.cfm?DocId=7845
    (accessed 4/4/06) http://www.unfpa.org/news/news.cfm?ID=80&Language=1
    (accessed 4/4/06).

38. http://www.unfpa.org/profile/palestinianterritory.cfm?Section+1 (accessed
    4/4/06).

39. http://www.unfpa.ps/main.cfm?sid=21 (accessed 4/4/06).

40. http://www.miftah.org/PrinterF.cfm?DocId=8003 (accessed 4/11/06).

Chapter 8

1. http://www.un.org/unrwa/refugees/index.html (accessed 8/22/06).

Chapter 9

1. http://electronicintifada.net/v2/article1708.shtml (accessed 8/22/06); Yehezkel
   Lein and Alon Cohen-Lifshitz, *Under the Guise of Security: Routing the
   Separation Barrier to Enable the Expansion of Israeli Settlements in the West
   Bank*, report prepared by BIMKOM and B'Tselem (December 2005).

2. http://www.acri.org.il/english-acri/engine/story.asp?id=171 (accessed 8/22/06).

3. http://www.phr.org.il/phr/files/articlefile_1108906478739.pdf (accessed 3/22/06).

4. http://www.btselem.org/english/Separation_Barrier/Jerusalem.asp (accessed 3/22/06).

5. http://www.btselem.org/english/Jerusalem/Infrastructure_and_Services.asp (accessed 3/22/06).

6. Menachem Klein, "Old and New Walls in Jerusalem," *Political Geography*, Vol. 24 (2005) pp. 53–76.

7. http://www.phr.org.il/phr/article.asp?articleid=73&catid=45&pcat=45&lang=ENG (accessed 3/23/06).

8. http://www.acri.org.il/english-acri/engine/story.asp?id=182 (accessed 8/22/06).

9. http://www.vopj.org/issues35.htm (accessed 8/22/06).

10. http://www.btselem.org/English/Maps/Index.asp (accessed 8/22/06).

11. Personal communication, Mustafa Barghouthi, MD, 2004.

12. http://www.acri.org.il/english-acri/engine/story.asp?id=185 (accessed 8/22/06).

13. http://www.phr.org.il/phr/files/articlefile_1108316859979.pdf (accessed 8/22/06); http://www.phr.org.il/phr/article.asp?articleid=73&catid=45&pcat=45&lang=ENG (accessed 3/25/06).

14. http://www.vopj.org/issues-e-the-western-wall%20.pdf (accessed 8/22/06).

15. http://www.miftah.org/Display.cfm?DocId=8253&CategoryId=5 (accessed 9/11/06); http://www.miftah.org/Display.cfm?DocId=10790&CategoryId=8 (accessed 8/24/06).

16. http://www.lrb.co.uk/v27/n21/roy_01_.html (accessed 9/11/06).

17. http://www.lrb.co.uk/v27/n21/roy_01_.html (accessed 9/11/06).

18. http://www.un.org/unrwa/news/incursion_oct04.pdf (accessed 10/27/04).

19. http://www.phr.org.il/phr/article.asp?articleid=347&catid=55&pcat=45&lang=ENG (accessed 8/23/06); Scott Wilson, "Gaza Clinic: A Lesson in Anatomy of Chaos," *Washington Post Foreign Service* (March 16, 2006) A 18.

20. http://www.phr.org.il/phr/files/articlefile_1151937195636.doc (accessed 8/23/06).

Chapter 10

1. Jad Isaac and Sophia Saad, *A Geopolitical Atlas of Palestine, The West Bank and Gaza*, Bethlehem, Palestine, Applied Research Institute – Jerusalem, 2004, p. 53.

2. http://www.un.org/unrwa/refugees/images/map.jpg (accessed 8/24/06).

3. http://www.lrb.co.uk/v27/n21/roy_01_.html (accessed 9/11/06).

4. http://www.lrb.co.uk/v27/n21/roy_01_.html (accessed 9/11/06).

5. http://www.gcmhp.net/eyd/stone.htm (accessed 4/13/06).

Chapter 11

1. http://www1.idf.il/DOVER/site/mainpage.asp?clr=1&sl=EN&id=7&docid=31524 (accessed 8/25/06).

2. http://www.mfa.gov.il/mfa/terrorism-%20obstacle%20to%20peace/palestin
    ian%20terror%20since%202000/Victims%20of%20Palestinian%20Violen
    ce%20and%20Terrorism%20sinc (accessed 8/25/06).

3. http://www1.idf.il/DOVER/site/mainpage.asp?sl=EN&id=7&docid=17482.
    EN (accessed 8/25/06).

4. http://www1.idf.il/SIP_STORAGE/DOVER/files/5/31365.pdf (accessed
    8/25/06).

5. http://www1.idf.il/DOVER/site/mainpage.asp?sl=EN&id=7&docid=22059.
    EN (accessed 8/25/06).

6. http://www1.idf.il/DOVER/site/homepage.asp?clr=1&sl=EN&id=-
    8888&force=1 (accessed 4/21/06).

7. http://www1.idf.il/DOVER/site/homepage.asp?clr=1&sl=EN&id=-
    8888&force=1 (accessed 4/21/06).

8. http://www.israeli-weapons.com/weapons/vehicles/engineer_vehicles/
    bulldozers/D9_D10.html (accessed 8/25/06); http://www.catdestroyshomes.
    org/article.php?id=101 (accessed 8/25/06).

9. http://www.hrw.org/reports/2004/rafah1004/1.htm#_Toc84676165 (accessed
    8/25/06).

10. http://www.imra.org.il/story.php3?id=20933 (accessed 8/25/06).

11. http://www1.idf.il/DOVER/site/mainpage.asp?clr=1&sl=EN&id=7&docid=
    31524 (accessed 8/25/06).

12. http://www1.idf.il/DOVER/site/mainpage.asp?sl=EN&id=7&docid=31531.
    EN&unit=12017 (accessed 8/25/06).

13. http://www.btselem.org/english/Razing/Rafah_Legal_Background.asp
    (accessed 8/25/06).

14. http://www.nytimes.com/2004/05/23/international/middleeast/23CND-
    ISRA.html?ex=1146024000&en=0f4a652c8d715321&ei=5070 (accessed
    4/22/06).

15. http://www.btselem.org/english/Razing/Rafah_Legal_Background.asp
    (accessed 8/25/06).

16. http://www.pchrgaza.org/files/PressR/English/2004/press2004.htm (accessed
    8/25/06).

17. http://www.hrw.org/reports/2004/rafah1004/ (accessed 4/22/06).

18. http://www.hrw.org/reports/2004/rafah1004/1.htm#_Toc84676165 (accessed
    4/22/06).

19. http://www.hrw.org/reports/2004/rafah1004/6.htm#_Toc84676183 (accessed
    4/25/06).

20. http://www.hrw.org/reports/2004/rafah1004/6.htm#_Toc84676180 (accessed
    4/25/06).

21. http://www.hrw.org/reports/2004/rafah1004/6.htm#_Toc84676180 (accessed
    4/25/06).

22. http://www.hrw.org/reports/2004/rafah1004/1.htm#_Toc84676165 (accessed
    4/22/06).

23. http://www.hrw.org/reports/2004/rafah1004/1.htm#_Toc84676165 (accessed
    4/22/06).

24. http://www.hrw.org/reports/2004/rafah1004/13.htm#_Toc84676203
    (accessed 8/25/06).

25. http://www.hrw.org/reports/2004/rafah1004/1.htm#_Toc84676165 (accessed 4/22/06).
26. http://www.hrw.org/reports/2004/rafah1004/16.htm#_Toc84676209 (accessed 4/26/06).

Chapter 12

1. http://www.phr.org.il/phr/article.asp?articleid=338&catid=55&pcat=45&lang=ENG (accessed 8/27/06).
2. http://www.nytimes.com/2006/05/08/world/middleeast/08gaza.html?ex=1156824000&en=f519749030840b00&ei=5070 (accessed 6/10/06).
3. http://www.oxfam.org/en/news/pressreleases2006/pr060711_gaza (accessed 8/27/06).
4. Frank Luntz, "Israel in the Age of Eminem: A Creative Brief for Israel Messaging," ClearAgenda, Inc. (March 2003), http://www.myisrael.com.
5. Frank Luntz, "Israel in the Age of Eminem," p. 3.
6. Frank Luntz, "Israel in the Age of Eminem," p. 14.
7. Frank Luntz, "Israel in the Age of Eminem," p. 3.
8. Frank Luntz, "Israel in the Age of Eminem," p. 20.
9. Frank Luntz, Luntz, "Israel in the Age of Eminem," p. 45–8.
10. Frank Luntz, "America 2020: How the Next Generation Views Israel," The Israel Project (June 2005), http://www.theisraelproject.org
11. Frank Luntz, "America 2020: How the Next Generation Views Israel".
12. Frank Luntz, "America 2020: How the Next Generation Views Israel," p. 4.
13. Frank Luntz, "America 2020: How the Next Generation Views Israel," p. 4.
14. Frank Luntz, "America 2020: How the Next Generation Views Israel," p. 24.
15. Frank Luntz, "America 2020: How the Next Generation Views Israel," p. 27.
16. Frank Luntz, "America 2020: How the Next Generation Views Israel," p. 30.
17. Frank Luntz, "America 2020: How the Next Generation Views Israel," pp. 31–2.
18. Frank Luntz, "America 2020: How the Next Generation Views Israel," p. 16.
19. Frank Luntz, "America 2020: How the Next Generation Views Israel," p. 3 4.
20. Frank Luntz, "America 2020: How the Next Generation Views Israel," p. 34.
21. Frank Luntz, "America 2020: How the Next Generation Views Israel," p. 35.
22. Frank Luntz, "America 2020: How the Next Generation Views Israel," p. 40.
23. Frank Luntz, "America 2020: How the Next Generation Views Israel," p. 44.
24. http://www.lrb.co.uk/v28/n06/print/mear01_.html (accessed 5/15/06).
25. http://www.lrb.co.uk/v28/n06/print/mear01_.html (accessed 5/15/06).
26. Michael Levenson, "Brandeis Pulls Artwork by Palestinian Youths," Boston Globe, Vol. 269, No. 123 (May 3, 2006) pp. 1, A19.
27. http://www.here-now.org/shows/2006/05/20060510_9.asp (accessed 8/27/06).
28. http://www.democracynow.org/article.pl?sid=06/05/10/1345208&mode=thread&tid=25 (accessed 8/27/06).
29. Michael Levenson, "Brandeis Pulls Artwork by Palestinian Youths," pp. 1, A19.
30. John R. Hose, email "Exhibit at Brandeis University" (May 4, 2006).
31. Daniel Terris, letter "Dear Members of the Brandeis University Community" (May 5, 2006).

32. Cindy Cohen, letter "Dear Students in *The Arts of Building Peace*" (May 2006).
33. Cindy Cohen, letter "Dear Students in *The Arts of Building Peace.*"
34. Arthur Neslen, *Occupied Minds: A Journey through the Israeli Psyche*, London, Pluto Press, 2006.
35. Arthur Neslen, *Occupied Minds*, p. 155.
36. http://www.haaretz.com/hasen/objects/pages/PrintArticleEn.jhtml?itemNo= 717653 (accessed 5/22/06).
37. http://www.haaretz.com/hasen/spages/711997.html (accessed 8/27/06).
38. http://www.thejerusalemfund.org/images/fortherecord.php?ID=257 (accessed 8/28/06).
39. http://www.counterpunch.org/halper10082005.html (accessed 8/26/06).
40. Amos Elon, "What Does Olmert Want?" *New York Review of Books*, Vol. LIII, No. 11 (June 22, 2006) pp. 53–8.
41. Sandy Tolan, *The Lemon Tree: An Arab, a Jew, and the Heart of the Middle East*, New York, Bloomsbury, 2006.
42. Sandy Tolan, *The Lemon Tree*, p. 212.
43. http://www.vopj.org/issues2.htm (accessed 8/26/06); http://www.vopj.org/issues3.htm (accessed 8/26/06).

References and Websites

Recommended Readings

Amiry, Suad, *Sharon and My Mother-in-Law, Ramallah Diaries*, New York, Pantheon Books, 2004

Beit-Hallahmi, Benjamin, *Original Sins: Reflections on the History of Zionism and Israel*, London, Pluto Press, 1991

Benvenisti, Meron, *Conflicts and Contradictions: One of Israel's Leading Commentators Reflects on Israel, the Arabs and the West Bank*, New York, Villard Books, 1986

Carey, Roane and Jonathan Shanin, editors, *The Other Israel*, New York, The New Press, 2002

Ellis, Marc, *Israel and Palestine – Out of the Ashes, the Search for Jewish Identity in the Twenty-first Century*, London, Pluto Press, 2002

Elon, Amos, *The Israelis: Founders and Sons*, New York, Penguin, 1983

Golan-Agnon, Daphna, *Next Year in Jerusalem*, New York, The New Press, 2005

Gorenberg, Gershom, *The Accidental Empire: Israel and the Birth of the Settlements, 1967–1977*, New York, Times Books, Henry Holt and Company, 2006

Grossman, David, *The Yellow Wind: With a New Afterword by the Author*, New York, Picador, 2002

Hass, Amira, *Drinking the Sea at Gaza: Days and Nights in a Land Under Siege*, New York, An Owl Book, Henry Holt and Co., 2000

Kushner, Tony and Alisa Solomon, editors, *Wrestling with Zion: Progressive Jewish-American Responses to the Israeli-Palestinian Conflict*, New York, Grove Press, 2003

Neslen, Arthur, *Occupied Minds: A Journey through the Israeli Psyche*, London, Pluto Press, 2006

Pappe, Ilan, *The Making of the Arab-Israeli Conflict, 1947–1951*, London, I. B. Tauris, 1994

Pappe, Ilan, *A History of Modern Palestine: One Land, Two Peoples*, Cambridge, UK, Cambridge University Press, 2004

Pearlman, Wendy, *Occupied Voices: Stories of Everyday Life from the Second Intifada*, New York, Nation Books, 2003

Reinhart, Tanya, *Israel/Palestine: How to End the War of 1948*, New York, Seven Stories Press, 2005

Reinhart, Tanya, *The Road Map to Nowhere: Israel/Palestine Since 2003*, London, Verso, 2006

Said, Edward, *The Question of Palestine*, New York, Vintage, 1992

Segev, Tom, *1949 The First Israelis*, New York, The Free Press, 1986

Segev, Tom, *The Seventh Million, the Israelis and the Holocaust*, New York, Hill and Wang, 1993

Shapira, Avraham, editor, *The Seventh Day: Soldiers' Talk about the Six-Day War*, New York, Scribner, 1971

Shehadeh, Raja, *Samed: Journal of a West Bank Palestinian*, New York, Franklin Watts, 1984

Shehadeh, Raja, *Strangers in the House: Coming of Age in Occupied Palestine*, New York, Penguin, 2003

Stone, Isidor F., *Underground to Palestine: And Reflections Thirty Years Later*, London, Hutchinson, 1978

Tolan, Sandy, *The Lemon Tree: An Arab, a Jew, and the Heart of the Middle East*, New York, Bloomsbury, 2006

Warschawski, Michel, *Towards an Open Tomb: The Crisis of Israeli Society*, New York, Monthly Review Press, 2004

Warschawski, Michael, *On the Border*, Cambridge, MA, South End Press, 2005

Recommended Websites

United States

Brit Tzedek v'Shalom – btvshalom.org
Foundation for Middle East Peace – fmep.org
Human Rights Watch – hrw.org
The Jewish Peace Lobby – peacelobby.org
Jewish Voice for Peace – jewishvoiceforpeace.org
Jewish Voice for Peace, Boston (formerly Visions of Peace with Justice in Israel/ Palestine) – jvpboston.org
Middle East Research and Information Project – merip.org
Refuser Solidarity Network – refusersolidarity.net
Tikkun – tikkun.org

Israel and Palestine

Adalah – adalah.org
The Alternative Information Center – alternativenews.org
B'Tselem – btselem.org
Coalition of Women for Peace – coalitionofwomen.org
Gush Shalom – gush-shalom.org
The Israeli Committee Against House Demolitions – icahd.org/eng
Machsom Watch – machsomwatch.org
MIFTAH (The Palestinian Initiative for the Promotion of Global Dialogue and Democracy) – miftah.org
The Other Israel – otherisrael.home.igc.org
Palestine Monitor – palestinemonitor.org
Palestinian Medical Relief Society – upmrc.org
Peace Now – peacenow.org.il
Physicians for Human Rights-Israel – phr.org.il
Rabbis for Human Rights – rhr.israel.net
Seruv, Courage to Refuse – seruv.org.il
Ta'ayush – taayush.tripod.com

Index

Compiled by Sue Carlton